ALIEN BEDTIME STORIES

Alien Bedtime Stories

Grant Cameron

All rights reserved.
No part of this publication may be reproduced, distributed, or transmitted in any form or by any means, including photocopying, recording, or other electronic or mechanical methods, without the prior written permission of the publisher, except in the case of brief quotations embodied in critical reviews and certain other non-commercial uses permitted by copyright law. For permission requests, write to the publisher, addressed "Attention: Permissions Coordinator," at the address below.

Printed in the United States of America
First Printing 2015

ISBN: 9781670532497

Library of Congress Control Number: 2015901984

Cover Design by Matt Lacasse
https://www.anomaligraphics.com/

Interior Layout and Design by Desta Barnabe
Editing by Desta Barnabe

Itsallconnected Publishing
445 Hudson Street
Winnipeg, Manitoba
Canada, R3T 0R1
whitehouseufo@gmail.com

Alien Bedtime Stories

CONTENTS

DEDICATION vii
ACKNOWLEDGMENTS ix
INTRODUCTION 1
CHAPTER 1 5
ODDS AND ENDS STORIES 5
    The Pole Deer Story 5

    Chris Bledsoe: A Good Alien Story 9

    The Roswell Live Alien Story 27

    The Aztec Live Alien 30

    Area 51 Live Alien 36

    The EBE Live Alien 37

    The John Lennon UFO Story 38

    The Barry Goldwater Alien Story 40

    The Dmitri Medvedev Alien Story 43

CHAPTER 2 47
THE CANADIAN GOVERNMENT AND FLYING SAUCERS 47
    The Flying Saucer Observatory 50

    The Government UFO Landing Base 53

    Wilbert Smith and Alien Hardware 57

    The 1952 Saucer Recovery 60

    The St. Lawrence River UFO-Recovery 63

The Roswell Piece Analysis 65

Wilbert Smith, In Defense of Talking to Aliens 71

Wilbert Smith on Disclosure: An Insider's View 76

The CIA Channels an Alien 77

The Aliens Send a Message 84

CHAPTER 3 91
UFOS AND THE GOVERNMENT 91
Why is the Government Covering Up the Truth? 91

Is There a UFO Government Control Group? 93

The Government Meets with the ETs 99

The Area 51 Story 101

Evidence for Cover-Up 105

The CIA Confirmation of Roswell 108

1973-1975: An Age of Awakening 110

Like to Talk to an Alien? 115

CHAPTER 4 119
CONSCIOUSNESS AND UFOS 119
Cleaning House 120

Consciousness and the Flying Saucer 126

The Story of the Modern-Day Computer: An Inspired Download 128

The Intergalactic Computer Network 132

UFOs and Fear 138

A Nobel Prize for Woo-Woo? 142

Amazing Right Brain Telepathy Tales 151

CHAPTER 5
PRESIDENTS TALES 159

President Roosevelt and the Battle of Los Angeles 159

Roosevelt and the First UFO Crash 160

Harry Truman and the Roswell Crash 162

Eisenhower and the Alien Meeting 166

President Johnson and the Official UFO Study 170

Nixon and the Alien Bodies..177

The Jimmy Carter UFO Sighting 185

The Carter ET and UFO Studies..186

Ronald Reagan Discloses ET Truth..200

Bill Clinton Talks UFOs 204

Hillary Clinton Talks UFOs 209

Hillary and the UFO Book 216

Obama and the Mars Jump Program......................................220

Obama Talks UFOs 221

Obama Denies ET Reality 224

Trump and the ETS 228

President Joe Biden 232

CHAPTER 6
THE ALIENS 237

The Alien Disclosure Playbook...237

The Technology...238

The Players..242

The Disclosure 244

The Alien Healings 245

The Alien Crystal Ball 249

The Alien's Melted Pictures 258

The Alien Hive 262

Are Aliens Commies? 265

The Aliens Use the Phone 268

The Aliens and the Pharmaceutical Industry 272

Aliens and Time Travel 274

CHAPTER 7 279
FAMOUS ALIEN ABDUCTIONS 279
   Moody Blues Abduction 280

John Lennon Abduction 282

Ace Frehley Abduction 285

Sammy Hagar Abduction 286

Cat Stevens (now Yusuf Islam) Abduction 288

Kary Mullis Abduction 289

Colin Andrews Abduction 291

Robert Salas Abduction 293

Jan Harzan Abduction 294

CHAPTER 8 297
WHERE THE STORY BEGINS AND ENDS 297
   Charlie Red Star and Nuclear Weapons 297

The Doubting Thomas Story 301

Alien Bedtime Stories

Two Wonderful Tales of Death from UFO Skeptics 306

ENDNOTES 313

DEDICATION

To my late father, a believer who played the skeptic, so that I would carefully follow the facts, stay on the straight and narrow, and not fall into a well of belief.

ACKNOWLEDGMENTS

Anyone who has taken the time to write a book and pursue the project through to publication will know that the process is a hard road and does not happen in a vacuum. I would like to acknowledge all the UFO researchers I have worked with for over forty years. Many of the stories in this book would not have been possible had it not been for their tireless unpaid work and willingness to tell their stories. If the concept of the soul contract is accurate, we all agreed to play these roles in the past, and I fully acknowledge that I am just part of a team playing in the Super Bowl of all stories.

Of particular note are the conference organizers and organizers of small and large UFO groups worldwide who have brought me in to speak. At these conferences, solid friendships with other researchers were formed. At these conferences, I realized we are all working together to find answers to why we were born and how reality works.

I would also like to thank and acknowledge the many podcasters and radio hosts who have had me on their shows. Like UFO researchers, most have done their shows without any monetary benefit. The podcasters talking about UFOs, consciousness, and paranormal phenomena will be the future of media. Here, the world's consciousness will be raised, and a new world will emerge. In the podcast interview venue, I realized people like a good story. I learned to tell the accounts found in this book in this venue. Thank you to Dr. Richard Feynman and Michael Shermer, two hardline skeptics who produced one of the best stories in forty years of research. Thanks to Betsy Platt for her manuscript editing and her past efforts to get my message out to the large UFO community in Las Vegas.

INTRODUCTION

In a UFO career that has now spanned 40 years, I have learned that the population is not yet ready to storm the White House demanding answers to what the government knows about the UFO mystery. To prove this point, it should be noted that the most protesters the UFO community has ever marshaled in front of the White House demanding UFO disclosures were in the early 1990s during the administration of George Bush Senior. The total amount who showed up to protest never exceeded nineteen people.

Despite this lack of interest in overthrowing the government over the UFO issue, the general population is still interested. In a 2002 Roper poll, 48% say that UFOs have visited the earth in some form over the years. How significant is that number? It is 300% higher than the number of people who believe in the random 'power-ball' theory of evolution that says there is no God. Everything in nature is an accident caused by random mutations in DNA over billions of years. The random theory of evolution is forced learning for our children in school, whereas the UFO proponents have no government or private financial support to promote their theory. Yet, it is evident that the UFO horse is winning the race for the minds of Americans.

In investigating why this might be so, I realized that the UFO message is getting promoted through storytelling. Some people tell others what they have seen or file a sighting report with some of the private groups that gather this material. The groups, in turn, promote the stories through their lectures, writings, and private documentaries. The biggest influence for promoting the 'UFOs are here' idea comes from the mass media. This does not mean that they believe what they are putting out. They are simply chasing the bucks, and there *are* bucks in UFOs when it comes to the media. Time and time again, you will see UFO documentaries being broadcast during sweeps week when the number of viewers will determine the advertising rate and, thus the bottom line. The UFO stories are usually put out as tales told in a TV reality show or Hollywood movie. Most of the time, the networks and studios revert to the same handful of UFO stories that have drawn in audiences before and can probably do it again. These stories that have been repeated time and again over the years include the Travis Walton abduction, the Betty and Barney Hill abduction, the 1997 Phoenix Lights sightings, the Rendlesham Forest story of a USAF officer actually touching a craft that landed outside the base, the overflight of the White House twice in July 1952, and the Lonnie Zamora - Socorro, New Mexico, UFO encounter.

One of the intentions of this book, then, is to play the game. To include some stories I have researched over the years that might interest the public. The core stories are ones that I have told in lectures or written about in other forums. Most of these stories I put out were read or heard by very few people. That is because the UFO research world is very small. For example, I usually take a few months to put a lecture together, and the usual audience for it when I present it is less than 100 people. The biggest audience might be 1000 people. This is almost no one when we consider that there are over seven billion people worldwide.

The other intention of this book is to document history. I make it a regular practice to tell the audiences I speak to that they should document their UFO story. The UFO story, despite the negative scientific dogma critical of it, is perhaps the most important story in history. If UFO stories were games, then the UFO story would be the World Cup of all stories. Those who are not sure that this is the case learn about some of the leading research into UFOs, which indicate that the UFO story seems to be tied into the question of what is the ultimate reality. These questions arise when researchers concede that something is here. As the phenomena do not mesh with our present physical reality it leads to the question of what aspects of reality do we have wrong. What laws of reality do we need to understand to come to grips with what we are seeing? The messages received by contactees, and high-level officials stating that ESP is tied into the phenomena, led to questions related to the hard consciousness problem. Is the mind separate from the brain, as this phenomenon and high-level officials seem to be saying?

The UFO mystery is, therefore, an area of research that will lead to most of the breakthroughs related to technology, consciousness research, and religious understanding in the next 100 years. The general population, however, does not have the time to chase these research challenges. Instead, they are busy living their personal lives. They spend long days at work, and most of their free time is spent driving their kids to extracurricular activities, interacting with their children, spending time with their spouse, going out to movies or sporting events, or just unwinding in front of the TV with their favorite show. After all this, there is not much time left to delve into the implications of the UFO mystery.

In light of a busy day for most people in the modern world, this book provides an opportunity to tell a bit of the UFO story and its possible essential implications for the world in a 5 to 10-minute bedtime story. Even one story at bedtime a couple of times a week will help raise the public's general consciousness. A rising consciousness is key because all major new ideas introduced into the world have come after many years of seemingly wasted time. Once enough people become aware of this reality, like a teeter-totter, it will shift, and the idea will suddenly become a consensus reality. The shift in all cases comes slowly.

This shifting reality can be seen by just time-shifting back 150 years. It was generally accepted in America that it was okay for people to own enslaved Black people, and it was a no-brainer that they should not be allowed to use the same washrooms as the whites. Those who think that consciousness changes overnight should consider that until 1978, The Church of Jesus Christ of Latter-day Saints (LDS Church) had a policy that prevented most men of African descent from being ordained to the church's lay priesthood or from participating in some temple ordinances.

Looking back over 150 years, it was a general belief by both men and women that only men should be allowed to vote. Women had limited access to education. Women's place was in the home and not in the workforce. It was their job to make babies and raise the family. They were subservient to their husbands. Who would dare say that in public today? Calls for gay rights 150 years ago were unheard of. Those participating in male homosexuality were convicted of sodomy which was a serious felony and often a capital crime. There were still many who believed that such people should be executed. Female homosexuality was unheard of (During the obscenity trial in 1928 for the first lesbian novel by Radcliffe Hall called 'The Well of Loneliness,' the judges asked to have lesbianism explained in court so that the jury would know what it was). Gay marriage was an issue that took even longer until the public consciousness changed. It was not until 2012 that Rush Limbaugh, the voice of conservative America, said it was over and that the conservatives should let them have it. The problem is that people want change yesterday because they live in a world of instant gratification. Consciousness does change, but it doesn't happen overnight. A look at any political or social movement over 150 years will drive that point home.

I hope the following tales will raise consciousness and entertain you simultaneously. If either is achieved, my 40 years of chasing this incredible mystery will not have been in vain.

-Grant Cameron

CHAPTER 1

ODDS AND ENDS STORIES

The Pole Deer Story

Over the years, I have written many articles. Like any author, I have written articles that I thought were very important and wanted the whole world to read. On the other hand, I have published articles that I did not see as important. I posted them on my website as odd stories I wrote merely to entertain. The strange thing is that the essential stories got the least attention. On the other hand, the stories that I regarded as insignificant set off a firestorm of interest from time to time.

The following is just such a story. It is a story I posted on my PresidentialUFO Website in 2003. The bizarre case of a deer ended up on top of a hydro pole just outside the city of Winnipeg, where I live. Besides the fact that the poor deer ended up on the pole, the pictures clearly show that the deer's back feet were also mysteriously missing.

The pole deer story set off an interest that continued for years, even though the most-read stories on my website were only read for a few days before people got distracted and move on to read other new stories. This account was linked from one website to another, and the numbers reading it every day continued to grow.

The group most interested in the story was not the UFO community but an association of people who work on the hydro lines. Until I saw that group's messages coming up every day, I did not even realize that hydro-workers would belong to an association that would follow such things in their off-hours.

I am sure those reading it now will probably be taken with the same interest, maybe because it is the kind of story people like to talk about at the water cooler. But unfortunately, no plausible explanation was ever found for this bizarre incident.

In Delaware County, New York, there was the strange story of State Wildlife Experts and hunters trying to figure out how a dead deer wound up in a tree 12 feet off the ground. A man hunting in a remote area stumbled upon the strange sight while lost in a snowstorm on the opening day of deer season on November 18th. According to at least one report, the deer reportedly had been shot with an arrow. Many, including the Associated Press, ran with the strange story. The UFO community loves a good mystery, so they also picked up the story. Like everything else in Ufology, a spirited variance of opinion broke out among researchers as to the true nature of the deer incident. Science reporter Linda Moulton Howe also covered this story on her website www.earthfiles.com.

The strange story may have occurred once again. This time the incident occurred just outside of Winnipeg, Canada. We are a city of 700,000 people, just 60 miles north of the North Dakota border. Just outside my prairie city, photos of a deer on top of a utility pole have gone viral over the past few days. People are puzzled at what might have happened. Only the local *CBC TV* and radio stations had pursued the story. They interviewed a fellow who made a videotape of the 2-year-old deer up on the 25-foot pole. He reported that there were many witnesses to the bizarre sight and that Manitoba Hydro had removed the deer with a cherry picker, "It was pretty shocking," he said. *"I had never seen anything like that before."* CBC also featured an interview with a conservation officer stationed in the area of the event. He stated there was a deer trail quite close to the track and plenty of deer. The CBC witness assumed that the deer had been hit by a train, but he still expressed great amazement at how this could happen. Others who have seen the photos have questioned how part of the rear legs are missing from the animal and how a deer could be thrown up 25 feet by a fast-moving train and not be ripped apart. The deer appears to be untouched except for damage to the rear legs. There was no visible blood.

After the CBC story aired, I received an email from someone who claimed to have been there. The email was very accurate in terms of location and events. It was dated January 6 (even though the event occurred in December) and read as follows, *"Ft Garry had a call this AM that there was a deer up a pole, right? Sure enough, there was! This is right beside the tracks a few miles west of Headingly station. So they figure a train hit it and launched it up there."*

No one ever came forward claiming to have mounted the deer on the pole. On January 9, 2004, the local Winnipeg CBC affiliate talked to Chris Rutkowski, a public relations officer at the University of Manitoba, looking for any story releases. During that conversation, Chris asked if CBC had looked into the unrelated mystery of the deer on the pole. Fascinated with the idea, CBC began an investigation. During that inquiry, the station found a witness who had been to the site and had taken a videotape. This video confirmed that the photos I received by email were not hoaxes. The witness spoke to a conservation officer in Headingly, Manitoba, who speculated that the deer had been hit by a CNR train and launched to its position high up on the pole. This conservation officer stated that there was a deer trail quite close to the location of the incident. Questions, however, remained. When questioned, the Canadian National Railway indicated that they had received no reports from train engineers about someone hitting a deer in that area. Secondly, the train story did not explain why parts of both back legs were missing from the deer or how a deer could be hit hard enough to be projected to the top of a 25-foot pole while remaining totally intact. Thirdly, and most importantly, the question of how the deer got up there remained unresolved.

Dr. Jasper McKee, a physics professor at the University of Manitoba, was asked about the deer by CBC radio as part of a science segment he did on-air each week. McKee cast grave doubts about the train theory, *"Whether you could get it up to 20 or 25 feet, I would doubt."* McKee said, *"And whether the deer would wrap itself conveniently around the top of a hydro pole and miss all the wires, I have no idea that that would be likely."* McKee said that *"Although the train theory is not entirely impossible, the deer would have to have been hit at just the right time, at just the right angle, for things to have happened this way."* McKee then proposed his best guess, *"I would expect someone very shortly to call you up and say, 'Yeah, he's right. We found this deer by the railway tracks with its legs off. We got a rope and a pulley and hauled it up to the top, and we've been chuckling ever since.'"*

The chances of finding a definite solution to this mystery are diminished by the fact that the Manitoba Hydro officials who removed the deer destroyed the animal. However, perhaps now that the story is out in the local media, someone will come forward with crucial new information. Maybe we will soon receive new explanations from other cases, such as the one in New York, that could shed new light on this bizarre new mystery.

Chris Bledsoe: A Good Alien Story

Every alien bedtime storybook needs at least one good story of an encounter between a man and an alien. The Chris Bledsoe story is one of the best tales that could be told. This was a story that I was lucky enough to have been involved in.

Chris Bledsoe is a quiet and unassuming man from North Carolina. His wife, Yvonne, is much more talkative. Both talk a lot about their family and their four children: Chris Jr., Jeremy, Ryan, and Emily. In January 2007, Chris and four other witnesses had a dramatic series of UFO experiences. Chris realized that something more than a UFO sighting had taken place, and he felt driven to go for help to get answers. He realized he had been abducted by creatures called "The Guardians," and he thought he had been chosen to share the message with the world. Chris would go on to convey the message in the future. This article will only detail the events surrounding Chris, which I believe indicate a dramatic series of incidents meant to share publicity along with the message.

When the 2007 abduction happened, Chris was sick with incurable Crohn's disease. He was taking over a dozen prescription medications each day. He had sold his 15-18 million dollar a year house-building business as he was told that he was too sick and would end up dead if he kept it. The one last house that Chris was helping build was for a brother-in-law. Three of the subcontractors had finished up and had come to Chris's place to get paid. They also wanted to celebrate, so Chris, his oldest son, who was 17 then, and the three men went fishing in a valley along the Cape Fear River in North Carolina, a few miles away from his house. Chris was not feeling well and did not fish. He instead decided to walk up the hill out of the valley and look for wildlife.

At the top of the hill, he saw two objects that looked like two setting suns. He became terrified and began trying to hide from the objects when a third object appeared through what appeared to be a "tear in the sky." At that point, Chris knew they had seen him. And suddenly, 15 minutes later, he was jogging back to the river where his son and the men were fishing. In reality, he had been gone for over 5 hours! The men were upset and asked where he had been. As he told them it was no big deal, that he had just been to the top of the hill, he noticed that Chris was not with the men. The men said he had gone into the bush two hours earlier looking for him.

Searching the bush, Chris found Chris Jr. crying and very panicked. He told his dad he had been frozen in place by two small creatures with red, swimming, goggle-type eyes. Chris led him back to the campfire without telling his son what he had seen. At the camp, the other three men joked about what Chris and his son were reporting when one of the men suddenly yelled for everyone to glance up. It looked like a constellation of 8-9 stars was moving toward them. Then, the lights began to drop, and three objects floated to the ground, landing in the woods just across the river from the shocked men. At that point, the panic set in. Everyone raced for the truck without pulling the fishing lines from the water or putting out the fire. They headed up the hill out of the valley as fast as Chris could drive in total terror. The road was very narrow, and the trees' branches were scraping the sides of the truck. One of the men was screaming that one of the tiny creatures was on all fours chasing the vehicle and was about to grab the tailgate. Chris Jr. told me the creature could move *"faster than any animal on earth."* They cleared the crest of the hill in the air, but their race to get away was over. The creature chasing them was gone, but one of the objects Chris had seen earlier was hovering a couple of feet off the road blocking their escape route.

The UFOs and at least one alien now surrounded them. The men noticed a small trailer with a TV visible through the screen door and cars in the driveway to their right. Knowing this was a chance to get a witness, they honked the horn and banged on the front door. No one answered, even though the man claimed the next day he had been there the whole time. The men were left staring at the object blocking the road when three gunshots went off. Someone was shooting at the object, slowly rising from the road and directly at the truck. The panic in the vehicle increased as the three workers fought among themselves about who would be dropped off first. Finally, the object shot off after barely clearing the truck's roof and the trees behind them. Chris said it was so close that he could have hit it with a slingshot.

The escape down the road to get home began, but the show was not over. Two objects appeared to the left over the trees that were pacing the truck. First, there was a large clearing where the trees had been cut down on the right. One of the men reported it was lit up like the 4th of July. The men were convinced that the world was coming to an end. They wondered why the military forces from nearby Fort Bragg weren't coming to their defense. Then they went to a familiar curve in the road. This spot was where Chris's first wife died in a rollover car accident, and Chris, at age 10, had been shot from six feet away with a shotgun. Near this spot, a vast triangle-shaped UFO was hovering 50 feet above the line over a set of high-tension lines. Chris was curious and wanted to stop and watch, but the truck's others had none. They yelled for him not to stop.

Once Chris had dropped off the three men, Chris and Jr. returned home to an empty house as Yvonne and the other children were out of town. There had been a total of at least 15 UFOs and three creatures seen. The show, however, was far from over. When he got home, one of the three subcontractors reported seeing the being with red eyes in the bush behind the house. Back at home Chris Jr. was turning the house into a fortress. All the outside floodlights were on. He had locked the doors, closed all the windows, and closed the curtains. This silence lasted about 30 minutes. Then, his father's hunting dogs began an unusual, strange barking next door. Something had spooked them. With Chris Jr. protesting, Chris Sr. headed out to see if someone had broken into his father's work shed.

The dogs were all looking toward the bush behind the two yards, so Chris sent his dog Rose into the bush to flush out the person. He quickly ran around to the north side of the bush area where the intruder would exit. He was utterly winded when he arrived at a large oak tree at the edge of the bush. He leaned against the tree to catch his breath. Rose was still barking and headed through the bush in his direction. Looking behind for Chris Jr., he saw the same 3-foot-tall creature his son had described hours earlier. Chris, at that point, spoke to the creature, *"I give up. You got me."* And for almost a minute, the two stared at each other. The alien vanished as Rose exited the bush and continued north, chasing something. Saying nothing, Chris returned to the house. Wanting to smoke a cigarette, he lifted the blind to open a window as Jr. insisted that his dad stays in the house. He didn't get the chance. In the floodlights of the house, there was a tall 7' human-like creature coming towards the window!

It was time to run again. The father and son ran for the truck. Before leaving, they pulled the vehicle up to the bedroom window of Chris's father next door to report what was happening. His awakened father, Ted, thought they had lost their minds and told them to go back to bed. The two spent the rest of the night in a hayfield four miles away.

At that point, Chris realized he had forgotten his Crohn's medication in the house. He, however, did not feel sick anymore, especially considering it had been many hours since he had last taken a pill. He would take no more pills from that day on. The incurable Crohn's had disappeared.

Despite the cure, Chris and his son's lives fell apart. Chris was holed up in the family room for the next ten months. Chris Jr. retreated to his bedroom with the door closed for the next six months. Yvonne was so concerned over what had happened to her husband that she had him committed to a mental unit. Chris finally got discharged, and he and Yvonne no longer discussed what had happened. Chris was not allowed to speak to the children either about the incident. At one point, Chris and Yvonne separated. Chris knew inside that he had to report the incident and filled one out to MUFON. He couldn't bring himself to submit the report for two weeks, realizing that his marriage might be over once he did that. The urge to report his experience, however, was overwhelming. Something was pushing him to get the message out. Finally, Chris gave in and pressed the send button. The healing began.

In July 2008, Dr. Michael O'Connor would do a regression on Chris, describing the same 7-foot tall bluish-green creatures he had seen outside the window the first night. During the session, he learned that the smaller creatures with red eyes were children. He would find out that he had promised the beings that he would take care of his family and deliver the message to the world. An extensive investigation by MUFON and a TV show produced by the Discovery Channel would set things back. Chris's Southern Baptist Pentecostal community's reaction was not positive. They interpreted the creatures as being demonic. Chris's children were bullied at school. Chris Jr. dropped out and ran away from home to escape the story. Chris stopped talking about the message he was given. That lasted until February 2012 and November 2012, when Chris had two encounters with the "Shining lady."

In the second series of incidents, four 7-foot aliens took him on a trip through space to meet with the lady. She was blond and beautiful, wearing a long white dress, and sitting upon a high platform in a darkened valley. Her radiance was lighting up the area. The four creatures bowed to the shining lady and then walked away, leaving Chris in front of her. *"You have a burden,"* she told Chris, *"and it is yours to carry."* While visiting him in North Carolina, I asked him what the burden was. *"The burden is the message,"* Chris told me. *"I have been given a message to give to the world. It is my burden to deliver it."* He began to deliver this message a couple of days after the first shining lady encounter at a MUFON meeting in Ashville, North Carolina. As he talked, something came into his mind, *"Tell them there will be an earthquake in Baja, California on Sept 25th, and a natural disaster will affect the upcoming election."* Chris did as he was told. Both the earthquake and hurricane Sandy arrived to fulfill the prediction. The unfortunate events gave Chris confidence in his mission.

Many more bizarre events will be part of the final story, told in a book and a Hollywood movie. These include an incredible account regarding a burning tree in Chris's backyard. The tree burning from the inside three times in six hours and after two days of rain. The tree started burning after a series of 'bottle rocket' type-events appeared at the bottom of the trees. Each time the tree began to burn, Chris and Yvonne would put it out with a garden hose, only to have it start up again a few hours later. The event is impossible by known physical laws. A UFO depression in the yard was discovered near the tree, which had caused it to die in 2007. Branches started falling off; the tree appeared to be dying. Then one night in October 2012, the tree started on fire. The outside of the tree received no fire damage. Only the inside of the tree burned. The flames shot 15-20 feet out of the top of the tree like a volcano during the event. Yet, there is nothing wrong with the tree. It grows just like all the other trees in the yard. It just has an inside that is all burned. A second oak tree that Chris had been leaning against when he encountered the small alien with red eyes on the first night of the 2007 abduction event did die. Not only did the tree die, but most branches fell off.

When Chris tried to photograph a nearby golden glowing object, a camera started to produce melted pictures. (See Chapter 6: *The Alien's Melted Pictures*)

In May 2013, during a visit I made to Chris's house, his dog Nellie suddenly started bleeding profusely from her neck as we entered the house. The blood was shooting out like an artery was hit. There was no evidence of anything in the yard that could have caused the cut. Both Chris and I were standing near the dog when the incident occurred. It stopped as suddenly as it had started. Nellie seemed unfazed by what had happened. Chris and his father checked Nellie's neck later and reported that they could find no wound.

The most bizarre event occurred in 2008 and involved a 4-foot-tall painting that Chris painted of the 7-foot tall bluish aliens. This was the clearest sign that the aliens wanted a message out. Yvonne didn't want it on the wall, so it had been in storage. I photographed it when I visited in May 2013. It looked familiar, but a couple of months later, I realized that it was precisely the same alien that appeared in the 2002 "Crabwood" crop circle along with the binary-ASCII message that accompanied it. Chris had never seen the crop circle until I showed it to him.

As various parties prepare to tell the Bledsoe story in a movie and a book, the sightings around the house continue to be experienced by all family members and visitors alike. There have also been reports of helicopters, as seen by Chris Bledsoe's father. He watched a helicopter hover only a few feet over the Bledsoe house for several minutes while sitting on his backyard swing, swiftly flying away. Many UFOs have been filmed on cell phone cameras, but few films have become public. *"I know they can hear us. I am positive. I know for sure, even our thoughts."* Chris said as he showed me a late 2014 video of an object moving near the house and just over the trees.

Grant Cameron

Figure 1 Chris Bledsoe discusses his experiences

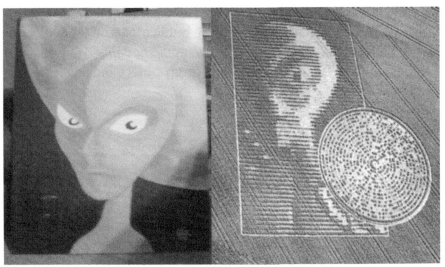

Figure 2 Left: A painting Chris did of one of the beings he encountered. Right: A very similar crop formation in Crabwood that appeared in 2002

Alien Bedtime Stories

Figure 3 The Burning Tree

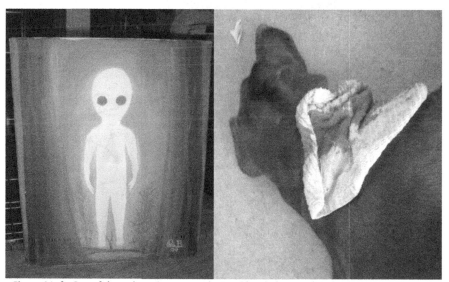

Figure 4 Left: One of the red-eyed creatures depicted by Bledsoe. Right: Chris's dog Nellie who started to bleed for no apparent reason during my visit

Grant Cameron

Figure 5 The Bledsoe Family

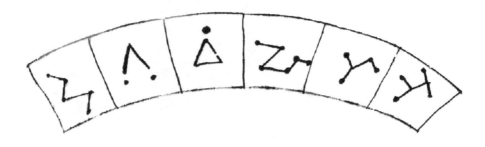

Figure 6 Symbols that Chris recalled from the console of an alien craft during his abduction

Alien Bedtime Stories

Figure 7 These 2 photos are some of the pieces of metal that Chris received from an orb flying 11 feet off the ground, dripping this molten metal.

Figure 8 This piece, which is flat on one side, is being analyzed now

Figure 9 "When it hit the concrete driveway, it was hot and cooled very quickly."

This is the transcript of the two-hour regression with Chris Bledsoe Sr. minus the induction.

Dr. Michael O'Connell conducted the regression on July 14, 2008. Chris had been suffering for 18 months from splitting headaches every time he tried to recall the events of January 8, 2007. Dr. O'Connell used five minutes of neuro-linguistic programming to eliminate the headaches, which miraculously disappeared.

Chris: (Sniffling softly) *Don't touch me* (sniffling more). *Get away.* (Frightened). *Don't touch me. Don't. Where are we going? Where am I? I'm in the sky. I am... It's high.*

Michael: You're OK. You're OK.

Chris: Is it awake? (More with parade and sniffling) ... *Don't... I don't know where I am... It's dark... Noise...*

Michael: Tell me about the noise.

Chris: Don't do it. I feel it. I feel it inside my body. It's vibrating... Dark... why me?... A cold walk... Where are we going? ... Where am I?... I am in the sky... A light... I couldn't move... It came over... I was hiding. It came over. I could reach over and touch it.... It paralyzed me... Somebody help me.

Michael: Can you see anything?

Chris: I could see the stars. I can see the stars. I made the stars. Like when I was 12. I'm in a row. It's dark, but it's like I'm looking through glass. I see stars there were around me. Around me, above me. I don't know how I got here.

Chris's description of where he was taken during the fishing trip was virtually identical to the description of where he had been taken after he was shot at age ten and was lying face down in the dirt.

Michael: Are you in a room?

Chris: I'm in a room. It feels like a room. I could hear the echo of, like, breathing. I don't know how I got here. They got me. There's a light. Orange bowls. There are two of them. They grab me. I got to know what it was that grabbed me. There's another one. It saw me. I looked at the other one, changing colors and shapes. It's over my head. Paralyzed me. Now, where I'm at, I see the stars. I could hear myself breath. It's echoing like there's a wall. There are like walls, and I can see through them. The light over my head is shining down on me. What's going to happen?

Michael: What do they look like?

Chris: I see them. They're tall. Tall and scary. I can't move. They're reaching for me. Tall.

Michael: What that they look like?

Chris: They've got long arms. Long fingers. There are not speaking. They're looking at me. Four of them.

Michael: They're looking at you with their eyes?

Chris: Uh-huh.

Michael: What are their eyes look like?

Chris: They are black. Big. I'm just... Scared. Tall. Very tall and skinny. I'm scared. I just wanna find my son.

Michael: Are they still touching you?

Chris: Yeah. They are around me.

Michael: Four of them?

Chris: Uh-huh. That is what it's called. I want to go. Oh, I see my son. See, he's OK. See, they are watching after him. What do you want? Why me? I love my family. Please take me home. They're talking with me.

Michael: What are they saying?

Chris: Strong. Promise.

Michael: Are they telling you to be strong?

Chris: Uh-huh. They're telling me not to worry. Why me? All my life? My son's life. Promise. All be strong for them. I know. I know. Tell them not to worry. Hard. OK. I love my family. I'll calm down. Why? Why? Why was I chosen? Where are we?

Michael: Are they telling you why you were chosen?

Chris: Uh-huh.

Michael: What reason was that?

Chris: Since birth. Before birth. It's possible. Everything is possible. They're my Guardians. Every time I get sad, they are here. I know I was sad. Promise. Promise.

Michael: Ask them if they helped you when you were shot as a little kid.

Chris: When I was shot, was it you? Uh-huh. I'm in the same place. So soothing. I can see the stars. Everything. I remember. I remember. Remember Montana. OK. Kids. Somebody's children. Those children too? OK. I'm trying. I'm trying to calm down. Tall. My children are tall.

The 'Remember Montana' reference was in reference to a hunting trip that Chris and his dad took in 2003. It was a family trip. It included Chris, his Dad Ted, Ted's brother and his two sons, Chris's wife Yvonne's two brothers, and a neighbor. They hired a guide for the trip. But the members of the hunting party and their guide were separated, and Chris wasn't in contact with any of them. While he was alone, he saw a very large UFO at a low altitude zoom over his head and disappear.

Michael: What are you promising them?

Chris: To protect and look after my family. I'll do everything in my power to help my mom and dad and the other people. I know I have to be strong. I'm just scared. I've had these dreams all my life. I couldn't sleep because of the dreams. Am I dreaming now? Un-huh. My son, my children. I just want to find him. I'll calm down. OK. And I'm scared. I don't want any harm to come to him. And I was sad. Is that why you come? I cried a lot. Cried a lot. I just want to go home.

Michael: Are they still talking to you?

Chris: Like, they're talking to one another. I can't understand.

Michael: Are they paying any attention to you now?

Chris: I know they are, but it doesn't appear they are. They are. Skinny.

Michael: How tall are they?

Chris: Real tall. 7 feet or better. They look almost human in the face. And their eyes. Their eyes are big. They are not human. Not human. They look greenish and blue. Grayish blue, maybe. Paying attention to me. And I'm nervous.

Michael: What did the room look like?

Chris: It is round. It's dark. There's lights and controls on one side to my right hand and ahead. Colored lights like a console. Like computers or something. It's like glass. You can see through it. Lights are not shining over my head like it was. I can see below, above, the stars in every direction. Glow from the controls. Nobody was sitting at them. They're just talking. Night.

Michael: What is their attitude towards you? How did they feel about you?

Chris: Feels like cares, concern. No expression. I can hear them talking. I don't see their mouths moving. I can hear the voices, and I know they're talking about me. They want me to calm down. They're trying to make me feel comfortable. You were assigned to me? They were with me before I was born. They take care of certain people. In my mind all along, I just didn't know it. Are you talking to me? Wow. They say in times of trouble, they are here for me. They are concerned, and they are here all along. I just never knew it. They're talking to me. Wow. I didn't know that. A voice. A silent voice. I always knew something was protecting me. I just felt that. I just knew things. Now, I better understand. Promise. I promise. I'll do my best. I promise, OK. I love my children; I do. All of them. I know these things. I've always been curious. I don't know. I just had a knack. Where are we? You're pure energy. How old are you? They've been here forever. That's a long time.

Michael: They've been here since before you were born? Were they with you in another lifetime?

Chris: Yes, before I was born. I didn't have to speak to talk to them. They're in my thoughts. Are you angels? Light. Creation. I believe in God. OK, I create you. Yes, they do everything. So, are you angels? Don't answer that. They just work for creation. Better. My son's fine.

Michael: Are they the same ones that you saw in your backyard later?

Chris: That's their children. They let them out to play.

Michael: In your backyard?

Chris: They come to take care of us. Teaching them. I want to go home. Why do they shine?

Michael: Are all their eyes black?

Chris: Uh-huh. They look alike.

Michael: To their children, do they look like their parents?

Chris: Yes, sort of. They're glowing. They have protection on.

Michael: Have they been in your home?

Chris: Regularly.

Michael: How long have they been there?

Chris: Since I was little. They're invisible.

Michael: If they're invisible, how do you know when they're in your home?

Chris: *I just knew. I wondered what I was.*

Michael: Are they with you now?

Chris: *Uh-huh. They're looking after me.*

Michael: Are they Guardians for your family? Are they looking after your entire family?

Chris: *Yes. And they have been for generations. I never knew that. I just wondered.*

Michael: How does that make you feel?

Chris: *Happy. Relaxed. It's like electricity. The hair stands up on my arms and legs.*

Michael: Were they the beings with the red eyes?

Chris: *The children have red eyes. That's protection. They have a suit on. Transparent. Glass. Learning. They're learning about us. Lifeguards.*

Michael: Why are they wearing them?

Chris: *They travel everywhere. It is a different world. They wear them until a certain age. Learn to use their abilities. There's not just one universe.*

Michael: There are other universes?

Chris: *That's what they say. Other dimensions.*

Michael: Do they come from other universes, other dimensions?

Chris: *They can go anywhere. Through time. Other dimensions. I promise*

Michael: Are they talking to you again?

Chris: *Yes.*

Michael: Where is their home?

Chris: *No place we know of. Dimension. Just a second away. Whenever they want to be here.*

Michael: Why did they come here to this earth?

Chris: *To learn. To learn balance. It's almost like a garden to them.*

Michael: What is it that they balance?

Chris: *Existing life of all kinds. Everything. To measure all the details. For eons, they've been doing that. Not just here. Lots* of places. In the blink of an eye. There in and out. I'm tired, and I wanna go home.

Michael: Where's your home, Chris?

Chris: Far away. Beyond Andromeda.

Michael: Do you have a family there?

Chris: It's sad, very sad.

Michael: You're still learning now.

Chris: Uh-huh. I want to see my son

Michael: Are they ready to let you go home?

Chris: They told me you can go whenever I can always go home.

Michael: How did you get from that place back to the road?

Chris: They brought me back.

Michael: How did they do that?

Chris: They brought me back to the ground.

Michael: Did they land?

Chris: No, it didn't touch the ground, but it was just above the ground. I see the spikes—the twinkle.

Michael: So, you are back on the road now?

Chris: Uh-huh.

Michael: What did you do then?

Chris: I was looking for my son. I was frightened. Walk through the mud. Everyone's frightened.

Michael: All the other men?

Chris: Yes, they're scared. They get in the car. We have to stay. Go, go, go. Let's go. Just leave it. Screaming. Quit yelling. I got to drive, so I'll get you home. I've seen it. This is what I was telling you about. Come down. The quiet. Calm down. I saw those lights. I saw them. They scared me. I got to drive. I'm going as fast as I can go. We're not going to get there no faster with your screaming. I would get us home. I'm doing the best I can. I want to get home as bad as you do. Lights everywhere. Huge. They've got to be following us. I'll take you home. Just be quiet. We've got all the children. I'm driving. I'll drop you off. Whichever one wins the fight goes *first. Just be quiet. Glad to be home. I just saw the white ones and the orange ones. Sit down. Catch my breath.*

The Roswell Live Alien Story

Some in the UFO community believe there is no good evidence that UFOs represent aliens from another planet. They assert that those who promote disclosure of the ET presence, such as Washington disclosure lobbyist Steven Bassett, are out of line and are damaging the possibility that science will ever take the subject seriously. The researchers claiming, *"There is no evidence,"* maintain that the word 'UFO' must remain the standard, as the objects are unidentified, and that is all we know. Whenever I hear this conservative dogma in public, I see it as a new type of 21st-century racism. It is a racism, not of skin color or religion but a belief that there is something intrinsically wrong with anyone who believes that they have experienced something that confirms that there is an extraterrestrial presence here on earth. Their stories can immediately be marginalized, and their claims require no further investigation.

When I hear the 'no evidence' statement, I immediately think, *"What about the people who claim that they have had an 'interaction with the live alien' story?"* There are scores of such people. This means that either everyone is deluded or lying, or they are like the rest of the people in society, just trying to tell as best as possible what they experienced. Most importantly, it only takes one person out of all the people telling the story to end the 67-year-old extraterrestrial debate. It only takes one of the ET stories to be true to establish that UFOs represent extraterrestrial visitation firmly.

There are many sources for the live alien story. The main collection of stories comes from the 1947 Roswell UFO crash story. The research was done by various researchers who have researched the crash report witnesses reporting that one alien survived the crash.

The story is consistent, involving the same number of live aliens being recovered; the number is always one. For example, there is a story about Herbert Ellis, a painting contractor at Roswell Army Airfield, who saw a live alien. He testified that he *"saw a live alien walking"* into the Roswell Army Airfield Hospital.

Then there is Sheriff George Wilcox, who saw the live alien at the crash site before it was taken to the hospital. According to what his wife, Inez, told her granddaughter, Barbara Dugger, *"There was a spacecraft, a flying saucer, that crashed outside Roswell,"* Dugger recalled her grandmother saying. *"There was a big burned area, and he saw debris. He also saw four 'space beings.' One of the little men was moving."*

Joseph Montoya, Lt. Governor of New Mexico, told Peter Anaya that he had *"Four little men."* One of them was still alive. He stated that they had oversized heads with big eyes. Their mouths were small, like a cut across a piece of wood.

Dan Dwyer claimed he saw the live alien as well. When he got home on the day of the crash recovery, he told his family about what he had seen that day. The story included an encounter with a live alien. His family asked, *"Were you able to talk to it?"* He answered that he could but:

> Not in the normal way. We talked to one another 'in our heads' without moving our lips. I wanted to know if it was all right. It told me not to worry, that it knew its comrades were dead and that it had accepted its fate of being stranded. It was more concerned about me than I was of it. It wanted to reassure me that it would be all right.

The four sons of Lt. Col. Marion M. Magruder said their father, on his deathbed for the second time, told the story of an encounter with a live alien at Wright Field, Ohio, in mid or late July 1947. He attended Air War College at Maxwell Field, Montgomery, Alabama, along with the best high-ranking officers in various services, including generals. They were flown to Wright Field, and the surprised officers were told about the recovery to Wright Field of an extraterrestrial spaceship that had crashed just two weeks previously. The wreckage was brought out for them to examine.

Then they were taken to another room and shown a surviving alien. Magruder first talked about this encounter with a live alien on the night of the first Moon landing in July 1969 while gathered around the TV set with his sons (there were five of them). The boys asked him about space and if he believed aliens were out there. He replied that he was sure because he had seen a live alien many years earlier. McGruder's deathbed account was told for the benefit of his granddaughter, Natalie, who had come to see granddad. He stated that the alien was under 5 feet tall, human-like but with longer arms and bigger eyes. The head was oversized with no hair, a slit for a mouth, and no real nose or ears. He said that he 'hooked up' mentally with the creature through no effort of his own. The experience was almost trance-like. Magruder stated, *"We had done experiments on the alien, and that we ended up killing it."*

It was the same story that another live alien witness, Roswell photographer Jack Rodden Sr, had told his son many years ago.[1] Another witness, Air Force JAG officer Griffin Stuart, in a death bed statement, stated that the alien had been held on the base for some time.

Authors Carey and Schmitt heard many stories about the live alien during their decades of research on Roswell. However, none of those stories had the live alien going along with his dead comrades. Instead, the stories had it going to White Sands near Alamogordo, where captured German V-2 rockets were being tested, to Los Alamos or Sandia near Albuquerque, where atomic research was being conducted, or that it never made it out of Roswell alive.[2]

Even before the Roswell live alien testimony was made public, Dr. Eric Walker, President at Penn State University from 1956 to 1971, hinted that there may have been a living alien.[3] He was being pressed in interviews about the alien bodies and autopsies that had been done, to which he replied, *"How do you know there were bodies? Maybe they walked away. You assume too many things."* When questioned about aliens walking away, he shot back, *"Most of the things are wrong."* Then he laughed again:

> *You jump to hasty conclusions. Maybe some walked away. Maybe some did not walk away, as I say. It is none of your business. Just to satisfy your curiosity is not going to do any damn good except to make you happy. Is it not true? Are we going to change the rules and regulations just to make you happy? If you say you are looking for the truth, you will never get it, so forget it.*

The Aztec Live Alien

Many may not be aware that Frank Scully, the Hollywood journalist who wrote the story of the 1948 Aztec flying saucer crash in his book, *Behind the Flying Saucers*, had received leads about live aliens. One story told of a 3.5-foot human-type alien held along with his craft at Muroc Air Base, where Eisenhower would have his famous rumored encounter with aliens in February 1954.

According to Scully's sources, in his book about the Aztec UFO crash, all 16 aliens died in the crash. Despite this, Scully received a letter in 1952 from Francis L Kelsey from New York. Kelsey tells a story about a live alien in New Mexico in the letter. Enclosed with the letter was a report entitled, *The story behind the book; Behind the Flying Saucers*.

The book *Behind the Flying Saucers* by Frank Scully has a sequel that is just as fantastic as any of the lines in the book and either bears out his statements if they are true or adds to the hoax if hoax it is.

> *Last July, my wife and my daughter Joan and I were motoring from New York to Reno, Nevada, and were in*

the eastern part of Nevada on the last leg of the trip, in the desert, when we saw a car stopped on the roadside. As it was miles in either direction to any town or even any habitation, we stopped to see if there was any trouble and if we could help. When I approached the stopped car on foot, a young man, about 27, crawled out from under it with an open-end wrench in one hand and a screwdriver in the other. He was dressed in well-tailored slacks and a sports shirt, both of which, as well as his face, smudged with dust and muddy grease. I asked if we could be of any help, and he replied that he had found the trouble and would be able to correct it himself. I then offered him a bottle of orange aide, with which we were well supplied, and we all had some with him. While we had the refreshments, Joan and the young man were having quite a chat. I noticed that the backseat compartment of his car contained one suitcase and several black and brown, rich leather cases, some with shoulder straps and some with substantial handles. The cases did not look like those carried by traveling salesmen but rather more like cases containing high-class photographic or other technical equipment. There was also a very unique-looking tripod in chrome, with elevation and angle adjustments. None of this seemed important to me at the time.

After we got on our way again, my daughter informed me that the young man, whom I shall call Mr. Fee, had learned from her where she was going to stay in Reno and had asked permission to call upon her during her stay there. Here I might add that we knew where she was going to stay, for I had sat in a lawyer's office in Ossining with her while he put a phone call through to Reno to make the arrangements.

I saw no more of Mr. Fee while out West as my wife and I stayed in a tourist cabin on the outskirts of town for the two-week period and then returned to our home in New York, leaving Joan behind there. A couple of months later, Joan returned to our home in New York and got a job in the city. It was then that she told me that Mr. Fee had called upon her several times in Reno and that he had taken her on tours to various resort places in the vicinity. I heard all this, and I was but mildly interested until she mentioned quite casually that Mr. Fee had said that he was formally in Army Intelligence. This information was a little more than mildly interesting to me because I, too, had been in Army Intelligence way back in the days when our only equipment was a pencil.

Another two months passed, and Mr. Fee showed up in New York and was invited to spend a couple of days and nights at our home. Again, he came dressed in slacks and a sport shirt, and although the weather was getting quite snappy, he did not wear a coat or tie. During his visit, I learned that he was a very personable young fellow and willing to talk briefly on almost any subject that came up. He never seemed to care to talk about himself, and if he did, it was in a reserved, even restrained manner. He had driven here from Nevada (or New Mexico) in his own car and was on his way to Boston on business. He had more trouble with his car on his way across the country, and, as before, he made his own repairs on the way with his own tools. He still had the very technical-looking equipment in the back-seat compartment, which I noticed he kept well locked at all times. At meals with us, he discussed the possibility of war, its possible course, and its outcome. To my untrained mind, he seemed exceptionally well-informed on the subject from every angle, particularly any angle involving military equipment such as radar, airplanes, and jets. I learned that he would travel in his car to

Boston and that later he would be required to make frequent long trips in the car, the nature of which I never learned. He mentioned that he had never traveled in any kind of public conveyance. This was easy to believe because I do not either if I can avoid it.

Sometime later, we received word from our friend in Boston that he would like to return here for a short visit. Of course, such a pleasant and informed young gentleman was perfectly welcome. He came, and in his car, which still possessed the leather case locked in the back. During this visit, we discussed everything from the latest vitamins and sulfas to the intricate working of hydramatic drives. The conversations certainly included flying saucers, and Mr. Fee did most of the talking, but as I was not extremely interested, I cannot remember to this day just what he said. But now, a story was getting ready to break. During the discourse on flying saucers, my daughter was unusually quiet. I thought at the time that her reserve was due to a lack of interest. I found out later it was no such thing but a determination not to betray a trust.

Later, Joan presented me with the book "Behind the Flying Saucers" by Frank Scully. I read the book twice before laying it down and then wrote a letter to Mr. Scully, mentioning some of the possibilities which I suggested that he may have overlooked. However, after studying the book for several days, I came to the conclusion that it was a hoax. Although very interesting reading, I could not swallow it hook, line and sinker without more substantial evidence than had been presented, and I think that a large part of readers felt the same.

During our friend's second visit, Joan invited him to return here for Christmas Holidays, and he accepted. So, it was all set, but just as we were getting ready to start the decorations, she received word from him that he would be unable to be with us as he had to return to New Mexico at once, but that he would be here again in about two weeks. At this time, I suggested to Joan that I felt our friend had not only been in Army Intelligence but, in my opinion, still was. She replied that she did not know but thought that he might be a very high-class accountant. I then commented that all FBI. Agents are lawyers or accountants, or they have some other special training; they are versatile and can shoot accurately from speeding cars, make repairs under adverse conditions, contrive and install secret starters, instantly render criminals' cars inoperative, and perform other various tricks that would have interested Houdini. Her eyes suddenly sparkled with enthusiasm and her face twisted into a peculiar sort of cunning; she began to slowly and hesitantly unfold a story about Mr. Fee, who was, as it turns out, working on highly secret assignments.

Frank Scully did not get all the facts. So, the story goes, the ship from outer space, which the lecturer at Denver College had mentioned as the 'one that got away,' had not gotten away completely with all its cargo and passengers. The little men had landed and left the ship and set up an elaborate signal system with which they planned to signal their home planet. Two of the little men were operating the signal set, and the rest of the crew had started back to the ship. Surprised by our field party, they embarked and took flight, leaving the two little men behind. The field force had found them after Mr. Scully's Mr. Fee had left the area, had captured them with all the signal equipment, and had taken them to a headquarters building for examination. The little men are still alive and thriving.

Alien Bedtime Stories

Mr. Fee was not a field man but spent his time in the building assisting in investigations after the field man had produced the evidence. There were ten scientists on the staff. Each was a specialist in his work. The little men were shown a drawing of our solar system and asked by sign language if their home was among our planets. They denied this and illustrated that they came from another solar system. Their radios could not be used over such a great distance and were only used to communicate from ship to ship when in flight. They did not use nor understand our nods and shakes of the head. Their eye expressions and facial movements served them for all ordinary conversations, which they spoke much as we do, but almost in whispers because they have very keen hearing.

The beings were astonishingly brilliant and mastered our language in a few days so that it became easy to exchange thoughts with them (Author's note: Consider what Dr. Eric Walker said in his Sept 23, 1987 letter to Steinman; "They were highly intelligent. They learned the English language in a few hours"). Compared to them, our own Einstein is a moron. They know the age of our planet and the age of the planet from whence they came. They have a full understanding of atomic science and used it more than ten thousand years ago but discarded it for magnetic power, which they have mastered completely. Magnetic power, they said, is easy to harness and inexhaustible. There never were any wars on their planet; there are but one people and no differences.

They were allowed to complete the signals to their planet and were requested to invite visitors from there to come and land at a designated secret spot (probably in Nevada). Although brilliant, they seemed unable to understand the government as we know it. It was

> *learned from them that they could not approve of a Communistic State or even our type of Democracy. Our investigators could not understand just how they live but thought perhaps in some sort of Anarchy, which would be possible among a people with the character and disposition of those little men. This story was told to my daughter Joan in confidence, and she was pledged not to repeat it, but she did, and I do, and I will repeat it again and again, true or false.*

Area 51 Live Alien

There are stories of a live alien being held at Area 51. These stories have come from a series of witnesses, including scientist Bob Lazar who claimed to have worked for a short time at an area known as S-4 just south of Area 51. He claimed he had been part of a back-engineering team flying saucers. In one trip to the bathroom accompanied by his security officer, Lazar caught sight of what appeared to be a smaller, grey-type alien through a window into a lab. The alien appeared to be talking to two lab coats wearing scientists facing him. When he returned from the bathroom, nothing was visible in the lab. It was the only encounter Lazar had with what might have been a live alien. In later retellings of the story, Lazar even questioned whether or not he had seen such a thing.

Lazar's story was backed up by a high-level Area 51 official who had been on the base since the first atomic bomb tests were being done. After six months of clandestine meetings with KLAS-TV reporter George Knapp, he finally confirmed that all the stories were true. There was work at Area 51 to back engineer saucers, and there had been a live alien on the base. The alien, who looked like Ross Perot, could not communicate with the scientists until they worked out a way to communicate. Area 51 officials were always afraid that the saucer work would get out but that the alien might escape. This witness went silent after being questioned by Dick D'Amato, who had gone to Area 51 on behalf of Senator Bird and other Senators on the Senate Appropriations Committee, who were curious if they were funding flying saucer research at Area 51. If they were providing the funding; no one had taken the time to brief them, so they sent in an investigator to check.

Later D'Amato would take Jesse Marcel Jr., whose father was the security officer at Roswell at the time of the crash, into a secure room in Senate Building 228. D'Amato said, *"I want to tell you something."* There was a book on the table called *Majestic* by Whitley Strieber. Pointing at the book D'Amato said:

> *This is not fiction, there is a black government, and they control the debris. These people answer to no one, and they collect it. They are not elected, and they have unlimited funds to spend. They are the ones who have it. They have control over it.*[4]

Others surfaced, stating they had worked at the base and had interacted with the live alien being stored there.

The EBE Live Alien

There are many stories told of the live alien that was a guest of the American government in the late 1980s. It appeared that United States intelligence wanted this story out, or they, for some reason, wanted everyone to believe it. The list of rumors surrounding this extraterrestrial biological entity (EBE) as it was being described began to grow.

Many people during this time were being offered interviews with the EBE. Included was Whitley Strieber, who published the prominent abduction book *Communion* in February 1987. Writer, reporter, and documentary producer Linda Howe was also offered an interview, but the two that got the closest to the discussion were Bill Moore and Jamie Shandera. They received information from a dozen government intelligence contacts in the late eighties.

Bob Emenegger and his producer partner Allen Sandler were also offered an interview. Still, later, Emenegger expressed skepticism over all the people who had been contacted to talk with this live alien. Furthermore, he evidenced that the interview never took place, so I asked him who had made the offer to him. He replied that his offer of an interview had come from Paul Shartle, the security director at Norton AFB, who had arranged for Emenegger and Sandler to do the 1975 UFO documentary: *UFOs, Past, Present, and Future.* "Was Shartle reliable?" I asked. Emenegger answered in the affirmative, meaning that his offer came from someone who had been reliable.

On an October 1988 live nationally broadcast documentary called *UFO Cover-Up Live,* which played to a large, live national audience, the UFO community sat on the edge of their seats watching the whole thing, which had been hyped as a major disclosure event. Richard Doty was taped for the show, backlit, and altered his voice. That was for the audience. He talked about an alien who was a guest of the United States government. The alien, he said, liked Tibetan music and strawberry ice cream. It was all very secret and very dramatic.

The John Lennon UFO Story

The Beatles will undoubtedly go down in history as the most significant musical group ever. John Lennon, who started the group in the fifties, will probably go down in history as the driving force behind the group. The group started as the Quarry Men. Paul McCartney was invited into the group by John, who was impressed with his talent, and Paul brought in George Harrison. Later, these three replaced drummer Pete Best with Ringo Starr; the rest was history. Many don't know that UFOs played a role in John Lennon's life, and

Alien Bedtime Stories

he may have been an abductee based on some of the things that have been reported about his experiences.

The first thing to consider related to aliens is the band's name. The band was initially called The Quarry Men, which changed to Johnny and the Moondogs, then The Rainbows. Most histories concede that the name Beatles came from John. John liked the name The Crickets (from Buddy Holly's band), and the story is that based on this, John's friend Stuart Sutcliffe suggested the name The Beetles. So they changed it to The Beatles with an A instead of an E. When Lennon was asked how the band got its name, he would reference a dream that he had, *"I had a vision that a man came unto us on a flaming pie and told us,"* Lennon would say, *"You are Beatles with an 'A.' And so we were."*

Those who have studied abductees or experiencers will immediately pick up the flaming pie as a screen image for a glowing red flying saucer used by the aliens to get across a message while masking the true nature of who they were. This interpretation is supported by John's later accounts of close encounters with UFOs. There was also the album produced in 1997 by Paul McCartney that continued the story of the man on a flaming pie. *Flaming Pie* was the tenth studio album by Paul McCartney. The album's first song talks about John's man who came on the flaming pie. The lyrics of the title song start: *"Making love underneath the bed, Shooting stars from a purple sky. I don't care how I do it; I'm the man on the flaming pie."* On the flaming pie album cover, there is a drawing of the flaming pie, which looks much more like a flying saucer than a pie.

John Lennon would also describe two very dramatic UFO experiences, not just lights in the sky. The first was a very close encounter. The second event was complete with missing time, and he had an object given to him by four 'bug-like' beings (See Chapter 7: <u>John Lennon Abduction</u>).

The Beatles were interested in UFOs. However, talking about UFOs was debunked and degraded at the time due to the "ridicule factor." Few editors would mention UFOs. Also, The Beatles were experimenting with LSD and other drugs, and for them to speak of off-world entities did not help anyone. During the 1977-79 worldwide UFO flap, the Beatles broke up and complained that their personal lives were micro-managed.

The Barry Goldwater Alien Story

Arizona Senator Barry Goldwater was a key US senator and a USAF Reserve General who was a part of the government for almost half a century. It is well known that Goldwater had a long-time interest in the subject of UFOs and that he corresponded with people related to his interest and his attempt in the early 1960s to get into the rumored Blue Room at Wright-Patterson Air Force Base (WPAFB).

In March 2012, I visited Arizona State University in Phoenix to review the Goldwater archive and find the UFO letters. Luckily most of the letters had been collected and put into a UFO file. The primary collection of UFO letters consisted of 143 pages. The Goldwater UFO letters ran from 1966 to 1996. Many of the letters answered questions about his request to his good friend General Curtis LeMay to get into the Blue Room at WPAFB. The Blue Room has long been rumored to be at 'Wright-Pat' where all the crashed alien hardware and bodies were supposed to be held.

In a 1988 New Yorker article found in the UFO file, Goldwater stated that he was getting 100 requests a year to look into the rumor of alien hardware and bodies at WPAFB. But, as Goldwater told the questioners, Lemay had said not only no but *"Hell no!"* Goldwater said he had never seen Lemay get so angry. LeMay added that if he brought up the subject again, he would make sure that Goldwater was court marshaled out of the Air Force.

Goldwater never again requested to go into the Blue Room, but he always maintained his interest in what was happening, as he had many Air Force pilot friends who had experienced sightings. Finally, near the end of his life, he concluded that it was a mistake keeping it secret then, and it's a mistake now. Here are some highlights of Goldwater's comments made to some of the people who wrote him letters about UFOs:

In 1967, Goldwater wrote back regarding a question about releasing sensitive files at WPAFB. If they were released, Goldwater stated, *"I think the information would be meager and not be substantiated fully. I can understand the sensitive and secret nature of these files."*

November 1974, Goldwater wrote:

> *I have no information that is not available to you, and I am not aware exactly of what the Air Force might have. I have tried in the years past to have the material collected by the Air Force to no avail. It is still classified above top secret. I have, however, heard that there is a plan underway to release some, if not all, of this material in the near future.*

It was this 'Above Top Secret' statement by Goldwater that would become the standard in the UFO community for describing the government UFO cover-up of the subject. Others were repeating this 'plan to release' material at this time, and there may have been a plan to get some stuff out. For example, the *documentary UFOs, Past, Present, and Future* was released at this time. The two producers of that document clearly stated that the Pentagon hired them to do the documentary, and they had received help during the production to talk to any government.

May 1977: *"If my secretary came into my office and said, 'there's a little man outside, he's green, he has three eyes and an antenna coming out of his head,' I would say, 'show him in,' because I wouldn't be surprised."*

February 1978: *"I made an attempt to get into the room at Wright-Patterson Field where information was stored, and I was denied this request, understandably. Frankly, I'm no expert on this subject; I've never made lengthy statements on it. What I've told you just about sums it up."*

June 1978: In a statement to former Blue Room (WPAFB) public affairs officer Col. Bill Coleman: *"I will argue either way about UFOs; I can't turn a blind eye to it. Something has to be there."*

November 1978: *"I truly doubt the Air Force has classified information on this subject not available to me."*

April 1980: *"He (LeMay) told me in no uncertain terms that I could not visit it and, furthermore, that he could not visit it either. After that, I just left it alone and forgot about it. However, I believe that the material has been spread around into different archives of the Air Force."*

July 1980: *"I have never been allowed to see the material that the Air Force collected, and I don't blame them. I think it should be kept a secret, but I hope one of these days we are going to know the whole story, and I hope I am around when it all comes to light."*

In 1981: Goldwater became Chairman of the Senate Intelligence Committee. The letters show that Goldwater doesn't reveal much about UFOs after this point. His letters seem more sympathetic to the government's position on UFOs.

May 1981: *"The reason I wanted to see the highly classified files on UFOs at Wright Patterson was not to see any remains because I don't know of any UFO that supposedly crashed."*

July 1981: *"Relative to your question about the accuracy of the details in The Roswell Incident, they are partially true, but not completely. I can't give you any other answer than that, so please don't push it."*

August 1981: *"I have been interested in this subject for a long time, and I do know that whatever the Air Force has on the subject is going to remain highly classified."*

In 1994: A scathing letter was written, which turned up in the Goldwater collection. It was a letter from Dr. Steven Greer, the head of Project Starlight, which began in July 1993. The Project Starlight Coalition (PSC) was a voluntary association of researchers, scientists, world leaders, and concerned citizens dedicated to affecting a non-harmful disclosure of the UFO/ETI issue. The 1994

Alien Bedtime Stories

letter was written from Greer to Goldwater. Greer reminded Goldwater of his promise to set up a meeting with Bobby Ray Inman in that letter. Inman had held many key intelligence positions, such as the Director of Naval Intelligence, Vice Director of the Defense Intelligence Agency, Director of the National Security Agency, and Deputy Director of the Central Intelligence Agency. More importantly, in the UFO world, Inman was rumored to be the man in charge of the back-engineering programs related to UFOs.

In a 1994 private meeting with Greer, Goldwater asked Greer to identify the people responsible for covering up the UFO technology. Of the many people Greer mentioned, Inman was a key figure. On hearing his name, Goldwater stated that he and Inman were good friends and would call him to find out and get to the truth. Greer reported that Goldwater eventually phoned Inman, but the call had not gone well, and he told Greer that he could not make any more calls like that. In a conversation with his daughter Joanne Goldwater, Greer was told, *"I don't know what Bobby Ray said to daddy, but he cannot make another phone call like that."*[5]

The Dmitri Medvedev Alien Story

The Medvedev alien briefing story is the type of UFO story that only comes along for a researcher once or twice in his lifetime. It was indeed a story I had longed for. What happened was the leader of one of the most powerful countries in the world stood up and stated that leaders are briefed on the extraterrestrial presence. What more could one ask for?

This is important because 'the briefing' is the truth. In theory, an officer responsible for the UFO program will approach an elected leader of a country, get them to sign a security agreement, and then brief them on the best evidence gathered. He will also answer questions. Therefore, when Russia Prime Minister Medvedev stands up in front of the top reporters in his country and says he has been briefed on an ET presence on earth, that story is essential and requires intense investigation. This is how the Medvedev statement unfolded.

At the end of 2012, there was a year-end news conference between Medvedev and Russia's top five TV networks. When the news conference roundtable ended, everyone got up and started to mill around talking. Medvedev assumed that the cameras had been turned off and answered questions. For example, Marianna Maksimovskaya, the top reporter for the most significant private TV network REN-TV, asked Medvedev whether the president is handed secret files on aliens when receiving the briefcase needed to activate Russia's nuclear arsenal.

It was at that point that, with a straight face, Medvedev dropped the extraterrestrial bomb. He stated:

> *For the last time, along with the briefcase with nuclear codes, the president of the country is given a special Top-Secret folder. This folder, in its entirety, contains information about aliens who visited our planet. Along with this, you are given a report of the absolutely secret special service that exercises control over aliens on the territory of our country. More detailed information on this topic you can get from a well-known movie called, 'Men in Black.' I will not tell you how many of them are among us because it may cause panic.*

None of the television stations that interviewed Medvedev broadcast the off-air comments, but the video was delivered to Reuters as a pool signal and placed on YouTube. As a result, the alien story went viral around the world.

In the investigation done by UFO researchers, it was discovered that the Russian documentary 'Men in Black' that Dmitry Medvedev may have been referring to was produced by the same TV network that employed Marianna Maksimovskaya, who asked the question. It was also later discovered that UFO researcher Dr. Bruce Maccabee was interviewed the month before

Alien Bedtime Stories

the Medvedev question, which may explain why the question was asked. The Maccabee interview and the Medvedev question may be intended for a second UFO documentary being created by REN-TV.

A poll was taken on the PresidentialUFO Website to question readers about what they thought of Medvedev's disclosure. The results were as follows:

18% Medvedev was joking with the reporter
63% Medvedev was telling the truth
18% Don't know
1% Other

Attempts were made to follow up on the question and answer with the reporter. A letter in Russian was sent to her asking why she had asked if she thought Medvedev was being serious and if they intended to follow up on the story. That letter was not answered. Questions were put to representatives of Russian Embassies around the world. The only comment that was received came from the Russian Embassy in Canada, where the spokesman said he had no comment to make about what Medvedev had said about aliens. Still, he did confirm that Medvedev did have the power to say what he wanted and was not answerable to Putin the President.

Finally, a letter was sent in Russian to the head of the world chess federation Kirsan Ilyumzhinov and the former governor of the Russian republic of Kalmykia. He is on record stating that on September 18, 1997, he was at home in his apartment when aliens came in and abducted him, taking him to their space ship where they communicated with him telepathically. Ilyumzhinov stated that he recalled the whole incident clearly without the help of hypnosis. He sent his case to Russia when Medvedev was the President, asking for an investigation. Ilyumzhinov did not reply to the letter asking what Medvedev had done about his case or if he had any insight as a leader of a former Soviet Republic as to the policy related to aliens inside Russia or the late Soviet Union.

Like all stories in the 24-hour news media cycle, the story that Russian leaders are briefed on an extraterrestrial presence faded after three days, and no amount of coaxing was able to bring it back.

CHAPTER 2

THE CANADIAN GOVERNMENT AND FLYING SAUCERS

"In 1950, I was attending a rather slow-moving broadcasting conference in Washington D.C., and having some time on my hands, I circulated around asking a few questions about flying saucers, which stirred up a hornet's nest. I found that the U.S. government had a highly classified project set up to study them, so I reasoned that with so much smoke, maybe I should look for the fire."
--Wilbert Smith, Interview CJOH radio 1961

"For your information, every nation on this planet has been officially informed of the existence of the spacecraft and their occupants from elsewhere. And as nations, they must accept responsibility for any lack of action or for any official position which they may take."
--Wilbert Smith, Letter 1956.

From December 1950 to August 1954, the Canadian government was very interested in the flying saucer phenomenon. Their chief radio engineer, Wilbert Smith, went to the United States and asked questions through channels to American officials. The main question posed was, what is the truth about flying saucers? The questions had been inspired by two bestselling books that had just been published. Major Donald Keyhoe's *Flying Saucers from Outer Space* and Frank Scully's book on a flying saucer crash at Aztec, New Mexico, called, *Behind the Flying Saucers*.

The Canadians were told five key things about flying saucers. Smith listed them in a Top-Secret memo written to the Deputy Minister at the Department of Transport asking for approval to run a program attempting to develop energy technology based on what the flying saucers were using as their propulsion. Smith wrote, *"This project is for the purpose of studying magnetic phenomena, particularly those phenomena resulting from unusual boundary conditions in the basic electromagnetic field. There is a reason to believe their discovery will open up new and useful technology."* That project, called 'Project Magnet,' was approved on December 2, 1950. The things that the Canadians were told were:

1. Flying saucers exist.

2. The matter is the most highly classified subject in the United States Government, with a rating higher than even the H-bomb.

3. Their modus operandi is unknown, but concentrated effort is being made by a small group headed by Vannevar Bush.

4. The entire matter is considered by the United States authorities to be of tremendous significance.

5. The United States authorities are investigating along a number of lines, which might be related to the saucers, such as mental phenomena.

Alien Bedtime Stories

Figure 10 Wilbert B. Smith

Figure 11 The restricted Department of Defense area utilized by Project Magnet at Shirley's Bay outside of Ottawa

The Flying Saucer Observatory

Without disclosing the secrets he had been told, Smith put together a group of top Canadian scientists and defense officials to discuss subjects related to outer space and emerging missile research. The first meeting took place on April 7, 1952. Smith wrote what appeared to be an introduction to the goals of the meeting. Considerable interest was expressed in the Flying Saucer phenomena, which, if accurate, might be a profitable line of study. It was generally felt that the group could undertake this work within its capabilities.

Smith also moved ahead with Project Magnet, hoping it would produce a new form of power for Canada. The program specifically outlined where the research would be headed. The initial program shall include the following avenues of investigations, to which others may be added from time to time as may appear expedient:

1. The theoretical study of electromagnetic radiation assumes boundary conditions different from those upon which the conventional theory was developed.

2. Laboratory study of mechanical forces associated with electron drift and electric currents in metallic masses.

3. Theoretical and laboratory study of magnetic domain resonance conditions in magnetic materials.

4. Investigation of the propagation of magnetic wave motion in magnetic materials.

5. Investigate the possibility of producing an effect such as a sink in a magnetic field.

6. Investigate the possibility of producing, in effect, single isolated magnetic poles.

7. Investigate the effects of a magnetic field on a rotating curvilinear metallic object.

The whole program would be classified *"In its entirety until such time as it can be assessed for its impact on our civilization."*

Alien Bedtime Stories

Project Magnet had two full-time and three part-time engineers employed. It was shut down quickly in August 1954 when it became public that the program detected a flying saucer over Ottawa. Part of the Project Magnet program, while it was active, involved a flying saucer observatory used to identify flying saucers. It was constructed in 1953 by the National Research Council and officially announced by the Hon. Lionel Chevrier, Minister of Transport. In his announcement, Chevrier stated, *"We are continuing to study new reports (of flying saucers) and are alert to the possibilities of discoveries of that nature."* The small 12-square-foot building run by the Department of Transport was placed in the restricted Department of Defense area at Shirley's Bay outside of Ottawa, where secret research into communications was conducted, and the Canadian government attempted to intercept Russian radio communications.

John C. Ross, a writer for *Fate Magazine*, described the station's equipment:

> *Tremendously complex and expensive equipment has gone into the tiny building at Shirley's Bay. The equipment is designed to detect gamma rays, magnetic fluctuations, radio noises, and gravity or mass changes in the atmosphere. Installed in the tiny little structure is an ionospheric reactor to determine the height, pattern, and conduct of the ionized layers of gases several hundred miles in the atmosphere. There is a new type of instrument called a gravimeter, imported from Sweden, to measure the earth's gravity, a magnetometer, to record the variations in the earth's magnetic field, a radio set running full volume at 530 kilocycles to pick up any radio noises and a counter to detect atomic rays from the outer atmosphere. Peter Dempson of the Telegram staff reports that all the instruments are connected to a control panel filled with lights, dials, and other instruments, which record the individual findings on paper. The station is not manned,*

> but is connected directly by an alarm bell system with the nearby ionospheric station at Shirley's Bay, where a staff of telecommunication experts is on 24-hour duty.[6]

Nothing happened until August 8, 1954. Then, young technician Ernie Epp stated that the bells had gone off, indicating something had been detected overhead. Smith later described what had occurred:

> The gravimeter began acting strangely. First, it waved, drawing a thin dark line on the graph paper being used to measure the movements of the instruments. Without further warning, the gravimeter went wild. All evidence indicated that a real unidentified flying object had flown within a few feet of the station. Alarm systems connected to the instrument panel began to ring, alerting us to the UFO. After watching the instruments for a few seconds, we ran outside to see what was causing the odd reaction. Unfortunately, our area was completely fogged in, and whatever was up there could not be seen visually.[7]

Smith reported to the media what had happened. He also requested the government to go full out or drop out.[8] Two days later, Project Magnet was wholly and quickly shut down after four years of promising research. Smith was forced to reverse his opinion on what had occurred. Later, however, he would confirm it was no mistake calling the article 'The Day Magnet Detected a Flying Saucer.'

Although the August 10, 1954, press release stated that the government was officially out of the UFO business, they still wanted people to forward their UFO information to Wilbert on an 'unofficial' basis. They even went to the point of including his mailing address in the press release. The shutdown was simply a closure of the public program that was causing public relations problems. The research continued, but now it was done far from the public's eyes. As Smith put it, *"The department decided that the investment in terms of personnel, laboratory facilities, and equipment would not be warranted, particularly in the light of the opinion that a great many people held flying saucers in ridicule."*

In 1969 the USAF did the same thing shutting down their UFO research, stating nothing was found, but at the same time, they continued collecting UFO data in secrecy. In 2011 the British did the same thing. It was a pattern started in 1954 by the Canadians. Do not air your laundry in public; do it secretly if you have to study UFOs.

The Government UFO Landing Base

The year was 1967, the 100th anniversary of Canada as a country. Many cities and towns built impressive buildings and tourist attractions to celebrate the Centennial. In St. Paul, Alberta, their idea was to create a UFO landing base. When the day came for it to open, Paul Hellyer, the Minister of Defense, showed up to cut the ribbon. During his time at the opening, Defense Minister Paul Hellyer would tell a story that would go down as one of the best UFO stories ever.

A Top-Secret Project had been set up in which UFOs could land at the Defense Research Board Experimental Station at Suffield, Alberta. The base is the Canadian equivalent of Area 51. Here is a one-thousand-mile restricted tract of land where the Canadian military carried out chemical weapons tests and all other secret things. The base was utterly isolated and, like Area 51, had a restricted no-fly zone. It was situated on flat ground, and there was no worry about people getting up on top of the mountains to look down at what they were doing.

According to the Canadian government story, as told by Minister Hellyer, there was a special committee attached to a Top-Secret UFO project. This is a revelation, as Smith's Project Magnet was always seen as the official top government program but was only classified at the 'secret' level. Furthermore, it appeared that the committee referred to by Hellyer had to be independent of Magnet.

Project Second Story, the Department of Defense Investigation into UFOs, was classified only at the Secret level. It appeared that it, too, could not be the committee Hellyer was referring to. Further proof that this was not the committee came from Dr. Peter Millman, the chairman of the Second Story committee, who denied he was involved. He told me in a letter, *"I certainly have heard vague rumors about some attempt to build a UFO landing site in western Canada, but that was absolutely all I knew about it."* The actual identity of the committee will probably always remain a mystery, as the Canadian government claimed the committee records were destroyed in 1957.

In 1979, despite the 1967 declaration of the landing base by the Defense Minister, even the story itself disappeared. Yurko Bondarchuk, a Canadian researcher, was told, *"We have no record of any such project, and from the information I have, we never had one."* According to Paul Hellyer, the Canadian government version of the story is as follows: "*Several groups became convinced that some unknown beings were trying to make contact with the Earth. One group made a strong representation to the committee because there had been attempts made by Canadian and U.S. Air forces planes to shoot down the UFOs, and the flying saucers were reluctant to land."* Therefore, it was argued, continued Hellyer, *"If there was ever to be any contact, the hazards had to be removed. The UFOs had to be provided with a safe place. Accordingly, in an effort to give the 'believers' a chance to demonstrate the existence of the flying saucers trying to make contact with the earth, the defense research board (experimental station) was designated as a landing area. The step brought no results, insofar as the committee was concerned, no evidence had been produced to prove their existence."* The story was printed in many papers in July 1967 and brought almost no reaction from the UFO community. Not until the late 1970s did people start to chase down the story.

I picked up on the story and began to put the story in front of Smith's inner circle members and write to Paul Hellyer. Unknown to me was that Arthur Bray, the man who held the Smith files, was also writing Hellyer asking him for a full explanation of what had occurred. Of the many people I put the story to, only Mrs. Smith knew the story entirely and was prepared to talk about what had happened. During my 1978 interview with Mrs. Smith, I showed her the Winnipeg Free Press article telling of Minister Paul Hellyer's statements at the UFO base opening in St. Paul in 1967. I asked Mrs. Smith if Wilbert had been involved. She read the article carefully and said, *"Yes, Wilbert was involved."* According to her, this is what happened. Smith had always wanted a chance to convince the government that the aliens existed. He believed strongly that the government should talk to the aliens face-to-face to learn all the elements beyond the simple reality of the aliens, such as where they are from and what they are doing here.

Smith believed that if the government would stop shooting at the objects, he might be able to get AFFA to land for a meeting. He approached what Mrs. Smith identified as 'the Government.' The three members, according to her, were the R.C.M.P., the Department of Defense, and the Prime Minister. This may have been the Top-Secret committee referred to by Hellyer.

In contacts made through Mrs. Frances Swan, a contactee in Elliot, Maine, Smith was informed by AFFA that to land, he would have to have protection against being shot down. This part of the story is told in an FBI document detailing the FBI's investigation of Mrs. Swan. According to Mrs. Smith, Wilbert Smith put this demand to the government or committee, and the committee agreed no one would shoot AFFA's ship down. Up to this point, both sides were telling the same story, and there are documents to prove these events did occur. Following this, AFFA, through Mrs. Swan, demanded that once he had landed and talked to whoever was there to meet him, he would be allowed to take off without any interference. The R.C.M.P. agreed to this, but when Smith approached what was described to me as "the Government," a cabinet meeting was held to discuss AFFAs demand. When the meeting was over, the government could not give a 100% guarantee that AFFA would be allowed to take off once he had landed at Suffield. Smith immediately called off the planned landing. That is the story Mrs. Smith told.

I placed many requests to the R.C.M.P. and the Defense Department for information or documents on the Top-Secret UFO committee. All requests came back that they had no information. I requested a ministerial inquiry from parliamentary representative Lloyd Axworthy. Axworthy never did spell out what actions he had taken to force action but told me on two occasions, *"I can't help you."* To resolve the story, Arthur Bray and I pursued Mr. Hellyer for further details. Some of the questions we wanted answers to were:

Canada is a big country. How did the aliens know where to land? The government version lacks this critical detail.

Who was the defense department expert who initially told Hellyer the story? The man had reportedly been an R.C.M.P. officer in 1954 and moved up to a senior high-level defense department official in 1967 (This confirms Mrs. Smith's contention that the R.C.M.P. was involved even though it is a federal police force).

In reply to the many requests for information, Hellyer did confirm that he had been briefed on the government UFO-related activities in 1967. He further remembered the top defense official who had briefed him and created quite a UFO file for Hellyer. However, he could not remember his name and could not find the UFO file. The cat-and-mouse game with Hellyer continued for years. Hellyer claimed at one point that he had even searched his files in vain at the National Archives in Ottawa searching for the UFO file. Try as he might, he could never remember the name of the official who told him the story. In a letter to me, Paul Hellyer concluded the affair this way, *"I can assure you there is no UFO cover-up, at least on our side of the border."*

Wilbert Smith and Alien Hardware

> *"You may recall a report about eight months ago about a saucer crash landing in Heligoland and taken by the Norwegians. AFFA says that is one of his ships, and it is possible that the British may eventually have gotten their hands on it. I think there are several in Earth people's hands, but I am afraid that they won't learn much about them from inspection. About as much as a 'Hottentot' would learn from one of our aircraft. One must go to kindergarten before one goes to college."*
> **--Smith's letter to David Middleton on June 12, 1955**

> *"I cannot comment on the 'True,' September '52 article as I just don't know. I do have knowledge from excellent sources that saucers HAVE crashed and fallen into the hands of earth people. I have handled some 'hardware,' but all this is deeply buried in classification and may as well be in the fourth dimension for all the good it is in establishing the reality of the craft or the people who manipulate them."*
> **--Smith's letter to 'Bill,' 1959.**

It is generally not well known that the Canadians were part of the American program to study flying saucers. As part of that program, they analyzed a lot of 'UFO hardware.' How much did they analyze? Most indications from those who might know are that it was a lot. One of the men who knew was Arthur Bridge, a young metallurgist attached to the Canadian Defense Research Board. He worked secretly with Smith from 1956 until Smith died in 1962. When I asked how much material he and Smith had handled, he used one word, *"Lots."*

Another person who knew was James Smith, about 17, when his father died. He stated that he remembered lots of hardware being handled by his father. In an interview with a Canadian radio show called 'Strange Days Indeed,'[9] James recalled the hardware that came for analysis:

James: *Many times, I do remember blue military cars pulling up to the house and leaving packages of things for him to do metallurgic analysis on. We asked him what they were, and he said they were chunks of unidentified things that the military had either shot down or found.*

SDI: Unidentified things, or did he actually use the word flying saucers?

James: *Yes, on a couple of instances, I remember packages about the size of a loaf of bread coming in. The box would contain a chunk of metal that he had been told that the Air Force had shot off a chunk of a flying saucer. They had already done some analysis of it and wanted him to have a go at it too.*

SDI: Now, was this the Canadian or the U.S. Air Force?

James: *Well, I don't recall what color the plate was. But it came from the States. Whether it was delivered to the house by the Canadian or...*

SDI: So, it came from the States?

James: *Yes.*

SDI: You actually saw some of these pieces as well, Jim?

James: *Oh yes, I saw them when he unpacked the boxes to see what is there and take a look at it.*

SDI: How old would you have been then?

James: *Well, looking back, 10 to 17, in that age group.*

SDI: Did you get to handle any of them? How would you know what was an unusual looking piece of metal at 17?

James: *I got to handle a few of them. One was a chunk about the size of a brick - semicircular in shape. It was a very smooth metal except for the jagged edges where it had been disconnected from whatever it belonged to. It was quite heavy in terms of its size. He had an analysis done of that one. I remember seeing that particular analysis sheet.*

Bob Groves was an Ohio UFO researcher who interviewed Smith in July 1962, a couple of months before Smith died. When he returned to Ohio, he made an audiotape of what he had learned. According to the audio, Groves stated that he had met with Smith and that he had been told that Smith was *"Constantly visited by Canadian government officials as well as American government officials who, of course, were upper echelon people with attaché cases that were chained and locked to their wrists to make sure none of the information would drop or be left behind in a bus station or something. He had a number of these visits. They had samples they wanted him to analyze, hardware and metal that had been found."* Groves continued:

> *According to Smith, let me cite this, in 1952, we had a noteworthy or a notorious sighting over Washington DC. During this time, an Air Force jet shot a piece right off of a UFO. It was found two hours later. It had a glow to it, a white glow to it; after two weeks, it had diminished to a brown texture. The part that was shot off was about as big as could be held in a couple of hands. It had a very distinct edge. It was curved. It had tapering sides so that it appeared that it had been shot off the edge of a double saucer shape which was the 'typical shape.' According to Smith,"* said Groves. *"The United States military intelligence has tons of hardware. They readily admitted this to Smith upon an interview with Smith when he was the director of the research project (Project Magnet 1950-1954).*

Smith also stated they had many films. Groves got the idea to ask about hardware based on an interview that had been done with another Ohio researcher C.W. Fitch and a letter to George Popovich. In that interview with Smith, hardware was a reality.

Grant Cameron

The 1952 Saucer Recovery

> *"In posting your representative with questions, please be sure the questions you ask are exactly what you want to know. If you ask, 'Does the Air Force have any saucer hardware?' you will get a "No," truthfully. The hardware is not held by the Air Force."*
> **--Popovich letter from Smith 1958.**

> *"Various items of 'hardware' are known to exist but are usually clapped into security and are not available to the general public."*
> **--Wilbert Smith, January 11, 1959.**

Wilbert Smith mentioned several times that he had handled a piece of a flying saucer that had been shot off a small saucer during the overflight of the White House in July 1952. He stated that the U.S. Navy had shot it off, but there is still some confusion at this point about whether or not there were one or two pieces involved.

Commander Alvin Moore, an intelligence officer with the CIA, recovered one piece that fits the story we know. It was transported back to Wilbert Smith by Canadian Defense official Captain Donald Goodspeed along with a sample of angel hair.

One of the key United States people to comment on the story was naval Vice Admiral Knowles, a friend of Smith. Knowles also sat on the Board of Directors at NICAP, the most significant UFO investigation group of the 1950s. He described the piece Smith showed him:

> *To the best of my recollection, the object was shot down by a plane and was seen to fall in the yard of a farmer across the river in Virginia. Upon searching the area, several pieces were found, one of which was turned over to Mr. Smith for independent research. On*

one of his trips down to see me he brought the piece along for inspection. It was a chunk of amorphous metal-like structure, brownish in color, with a curved edge, the whole thing to have been not over 2' in diameter. The edge was rounded in cross-section, perhaps a quarter-inch thin, and obviously swelled to a considerably greater thickness at the center. The outer surface was smooth but not polished, and at the broken sections, there were obviously iron particles and even some evidence of iron rust. I would say that the weight was somewhat lighter than that of solid iron, but it was not 'extremely light.' Mr. Smith told me that a chemical test had been made on the piece at hand. That iron had been found in it but little if anything else could be identified.

Smith's main comment on the 1952 piece came in an interview that occurred a month before his death. Smith knew he was dying and seemed very open in the interview about other recovered artifacts besides the 1952 fragment. The interview took place in November 1961.

FITCH: Have you ever handled any of this hardware yourself, sir?

SMITH: *Yes, quite a bit of it. Our Canadian Research Group has recovered one mass of very strange metal; it was found within a few days of July 1, 1960. There are about three thousand pounds of it (see; <u>St. Lawrence River UFO-Recovery</u>). We have done a tremendous amount of detective work on this metal. We have found out the things that aren't so. We have something that was not brought to this Earth by plane, by boat, nor by any helicopter. We are speculating that what we have is a portion of a very large device that came into this solar system; we don't know when, but it had been in space a long time before it came to Earth; we can tell that by the micrometeorites embedded in the surface. But we don't know whether it was a few years ago or a few hundred years ago.*

FITCH: You mean then that you have about a ton and a half of something metallic, of unknown origin.

SMITH: *That is correct. We can only speculate about it at this time, and we have done a great deal of that. We have it, but we don't know what it is!*

FITCH: You're a friend of Admiral Knowles, Mr. Smith?

SMITH: *Oh, yes. Admiral Knowles and I have been very good friends for many years.*

FITCH: I have been told by a mutual friend that in 1952 you showed Admiral Knowles a piece of a flying saucer. Is that statement correct, sir?

SMITH: *Yes. It is correct. I visited with Admiral Knowles, and I had with me a piece which had been shot from a small flying saucer near Washington in July of that year, 1952. I showed it to the Admiral. It was a piece of metal about twice the size of your thumb, which had been loaned to me for a very short time by your Air Force.*

FITCH: Is this the only piece you have handled that definitely had been part of a UFO, Mr. Smith?

SMITH: *No. I've handled several of these pieces of hardware.*

FITCH: In what way, if any, do they differ from materials with which we are familiar?

SMITH: *As a general thing, they differ only in that they are much harder than our materials.*

FITCH: What about this particular piece from that UFO near Washington? Did it differ from conventional materials? Was there anything unusual about it, sir?

SMITH: *Well, the story behind it is this. The pilot was chasing a glowing disc about two feet in diameter.*

FITCH: Pardon me, sir. But did you say two feet?

SMITH: *That is correct. I was informed that the disc was glowing and was about two feet in diameter. A glowing chunk flew off, and the pilot saw it glowing all the way to the ground. He radioed his report, and a ground party hurried to the scene. The thing was still glowing when they found it an hour later.*

The entire piece weighed about a pound. The segment that was loaned to me was about one-third of that. It had been sawed off.

FITCH: What did the analysis show?

SMITH: *There was iron rust; the thing was, in reality, a matrix of magnesium orthosilicate. The matrix had great numbers; thousands of 15-micron spheres scattered through it.*

FITCH: You say that you had to return it. Did you return it to the Air Force, Mr. Smith?

SMITH: *Not the Air Force. Much higher than that*

FITCH: The Central Intelligence Agency?

SMITH: *(Chuckles) I'm sorry, gentlemen, but I don't care to go beyond that point. I can say to you that it went to the hands of a highly classified group. You will have to solve that problem, their identity for yourselves.*

The St. Lawrence River UFO-Recovery

The piece of metal that Wilbert Smith talked about the most was the one that came to be called the 'Saint Lawrence Slab.' Nothing was really resolved about it except that the stuff was pretty strange. Two pieces found way up on the rocky shore above the river. The pieces were 3000 lbs and 800 lbs. The discovery occurred in 1960 when the metal suddenly appeared on the shore of the St. Lawrence River. It was composed of high-strength manganese steel, fabricated in layers of 0.01 to 0.8 inches thick, and according to Smith, "It looked like the whole thing had been subject to an impact as it fell on a hard surface with very high velocity. The flat surface was embedded with myriads of particles tentatively identified as micro-meteorites. The analysis showed it to contain known elements but such as we do not normally use in steels." It was analyzed for at least ten years after Smith died by the Ottawa Flying Saucer Club. Their conclusions were:

1. The object was subjected to a great deal of heat.

2. The piece underwent a severe impact.

3. The metal had a low magnetic nature.

4. No aluminum, calcium, or copper traces are usually found in manganese.

Smith described in one letter how his metallurgist had worked on the metal:

> *Art Bridge took it and has been working on it for the past two weeks. His first try was like mine, to cut off a piece of the power saw. All that happened was a shower of sparks and broken saw teeth! He eventually had to use a tungsten wire saw and abrade off some samples. He got a friend in Mines and Technical Surveys to make a spectroscopic analysis of the sample and got the verdict that it was magnesium ferrite. Now, this material is a purely artificial product made with some considerable effort and does NOT occur free in nature to the best of your knowledge, nor is it a 'byproduct.' The only use for it that I can find is in missile nose cones and rocket motor linings, as it is reasonably resistant to ablation. A close inspection of the surface shows the inclusion of large numbers of very small particles, most of which seem to be light metal silicates. The density of these particles (on the outer surface only) is about 30 per square centimeter. Dr. Peter Millman advises that micro-meteorites of this size would occur through a square cm. section at about 10'6 second, so it would take about a year to accumulate such a density.*

The Roswell Piece Analysis

The final story surrounding the work Wilbert Smith did on UFO hardware deals with the possible metal analysis from the 1947 UFO crash in Roswell, New Mexico. In 1987 after the MJ-12 document story broke, I sent a copy of the documents to Art Bridge. I also sent a copy of an interview between Smith and U.S. engineer Dr. Robert Sarbacher. With this interview, I added a letter that Sarbacher had sent to UFO researcher Bill Steinman about light material from a flying saucer that had been analyzed at Wright Field in Dayton, Ohio. Bridge trusted no one and hated using a phone. Usually, he would phone me and tell me to come out to where he lived. This time it was different. The first comment he made was about the material Sarbacher had described on the phone. *"I'll tell you flat out, Grant,"* said Bridge. *"I analyzed a piece that was 'pulled off that New Mexico thing. I know that thing was analyzed. It was a super light material."*

Bridge had told me that there were tons of material on more than one occasion, and he had done a lot of analysis. However, I knew that Bridge had no documents or records of the analysis work in his house. He had also stated that he was unfamiliar with most of what was in the MJ-12 document, so I never pursued the Smith-Roswell connection.

That, however, is not where the possible Smith connection to Roswell ends. All of the Smith documents and Smith's testimony show that he did have high-level access to people in the United States, including Vannevar Bush.[10] Part of this story involved Smith being given access to both the bodies and the craft. Now, add to the report the theory that some have proposed, that the Aztec story may have been about the Roswell crash. The story may just have been changed to allow the telling of the story without violating the law by revealing classified information (this is often done with books in the intelligence field. A fiction book is put out which contains a classified story with names and locations altered).

If Aztec was Roswell, then another stronger report shows Wilbert Smith may have been involved.

The genesis of this body story goes back to the Hotel Algonquin in 1972. Psychiatrist and paranormal researcher Dr. Berthold Schwarz met with Harold Sherman, a renowned paragnost, psychic researcher, and author of more than 90 books. Sherman was also prominent for his experiments in telepathy conducted between himself in New York City and Sir Hubert Wilkins, who was in the Canadian arctic. During the conversation with Dr. Schwarz, Sherman began discussing his friendship with Mr. Silas Newton. Newton was the geophysicist and oil businessman who gave the original lecture about the 1948 Aztec, New Mexico crash at the University of Denver on March 8, 1950. Silas Newton also approached prominent Hollywood writer Frank Scully with the story of the Aztec crash, which Scully wrote up in a bestselling book, *Behind the Flying Saucers*. The book created controversy and was generally written off by most researchers as a hoax. Part of the book's problems was that despite many attempts from researchers, reporters, and people offering movie deals, neither Newton nor Scully would reveal the eight different sources that had provided the details of the Aztec crash. Harold Sherman had met Newton through Frank Scully, a long-time friend. He went on to know Newton for 30 years and gained great respect for him. He called him *"an altogether extraordinary person who probably was misunderstood in many fields, but he had an awful lot to him."* [11]

According to Schwarz, during the 1972 discussion, Sherman had told him Wilbert Smith had provided access to the Aztec crash bodies for Silas Newton. In his 1983 book, *UFO Dynamics,* Schwarz wrote that *"through the intervention of Wilbert Smith, electronics expert, and organizer of Project Magnet, Newton later actually saw the humanoids himself."*[12]

The significant part of this disclosure is that Newton, although accosted by many researchers as an untrustworthy con man, ended up describing an event that now fits with what we know about Smith. In 1972 there were no public stories that Smith had access to the alien bodies and craft. In fact, in 1972, there was no discussion at all about dead aliens and recovered crafts. Those crash stories had died in the 1950s and were not discussed again until 1978 when Leonard Stringfield gave a lecture at the MUFON yearly conference in Dayton, Ohio. Stringfield received a death threat and moved to a different hotel room before the lecture, and the story of crashes and alien autopsies was off and running.

As well as telling an alien body story that others would later tell, the Newton story rings true because if he had made up the story about seeing the bodies, it makes no sense that he would claim to have been given this ultimate Top-Secret access through a foreign national. He would surely have claimed access through some high-level U.S. official or his mysterious group of eight scientists known as 'Dr. Gee.' Another fact not known in 1972 when Schwarz and Sherman spoke is that Smith was very interested in the Aztec crash and had received a confirmation of a flying saucer craft through classified channels.

In 1983 a transcript of a September 1950 interview between Wilbert Smith and a U.S. military scientist named Dr. Robert Sarbacher was released. In this interview, Dr. Robert Sarbacher had told Smith, *"The facts in the book (Frank Scully's book on the Aztec flying saucer crash) are substantially correct."*[13] Smith would, therefore, have been operating under the assumption that the Aztec crash did take place despite the numerous debunking articles that were being written about the Scully book in the early fifties. Furthermore, there is little doubt that Smith would have followed up on the Aztec case with other high-ranking U.S. officials.

There was no correspondence between Smith, Scully, and Newton in Scully's files at the University of Wyoming or the Wilbert Smith files found at the University of Ottawa. Any contact with Newton by Smith would have been via phone or channels.

The evidence that Smith had seen the bodies continued to surface in a 1997 message published on the Usenet from a former President of the Montreal Flying Saucer Club. This group was very active during the sixties and connected with the Ottawa Flying

Saucer Club just down the road. The two groups had also done work together on two large objects that had been recovered from the shore of the St. Lawrence River in 1961. The story told by the former president, who identified himself only as 'The Observer,' is that four members of the Montreal group had been visiting Ottawa in early 1964 and had stayed overnight at Mrs. Smith's home. During supper in the evening, Mrs. Smith told tales about her former husband. One of the stories included that Wilbert Smith had personally viewed dead alien bodies. In an email to this author, The Observer wrote:

> *We were told about the bodies that Wilbert Smith had seen when he was personally invited by the US military. We were simply told that he saw the bodies, and from the impression that I received, it was for only a short time, minutes, not hours.*[14]

This Montreal Flying Saucer Club member further described the bodies. According to what he recalled, Mrs. Smith had stated, *"Mr. Smith described (to his wife) the dead occupants as having been approximately 4.5 to 5 feet in height, grayish-blue tint to the skin, large eyes, small slit for a mouth and four long fingers with no thumbs."*[15] This" large eyes and four-finger" description is the only time a 'Grey type' description of the alien was ever associated with Wilbert Smith. The Observer, in relating what Mrs. Smith had told the four Montreal members, might have added more than what they were told. For example, in a separate article written by The Observer concerning the disclosures made by Wilbert's wife, the claim was made that the Smith description was associated with Roswell. The report also stated Smith had been invited to the crash site. Smith did not get involved in flying saucers till 1950, so there is no way he was at the Roswell crash site in July 1947.[16]

The large-eyed grey alien idea was not only unknown to Wilbert Smith but also unknown in the UFO world before the 1961 abduction of Betty and Barney Hill. There were tall 7' 8' or 10' beings, little men, tiny hairy dwarf-like beings, dwarf-like beings

Alien Bedtime Stories

with large heads, entities shaped like potato bags, robot-like creatures, entities without heads, and many humanlike figures.

Contactees dominated Wilbert Smith's research timeframe, and Wilbert Smith was one himself. In a letter to a man named Mr. Milne in 1957, for example, Smith stated, *"It is my opinion that the people from outside are so much like us that they could mingle with us, and we would be none the wiser."*

Once Smith died and the Hill abduction gained widespread publicity, all the alien encounters from 1947-1961 were removed from UFO histories as if they had never occurred.

Most present-day researchers, for example, would probably agree with J. Allen Hynek (Scientific Consultant to the United States Air Force Project Blue Book), who described most contactees as *"pseudo-religious fanatics of low credibility value,"*[17] or with abduction researcher David Jacobs who stated, *"Basically contactee followers were gullible people who, through lack of adequate factual information about the UFO phenomena, formulated a belief system that easily incorporated the contactees claims as fact."*[18]

The usual telling of the Smith body story was the one related in 1998 when researcher and author Palmiro Campagna wrote the following in the Postscript section of his 1998 softcover edition of *'The UFO Files.'* He wrote, *"According to James Smith, on one of his many trips to the U.S., Wilbert Smith told his son that he was shown recovered bodies from a recovered craft. Wilbert Smith described the bodies as small and humanoid in appearance."*

In July 2000, I interviewed James Smith by phone and revisited the issue of the alien bodies that Smith had seen. James stated that he had been told about the bodies as his father was near death. However, James did not recall that the body description involved Greys, simply small people.

In March 2002, James Smith was a guest on *Strange Days... Indeed* radio show where he described the UFO hardware his father had received from the United States to analyze, and he again was asked about the alien body story. James Smith described the aliens as *"Small humanoids"* and *"like descriptions of the time."* These descriptions agreed with reports made by many other people having alien encounters in the fifties. They would also agree with Smith's notion that aliens were not much different from us and might even be distant relatives.

If Smith saw the bodies and craft, it probably occurred in the early fifties. The reasons for that would include correspondence from the Canadian Embassy in Washington during 1951 that indicates that during that period, Smith was dealing, at least indirectly, with Vannevar Bush at the Research and Development Board in Washington, D.C. Bush, being the head of the U.S. flying saucer effort, would have been able to give Smith access to craft and bodies. Most importantly, Smith directed the classified Project Magnet from December 1950 to August 1954. With his clearance, he would have been in a position to be shown the craft and body. Bridge told me that Smith had an extremely high-security clearance. Once the classified saucer program was closed in August 1954, Smith's clearance and 'need-to-know' on flying saucers probably went with it.

Before the CIA Robertson panel in January 1953, flying saucers was more openly discussed. It is then more probable Smith was shown the craft and body before the CIA began the debunking campaign. The report from Sherman that Silas Newton was given access to the bodies through Wilbert Smith's help also indicates an early fifties date. The Musgrave story concerning the Washington crashed saucer viewing mentioned the early fifties.

The tone of Smith's writings near the end of his life in 1962 was not upbeat. Smith had not received a message from AFFA for almost two years. He had taken his anti-gravity experiment apart, telling his wife that the world was not ready for it. His writing began to reflect his strong belief that the important part of the UFO mystery was in the philosophy of the aliens rather than in their technological hardware. In the early fifties, Smith's writing had shown a keen interest in discovering the propulsion of these strange new objects.

Alien Bedtime Stories

Wilbert Smith, In Defense of Talking to Aliens

> *"Certain officials in my government are aware of my contact with these people and are willing to let me play it my way."*
> **--Wilbert Smith's letter to Major Donald Keyhoe 1955.**

> *"I do not agree with NICAP policy on contact stories. I have spent too many hours conversing with people from elsewhere to have any doubt about their reality or that they are what they claim to be. Those of us who have been fortunate enough to have made contact with these people have learned a great deal and profited greatly through their knowledge in those things which really count, which we can take with us."*
> **--Smith's Letter to Keyhoe October 4, 1958.**

Wilbert Smith was a contactee who headed up the Canadian government investigation into flying saucers. He said that he had established ways of communicating with the entities who were in the flying saucers. He would refer to them as the 'Boys topside.' There are many people who, after hearing the Wilbert Smith saga about attempts to talk with the aliens, will feel that Smith was nothing more than an earlier version of Steven Greer or Billy Meier. They denounce any effort to consider seriously the possibility of mutual, bilateral communications rather than the passive notion that only the aliens can initiate contact, or worse yet, that no alien contacts are taking place. Such views are shortsighted and uninformed.

Firstly, on the issue of signaling UFOs with flashlights, I stand as a testimonial and will argue with anyone, anytime or place, that this is a legitimate pursuit. A hundred witnesses I can call to testify, and I will confirm that UFOs are very responsive to lights. While investigating the UFO flap in Manitoba for 18 months, we had many occasions to test such theories.

On the more important concept of contact between humans and aliens, which Wilbert spent a great deal of his life pursuing, people should note a couple of points before they begin throwing stones. Firstly, many UFO researchers' goal is to confirm the reality of the extraterrestrial presence on earth. Calls of, *"Give us alien bodies, hardware, crashed flying saucers, and statistical reports based on sighting reports,"* are often heard. There is nothing wrong with this noble goal, but it is only part of the overall UFO reality. Establishing the reality of the extraterrestrial phenomena goes almost nowhere in explaining what has been happening since 1947 and why. For people who claim that physical evidence such as hardware and bodies should be our only consideration in our UFO studies, I present to them the same question that Dr. Eric Walker (former President of Penn State University and a man who knew exactly what the government's knowledge of the phenomena was) asked us in response to our constant demands to help us prove the UFO reality. *"When you finally get the answer (the proof), what will you do with it?"* he demanded to know. He had made a valid point, but one that took this author 15 years to figure out. Walker's question was simple; if you do get a body or crashed flying saucer, what will your next step be? What will you do once you have established the reality of the phenomena?

Wilbert Smith was in the position of having had the answer to the question concerning the reality of the phenomena. He had been shown a crashed flying saucer in Washington, D.C. He had seen the bodies. He had handled piles of mysterious hardware. He had handled all the sighting reports coming into the government for 12 years. He knew the reality of the flying saucers and their extraterrestrial occupants. Yet he described his position as frustrating. Smith realized that he was now at a dead-end in uncovering the fundamental questions of where visitors were from, why they are here, and what they have planned for our future. Smith further stated that high government officials were in the same dilemma he was in. Despite their collections of hardware and bodies, they were at a dead-end in searching for an answer to the UFO phenomena.

Consider, for example, the case of what Dr. Robert Sarbacher said when asked a question that went beyond the reality of the phenomena. Asked by Wilbert Smith where they came from, Dr. Sarbacher stated, *"We don't know. All we know is we didn't build them."* Consider what Smith wrote in the Top-Secret memo, *"Their modus operandi is unknown, but concentrated effort is being made by a small group headed by Doctor Vannevar Bush."* The American officials that Smith talked to had bodies and crafts, but they could not answer the questions about where they were from and why they were here. Smith wrote that the reaction to the dead end situation the government found itself in was that nothing more could be done and that they should do nothing. Smith explained it this way, *"Fact is, when certain government people came face to face with the reality of the space people and realized there wasn't anything they could do about it, they promptly closed their eyes and hoped the whole thing would go away!"*

Dr. Eric Walker, who was at one time a high government official, expressed the same 'dead-end' evaluation of the situation, *"You are up against the windmills. Leave it alone; there's nothing you can do about it,"* he told us on several occasions. *"Study something else. Leave it alone."*

The 'dead-end' conclusions reached by the government were accurate as far as the government had taken the evidence. Bodies and hardware do nothing but establish the reality of the situation, and they do nothing to explain anything else. With a body, we know the phenomenon is real, but to evolve our knowledge of the phenomena, we must take another step. Smith understood that these physical reality items were of no use in explaining the phenomenon, and he was right. *"It might as well be in the 4th dimension for what it's worth,"* he once said of a recovered crashed flying saucer. If you have an alien body, what does that tell you about who they are or why they are here? It tells you nothing. All it does is prove the reality of the phenomena and little else. So, what is the answer? As much as it might hurt to admit it until we talk to the aliens, we will never understand why they are here, where they are from, and the nature of the phenomena.

After receiving the proof for himself, Smith knew that contact with the craft's occupants was the next step. Smith had been shown a crashed flying saucer at an airbase outside of Washington, D.C. He had been shown the bodies. He had handled piles of mysterious hardware sent to him by U.S. officials. He had handled every UFO report to come into the Canadian government for 12 years. He knew the reality. Discussions with U.S. officials would not help, as all they had were bodies, crafts, and sighting reports which would tell them little about the true nature and intent of the phenomena. They didn't know what was going on either. Smith had faced Walker's question, *"When you finally get the answer, what will you do with it?"* In his answer to the question, he decided putting his head in the sand was not an option. For Smith, it was either trying and talk to the people flying the crafts or making Ufology a hobby to see how many reports, bodies, crafts, and hardware pieces he could collect. Smith took the logical next step to Walker's question and moved to try to find out why the aliens were here, where they were from, and what we could learn from them.

Let me make a point to illustrate this. I will bet the farm on the fact that one of the key reasons that the government is withholding the UFO story from the public is what they know and, more specifically, what they don't know about abductions. If the President were to stand up and say, *"UFOs are real, and they are extraterrestrial,"* I can guarantee that one of the first questions that would come his way from the press would be, *"Mr. President. There are estimates that these aliens have possibly abducted millions of people. What are you doing to stop this?"* So, what does the President say to that? He can say nothing. Not only does he not know how to stop it, he also does not even understand what they are doing. So how does he, as Commander-in-Chief, find out? Does he go to Area 51 and get a body, a downed craft, or a piece of hardware? What will those items do to help provide an answer? They do nothing to provide an answer. They simply, once again, confirm the reality of the situation. Sighting reports will not ever prove the reality. They will merely describe the phenomena. Not until someone talks to an alien will he find out what they are doing. Not until someone negotiates with an alien will the abduction phenomena stop.

Smith worked hard to find a scientific way to evaluate and create alien contacts. He stated that when contact was finally made with the aliens, the answers to what was going on would come. It was the key to his research after that, and he was right in what he did. Undeniably, a live alien will provide many more answers than a dead one.

People may question the quality of alien messages, which is a valid concern. It is, however, a problem of inadequate information or poor evaluation techniques. That, however, is not the problem of the contactee whom we have chosen to kick in the head. Instead, it is a problem for researchers who have not spent the time to set up appropriate protocols to deal with collecting contact evidence.

One must simply find a way to get reliable messages from aliens, as I will guarantee the government has tried to do from day one. The argument that there is too much noise compared to the message is no reason to quit the search. It is similar to the cure for cancer, where there is a lot of noise from inventors and drug companies claiming cures almost daily that do not pan out. Because there is a lot of noise in the cancer cure search, does that mean we should stop looking? Of course, not; it is our job to find the signal in the noise. Smith, inspired by the American Top-Secret information that 'mental phenomena' was involved, was fully justified in attempting to talk to aliens, just as the American officials were doing quietly in the background across the border.

Grant Cameron

Wilbert Smith on Disclosure: An Insider's View

Wilbert Smith, despite claims to the contrary by people who were not there, was the official head of the Canadian government's investigation into flying saucers. The investigation, Project Magnet, ran from December 1950 to August 1954. Mr. Smith was quite open about his assessment of the UFO phenomena. He almost never used the word UFO, a term that the United States Air Force created in 1952. To Smith, they were always either flying saucers or flying discs. Smith was quite blunt about what the phenomena were. Flying saucers are real, which he relayed to the Canadian government from official sources in the United States. According to Smith, the flying saucers were piloted by extraterrestrials, and he was not afraid to disclose that he and others had received communications from the aliens.

Smith was also very open about the fact that there was a cover-up of the facts by United States officials. When he was in his later days of life-fighting cancer, he told his son that he had seen a downed craft and the alien bodies at a location outside of Washington, D.C.

In his final days, just weeks before he died, Smith's hand wrote a note to C.W. Fitch, a researcher from Ohio, who was insisting he gets an answer on hardware. Smith appeared so sick at this point that he could no longer type, as was his practice through hundreds of letters. Smith told Fitch that there were tons of hardware and that US officials and not the USAF held it. In light of Smith's openness on the subject, it, therefore, came as a bit of a surprise, while reviewing 4 DVDs I have that hold all his files that he spoke against disclosure in letters written shortly before his death.

Speaking of gravity control, his main research interest related to flying saucers, Smith stated in a letter to Mr. Rogers, *"The possibility of gravity control has very great significance with aspect* to our civilization since it would virtually revolutionize it almost overnight. Railroads, highways, and even ship travel would be obsolete, and even national borders would rapidly dissolve. Consequently, neither I nor others working in this field are going to make any disclosures until we are very sure that it will be in the interest of humanity to do so." In another letter written in the same time period (to Mr. Bunting), Smith reiterated, *"We must be certain that disclosure will not add further to the present world unrest and instability before we can seriously consider divulging anything having the ramifications of Gravity Control."*

The CIA Channels an Alien

"Am busy saving your planet; what more do you want in the way of friendship?"
--An alien by the name of AFFA answering questions posed by US Naval Intelligence in 1954.

"He came in contact with the bad (Grey) ones. I told him to keep away from them, but he thought he knew everything. He didn't know how to be quiet. At least he was asking for help, so I told him how, but I think it was too late."
--Francis Swan confirms that Naval Intelligence officer Julius Larsen came back to her in the 1980s looking for help from aliens who were haunting his world.

This is one of the longer stories. It is that way because the story has many vital components that cannot be left out. It is one of the wildest and most well-supported stories in Ufology. It has been told in part by three different sources: The Canadian government, Major Robert Friend, who headed up the USAF Project Blue Book investigation into UFOs, and Arthur Lundahl, who was the Director of the CIA's National Photographic Interpretation Laboratory

(NPIC) in Washington D.C., and also rumored to be the UFO expert inside the CIA for four White House administrations.

This story involves the channeling of an alien on July 6, 1959, at the National Photographic Interpretation Center (NPIC) in the slums of Washington, D.C. The reason the building was in the slums is that it was the CIA building where all the U-2 spy plane film was processed. It was one of the most Top-Secret places in the country. It was in the slums because it was figured that was the last place the Soviet spies would look for it. Those living around the building knew something was happening because of the security, but they thought someone might be printing money in the building.

The channeling part of the story goes back to the fall of 1953 in the small town of Elliot, Maine. There, while putting up decorations for a Halloween dance at the Grange Hall, a woman by the name of Francis Swan encounters an alien by the name of AFFA. At that point, she did not know he was an alien. She just knew that there was something unusual about this man who wasn't from town. She thought he was *"a very distinguished and very intelligent"* fellow. He walked into the room, walked out, and then walked in again. *"I was the only one who talked to him,"* Swan said. *"That seemed strange. He didn't tell me anything then. He just walked out. But even after that night, if I looked in the direction he came in, I could almost see him."*[19]

Six months later, in May 1954, Swann started getting messages. The notification would be a soft shrill whistle or a flat musical note in her left ear. The first message was, *"We come...will help keep peace in EU. Do not be frightened."* This would start a series of messages arriving at all times of the day and night. The sharp ringing in Swan's ears was loud and caused great discomfort. However, they could sense her feeling and read her thoughts. She complained, and eventually, the messages came without all the discomfort.

Swan had always been interested in the paranormal. Despite only a couple of years in school, she looked up everything she could find on the subject. She went to séances, sought out spiritualists, and used an Ouija board to help farmers in the area with problems like lost sheep. She was also a strong Christian. She was a member of the Congregation church, read the Bible daily, and interpreted everything that happened daily to what was written in the good book. Swan was among only a few well-known female UFO contactees in the 1950s. The others were Elizabeth Klarer of South Africa, Dana Howard and Gloria Lee, who claimed a telepathic contact with J.W. from Jupiter. The rest of the contactees of that era who were publicly discussing meetings and rides with people from flying saucers were all men.

Days after the messages began, the entity identified himself as AFFA, a representative of the Universal Association of Planets, Bell Flight Signal M4, cruising above the Earth in a spaceship 753,454 feet across. AFFA also identified himself as the man who had met her in Grange Hall the October before.

On May 18, AFFA told Swan to write a letter to the Navy. AFFA said they had the short-wave radio to tune into their messages. AFFA wanted the world to know that aliens are friendly. This is how the Navy and CIA became involved in the case. The FBI documents on the Swan case indicated that the Navy had a file on Swan, but FOIAs could not find it. The CIA part of the story became public, and surprisingly, the CIA leaked the report to the public.

In a synchronistic world, Swan's neighbor was Admiral Herbert Knowles. Knowles had just retired from the US Navy and happened to have picked up an interest in UFOs and had been recruited by Major Donald Keyhoe to the Board of Directors of the most significant UFO group in the nation, the National Investigative Committee for Aerial Phenomena (NICAP). Swan contacted him on May 26th, and the same day, Knowles came over to Swan's house to host a question-and-answer session with AFFA. Mrs. Swan produced the answers through automatic writing.

AFFA and a second commander named Ponnar stated they were in two large crafts circling the Earth (a story about two mysterious satellites would appear the same year in the New York Times, Aviation Week, and other prominent American publications). During the initial communication, AFFA asked for a base to be opened so he could have and make contact with political leaders. This was the same year that Eisenhower allegedly met with aliens at Muroc and the same year the Canadians opened Suffield Base in Alberta, Canada, for a UFO to land.

A long series of meetings with Knowles and Swan began where long question and answer sessions took place. Meanwhile, Knowles sent his discoveries to the White House and Navy Intelligence. However, it was the material that was sent to Navy intelligence that prompted them to action. The Director of Naval Intelligence, Admiral Espy, sent Captain John R. Bromley and Captain Harry W. Baltazzi to Maine to investigate Swan and watch the conversations with AFFA. During their session, they asked for AFFA to show himself, and the reply came back, *"This would not be possible at this time."* So the two investigators returned to Washington.

More investigators from Naval Intelligence came to see Mrs. Swan in 1954. John Hutson made one visit from the Bureau of Aeronautics, which was 'unofficially involved' in the case. He, Knowles, and Wilbert Smith from the Canadian government met with Swan on July 24, 1954. Hutson was there for three days investigating and asking AFFA questions. They also wanted to receive messages but couldn't, even though they could hear the buzzing sound that Swan was getting in her ear. Although Hutson stated to the FBI that he was in Maine talking to Swan 'unofficially,' Mrs. Swan would report that he was still in contact with her 25 years later. Randall Fitzgerald confronted Hutson, who admitted the contact but refused to talk about it on the grounds of national security, *"I'd rather not go into my involvement. She (Swan) still feels a religious connotation about her experience. I would honor that. I have never said anything to anyone in public relations about my own experience with her, partially because I was part of national security. But I just don't want to get into that."*[20] What was strange about some of the later visits, according to Swan, is that the intelligence officers did not ask her about technical things but religious matters. This did not please Swan or AFFA, for that matter.

Alien Bedtime Stories

"*AFFA refused to answer any more questions,*" Swan told reporter Randall Fitzgerald. He had *"Gotten sick of it."*[21]

In 1959 Naval Intelligence was again at Swan's door. This time it was Julius Larsen, a naval liaison to the CIA and a fellow pilot. They flew up to Maine to talk to Swan. It was at this point that things began to really happen. The two men posed technical-scientific questions to AFFA, and Swan again provided the answers through automatic writing. During the session, Larsen asked to be taught how to do it. According to Swan:

> *He was all for spiritualism. He swallowed everything. He decided he'd like to do automatic writing and would you show me how. I said sure. I just put my hand on his shoulder, and he could write. But that wasn't flying saucers because you know what they are going to say before they say it. With one try, he began writing, and right away, someone named AFFA started writing.*

Swan insisted that it wasn't AFFA as the writing was different, and AFFA always signed off, *"God bless you."* This signoff was signed *"AFFA."* Swan tried to tell him, but he wouldn't listen. Finally, the other officer stormed out of the room. To back up her story, Swan stated that Larsen had gotten into trouble and came to her 20 years later looking for help, *"He wrote me a long letter pleading with me to get them off his back. He couldn't think. He couldn't do anything. He was a total wreck. And so, I told him, you've got to pray, and you have to be as mean to anyone who's trying to control you. You have to be mean and negative and drive them out."*

Six days later, Larsen approached Arthur Lundahl and his deputy at the NPIC, Robert Neasham, to tell them about the channeling session. Both NPIC men were interested in UFOs. Lundahl had overseen the photo analysis for the famous CIA-sponsored 1953 Robertson Panel, which looked into UFOs. So, they were very interested and set up a July 6, 1959, channeling session.

The story of the 1959 channeling was given to Robert Emenegger and Allan Sandler for inclusion in the 1974 TV documentary, '*UFOs, Past, Present, and Future.*' The two key government officials involved were Major Robert Friend from the USAF and Arthur Lundahl from the CIA. To support the story, they were told they received a document that describes the whole story. It has been called the '*CIA memo*' or the '*Friend memo.*' However, some confusion still exists as to its actual origin. One version of the story states that J. Allen Hynek, then a consultant to the USAF UFO Project Blue Book, said that he had obtained a copy of the document. In contrast, on a visit to ATIC at Wright Patterson AFB in July 1959, just days after the document had been written. Hynek saw the typed document on Friend's desk and made an 11-page handwritten copy of the document at the time in possession of acting Blue Book head Major Robert Friend.

The other version of the story was Friend's handwritten recollection of his involvement. The information in the memo was the basis of a letter that Major Friend sent to his boss, National Air Intelligence Center Commander Major General Charles B. Dougher. It told him that the USAF should pursue this dramatic case involving Mrs. Francis Swan. Dougher notified that the USAF would stay out because another agency (the CIA) was dealing with the issue. Emenegger reproduced this memo, minus the names, in his 1974 book, *UFOs, Past Present, and Future*. He referred to the memo as the CIA memo. He claimed that he had analyzed and confirmed the original CIA memo that NPIC Assistant Director Arthur Lundahl had written.

Years later, researcher Jacques Vallée would provide this author with a copy of the documents, complete with the names of the CIA officers who had been called in to investigate the alien channeling. Major Friend and the handwritten document tell the bizarre story of the CIA's effort to talk to Larsen's new alien friend. First, Larsen sat in a room at the NPIC and went into a trance. Then, using automatic writing, he began to answer the questions that Lundahl and Neasham were asking him, such as, *"Will there be a third world war?"* and, *"Do you prefer any religion?"* At one point in the interview, one of the two men[22] asked that AFFA produce some proof, to which AFFA replied, *"What would you like?"* Finally, the men said that AFFA should show himself, at which point Larsen went from automatic writing to a verbal command, *"You to the window."* Neasham and Lundahl raced to the window, and according to the Memo, a flying saucer flew by in broad daylight and over the Capitol. Amazed and looking for confirmation, Neasham immediately contacted Washington National for radio confirmation but was told that that section of radar section was blocked out during that time.

The next thing that happened is that Lundahl and Neasham contacted Friend at Wright Patterson, heading up the USAF flying saucer investigation, and ordered him to come to Washington immediately. Friend arrived on July 9th, and although Lundahl would later claim it was no big deal to bring Friend in, there was a roomful of CIA agents in there this time with them as he briefed Friend on what had occurred a couple of days earlier. Then they again sat Larsen down to talk to AFFA. The session went for 15-20 minutes. Friend would often talk about this case when asked in the coming years. He told Jay Gourley:

> *He was obviously in a trance. I saw it. There was no doubt about that in my mind. I would see his pulse quicken. I could see his Adam's apple move up and down rapidly. His handwriting was entirely different from his normal handwriting. The muscles in his torso did not appear to be strained, but the muscles in his arms were obviously stressed, as were the muscles around his neck. I tried to ask questions, but he did not respond to me. Others asked questions. He responded to only one man. I asked the man to whom the Navy officer was responding to ask AFFA if he would arrange a flyby. The officer's arm jerkily wrote out, 'The time is not right.' I was convinced that there was something there. It didn't make much difference whether they (Larsen and Swan) were in contact with some people in outer space or in contact with someone right here on*

Earth. There was something there, and we should find out more about it.

When Friend asked his commanding General at Wright Patterson about it, he was told another agency was dealing with it, and the Air Force would be hands-off. However, the evidence shows that many others in the Canadian and United States continued to contact and deal with Swan and AFFA until the 1980s.

The Aliens Send a Message

On August 23, 1954, the technology magazine *Aviation Week and Space Technology* released a story that stirred the American population. It also angered Pentagon officials trying desperately to keep the story secret. The short one-paragraph article in the 'Washington Roundup' section stated:

> *Pentagon scare over the observance of two previously unobserved satellites orbiting the earth has dissipated with the identification of the objects as natural, not artificial satellites. Dr. Lincoln LaPaz, an expert on extraterrestrial bodies from the University of New Mexico, headed the identification project. One satellite is orbiting about 400 miles out, while the other track is 600 miles from the earth.*

The Pentagon momentarily thought the Russians had beaten the U.S. to space explorations. However, the next day the New York Times, basing their story in part on the Aviation Week story, wrote their version telling of the discovery of two large objects orbiting the earth. In a matter of days, the story was all over the country. Wilbert Smith, in charge of the Canadian flying saucer investigation, had also heard about the discovery and was alerting researchers to look for the two objects in the night sky.

Despite the official explanation that the objects were just new natural satellites like the moon, not everyone was buying the answer. The chances of capturing two asteroids in the earth's gravitation field were almost impossible; if it did happen, they would still be there. So many in public would assume that the two objects were artificial and might have been tied into the close approach of Mars, which always seemed to bring many more UFO sightings than the norm.

On the evening of November 28, 1954, at radio station WGN in Chicago, the two mysterious satellites were the topic of conversation. The radio host Jim Mills and his guest for the day, UFO researcher John Otto (referred to in CIA documents as a villain and scoundrel), got an idea to try and communicate with the orbiting satellites. The plan of action was carefully planned and kept secret until the day of the plan.

At exactly 11:15 during the radio show, Mills announced that they would attempt to send a signal to the orbiting satellites and get the aliens to send back a message for the radio listeners. Mills said that in ten minutes, at 11:25, they would prompt the aliens to send their message with the words, *"Come in Outer Space."* Only a 10-minute warning was given to prevent someone in the audience from getting a truck with the proper radio equipment and broadcasting a signal. Mills announced that once they had prompted the spacemen to talk, they would shut off the microphones in the studio for fifteen seconds. They would, however, continue to broadcast their signal to the Chicago audience. The aliens were expected to tap into the WGN transmitter and send their signal to the radio listeners. All the radio listeners were encouraged to run and get a tape recorder to record the signal if it did come through.

When 11:25 arrived, Mills said, *"Come in Outer Space,"* and turned off the microphones. The two men had a radio in the studio, so they, too, could hear the alien message. They sat and waited the appointed fifteen seconds but heard nothing coming over their radio. The show ended, and the two men left the studio.

Mills and Otto were away from the studio when the calls came in. There were four calls in total coming from people who claimed that they had heard the alien message. They were from varying places around the radio-listening audience. Later, CIA documents revealed five Chicago ham radio operators also claimed to have taped *"These weird, coded messages from outer space."* One more listener in Wisconsin stated they, too, had made a tape recording of the message, but it was never recovered.

Two of the callers who claimed to have received a message were two older sisters who lived north of the studio. The two sisters, Marie and Mildred Maier, phoned and were upset about the joke the station had just played on the listeners. They stated it was not funny to be playing "Jingle Bells," pretending it was a message from space. They were told that "Jingle Bells" had not been played, and arrangements were made to visit with the ladies. John Otto met with the women to get their story and was able to make a copy of the tape. The tape was then played a number of times over the air. It apparently sounded like jingle bells with some strange telex noise in the background. In early 1955 the Maier sisters reported on their UFO experiences, along with the story of the message from space, in the *Journal of Space Flight*. The Office of Scientific Investigation at the CIA saw the article and contacted the Scientific Contact Branch to recover the tape.

Two men from the Chicago Contact Division, Chief George O. Forrest and Officer Dewalt Walker met with the sisters to recover the tape. Because the CIA was on the record as not being involved in the UFO phenomena beyond their short involvement with the 1953 Robertson Panel, they could not tell the Maier sisters they were from the CIA. To overcome this problem, they dressed up as Air Force officers to make the Maier sisters believe they would be dealing with the Air Force. They did this as the Air Force was publicly known to be working on UFOs. The CIA had always publicly denied they were involved in the investigation of UFOs, so any involvement by the CIA had to be hidden. Their first attempt to recover the tape from the two women was unsuccessful. The women were impressed that the government was interested in their tape, but they would not part with it. On the second visit, the two intelligence officers were able to get not only a copy but the original tape. They forwarded it to CIA headquarters. Forrest wrote that he felt the case was not a hoax. *"In all seriousness,"* he wrote. *"We don't think that the sisters themselves are trying to fake anything."* He then wrote that he hoped the Chicago office would be informed if there should be an answer.

It was over until 1957 when NICAP researcher Leon Davidson spoke to the Maier sisters and decided he would like to talk to the Air Force officer who had recovered the tape. Furthermore, he was very interested to see the analysis the Air Force had done on the tape. Davidson wrote to the address Dewalt had given the sisters and received a reply from Walker stating that he had forwarded the tape to the proper authorities and had no further information. Not satisfied and now assuming Walker might be CIA, he wrote to Eisenhower's Director of Central Intelligence, Allen Dulles, demanding the results of the tape analysis and the real identity of Dewalt. Dulles then did what the CIA normally does in such cases. Firstly, he reported Davidson to the FBI as a possible subversive; secondly, he created a new lie. The Air Force was contacted by the chief of the Chicago Contact Division and told to write a letter to Davidson, falsely telling him that Dewalt was, in fact, an Air Force officer and that the tape had shown only identifiable Morse code from a known U.S. licensed radio station.

Next, J. Arnold Shaw, the assistant to Allen Dulles, wrote Davidson on May 8, 1957, with a carefully worded statement. It deflected involvement away from the CIA to the Air Force, *"A survey of the intelligence community has resulted in the determination that another agency of the government analyzed the tape in question,"* wrote Shaw. *"We believe you will receive another communication shortly from the Air Force, which will answer your query as to the nature of the recording."* Armed with this new information Davidson again contacted the CIA, demanding to know the identity of the Morse code operator and the name of the agency that had done the analysis claimed by the Air Force. As the CIA had claimed the tape was not analyzed, they were in a situation where they didn't know what to do. So undercover CIA officers contacted Davidson and promised to try and get him the Morse operator's name and the transmitter's identification if possible. This, of course, was just a stall tactic.

When this did not appease Davidson, the CIA again dressed up an intelligence officer who met with Davidson in person in New York City. This officer tried to talk Walker out of pursuing the case any longer. He told Davidson that the Air Force could not *"Disclose who was doing what."* Davidson would not accept the argument and pressed on. The officer then agreed to see what he could do.

The general rule for the CIA seemed to be to keep lying until you get it right. When confronted with a letter from Congressman Joseph Karth related to Davidson's claims that he was being lied to by the CIA, the CIA chose to lie outright to the Congressman. Karth was told that besides a brief involvement with the Robertson panel, the CIA has not participated in any flying saucer activities and referred all correspondence to the Air Force. As to Mr. Davidson's charges, the CIA wrote to the Congressman:

> *Mr. Davidson's belief that this agency is involved in the 'flying saucer furor' and is using this as a tool in psychological warfare is entirely unfounded. His indication that the CIA is misguiding persons in leading them to believe in Flying Saucers is also entirely unfounded.*

The next lie in store for Davidson involved a CIA officer pretending to be an Air Force officer, who then phoned Davidson back and told him a thorough check showed that the signal had been of U.S. (not outer space) origin. The tape and notes had been destroyed to conserve space. Knowing now that he was getting the runaround by the CIA, Davidson warned the agent that he and his agency, whichever it was, were acting like Jimmy Hoffa and the Teamster Union in destroying records that might indict them. This statement led to a funny series of messages inside the CIA. People dealing with Davidson were warned that he had already been given too much information and many names. Unless the letter was registered, no one was allowed to answer anything from Davidson. They were reminded that they were under no legal obligation to answer questions from the public. Strangely, this technique of simply ignoring Davidson worked.

Eventually, Davidson seemed to give up on the case, and the tape from outer space was forgotten until 1997 when the CIA retold part of the story in their 1997 report, 'A Die-Hard Issue: The CIA's Role in the Study of UFOs, 1947-90,' which was published in *Studies in Intelligence* in 1997 (*Note: This author has spent over two years trying to recover the documents used to footnote 'A Die-Hard Issue: The CIA's Role in the Study of UFOs, 1947-90,' related to the Maier case*).

The first FOIA gained a couple of documents from the numerous footnotes. An appeal brought forward several new ones, but some were still missing. Searches on the CIA website when searching 'Davidson' and 'radio code' turned up other information that had not been released to me. I then filed for the entire file on the Maier sisters, which ended the meager CIA cooperation I had received to that point. The CIA demanded that I now pay for search fees as a new search would be required, and the material would not add to understanding how the government operated. An appeal to that decision was filed and ruled against by the CIA.

CHAPTER 3

UFOS AND THE GOVERNMENT

Why is the Government Covering Up the Truth?

> *"I do have knowledge from excellent sources that saucers have crashed and fallen into the hands of earth people. I have even handled 'hardware,' but all this is buried deep in classification and may as well be in the fourth dimension for all the good it is in evaluating the reality of the craft or the people who manipulate them."*
> **--Wilbert Smith, who headed up the Canadian investigation into Flying Saucers**

> *"Whoever makes the first major breakthrough in this field will have a quantum lead over his opponent, an advantage similar to sole possession of nuclear weapons."*
> **--Colonel John Alexander spoke about advanced weapons such as psychotronic weaponry.**

The question of why the government is covering up the truth of the extraterrestrial presence is one of the most asked questions to me when I appear on radio talk shows. I have wondered about this and therefore set about to find out why there was a cover-up after almost 70 years. The way I approached the problem was to use the model of Kremlinology, which was the study during the cold war of the Kremlin, which was the seat of government for the former Soviet Union. Because everything that happened inside the Kremlin was secret, Kremlinologists would have to read between the lines of every statement and watch every movement inside the Kremlin to figure out exactly what was happening. If there is a cover-up of an extraterrestrial presence, the government or secret cabal that is the governing body over UFO policy is operating in total secrecy like the former USSR Kremlin.

The position I took in my investigation was to assume not that the secret keepers were evil people determined to destroy the world for their children and grandchildren but rather a group that believed they were doing the best for future generations. They may be deluded, but they were doing things they thought would save the world. This approach to the cover-up problem explained a key fact of UFO history that really disturbed me. That problem involved former Presidents Gerald Ford and Jimmy Carter. Both had been strong supporters of UFO disclosure. Ford had made many speeches demanding openness and a congressional investigation where government officials could be brought forward under oath and forced to tell the truth. Jimmy Carter had campaigned for President, and part of his campaign promises was that if elected, he would release all the UFO files held by the government. Yet, when both were elected, they failed to support their belief that the truth behind the UFO mystery should be made public. Neither man disclosed what the government knew on the subject nor ever uttered the word UFO while in office.

So, what happened? Something had changed when they became President. What had they been told in briefings that made them change teams and decide that a continued UFO cover-up was best for the country? But after Carter took office in January of 1977, his promise of announcing UFO information was not to be. Walter Wurfel, the administration's Deputy Press Secretary, told the press,

"There might be some aspects of some sightings that would have defense implications that possibly should be safeguarded against immediate and full disclosure."

The mental capabilities exhibited by the aliens also present possible weaponization capabilities. Col. John Alexander wrote about some of these weapons that were being developed in 1980, *"There are weapons systems that operate on the power of the mind and whose lethal capacity has already been demonstrated. Clearly, psychotronic weapons already exist; only their capabilities are in doubt."*[23]

Is There a UFO Government Control Group?

In my book *UFOs, Area 51, and Government Informants*, I spent a lot of time looking at the evidence that backed the idea of an inside control group known as 'MJ-12.' The idea of this MJ-12 group started to appear in the early 1980s through a researcher known as Bill Moore. Moore had written a book entitled, *The Roswell Incident*, which sold many copies and was the forerunner of the modern obsession with the Roswell crash. Days after Moore released the book, he was contacted by US intelligence which started to tell him the story of MJ-12, the super-secret group that President Harry Truman had established to deal with the extraterrestrial presence on earth. Moore was fed information by USAF master sergeant Richard Doty and a second person attached to the CIA that Bill Moore gave the code name Falcon. Later ten more intelligence sources would come forward to provide information to Moore. It is believed that some of these may have been ex-CIA directors.

Moore's involvement with the MJ-12 story culminated in a document release made in 1987 by Moore and two other researchers named Jamie Shandera and Stanton Friedman. The document marked "Top Secret Restricted," purported to be a briefing document presented to then-President-elect Dwight

Eisenhower about the 12-person group of high-level scientists and military officials who made up the elite Top-Secret MJ-12 committee. In *UFOs, MJ-12 and Government Informants,* I wrote that I believed the document had been a leak of true and false material that a present-day MJ-12 type group had authorized to desensitize the public about how the White House had handled the flying saucer problem. I also wrote that although some of the material in the document did not appear correct (like the failure to mention that there was a live alien recovered at Roswell), there was lots of evidence that indicated this mythical MJ-12 group mentioned in the document had existed. The document was altered to avoid breaking the law by releasing classified material and to protect the overall UFO program that needed to remain classified.

The evidence indicating that there actually *was* an MJ-12 group included the following information. My co-author T. Scott Crain had come across a woman (USAF NCO) who had been on a 1979 declassification team in Okinawa, Japan. While declassifying documents in a general's office, the team came across a document that she told us may not have been the same document. Still, it appeared to contain all the same material. This woman was hassled when we first released the book in 1991.

In conversations with the former President of Penn State University, he confirmed the MJ-12 group. His first confirmation came in 1987, just days after Moore made the MJ-12 document public. Walker said, *"Yes, I know of MJ-12. I have known them for 40 years. I believe that you're chasing after and fighting with windmills!"* Moya Lear, the wife of Lear Jet inventor Bill Lear, phoned her friend, four-star General James Doolittle, to ask if the group had existed. Doolittle confirmed the group had existed but said that was all he could say. She was prodded to do this by her son John Lear who had just become aware of the MJ-12 document.

Edgar Mitchell, the Commander of Apollo 14, is another high-level person who confirmed that the group MJ-12 did exist based on sources he had. General Arthur E. Exon, who was at Wright Field in 1947 when the alien bodies were shipped from the Roswell crash site, said he was aware of a UFO controlling committee made up primarily of high-ranking military officers and intelligence people. He did not know the group's name but called them the 'Unholy Thirteen.'

In July 1989, Bob Oeschler provided some of the most dramatic evidence supporting the existence of a group known as MJ-12 when he taped a conversation on the MJ-12 subject with Bobby Ray Inman. Inman stated that MJ-12 *"meant something to him."* And that he *"has been aware of a program to 'indoctrinate the public' in UFO matters prior to his retirement."* And that he had 'some expertise' around UFOs, but his information was out of date at the time of the conversation.

Another person who confirmed the existence of MJ-12 was an archivist at the National Archives in College Park, Maryland, who approached me after a lecture in Eureka Springs, Arkansas, in 2005. His job was to declassify documents for release, which meant he worked inside the classified vault and saw all government documents before their release. He stated that a colleague had reported seeing documents with the MJ-12 designator on them years before while doing declassification on Joint Chiefs of Staff documents.

Harold Stuart, a former member of the Truman administration, had been listed as a member of an advisory committee for MJ-12 in Robert Collins' 2005 book, *Exempt from Disclosure*. In replies to letters from researcher Brian Parks, Stuart stated:

> *I have a vague recollection of MJ-12, but not significantly specific to make a comment. I was not on the MJ-12 Advisory Board and only had a faint recollection of this project or group. I did know most of the Generals you mentioned in your letter, but sorry I cannot shed any light on your request.*

Researcher Lee Graham wrote many letters and filed dozens of FOIA requests to try and validate the MJ-12 document. Finally, on May 24, 1990, the Defense Investigative Service (DIS) responded to one of Graham's FOIA requests by sending him back a copy of the MJ-12 document, each page of which was stamped 'Unclassified' across the lower part of the page. This indicated the document had been declassified. Unfortunately, Graham was never able to clarify who had done the declassification.

In a 1987 letter written by John Andrews to his good friend Lockheed Skunk Works President Ben Rich, Andrews stated that he had known about MJ-12 for years, *"Even though officially it didn't exist."* In a discussion with Lee Graham, he said he had heard of MJ-12 in early 1984, almost a year before researchers Moore and Shandera reviewed copies of the MJ-12 briefing document for President Eisenhower in the mail.

Since the release of the book in January 2013, there have been two new pieces of evidence that help to confirm that there was an MJ-12 control group. The first piece of new evidence came from a story told by Jesse Marcel Jr., the son of the intelligence officer at the Roswell Army Airfield that handled the July 1947 UFO crash. Marcel, who told his story in front of the May 2013 'Citizen's Hearing on Disclosure' in Washington D.C., stated that several years ago, he was called to Washington D.C. by Dick D'Amato for a meeting in a secure room in the Senate Building. D'Amato was the chief counsel and chief investigator for Senator Bird's Senate Appropriations Committee. When the Area 51 story broke in 1989 in Nevada, Bird, and other senators on the committee responsible for all budget spending wondered if they were financing the back-engineering of flying saucers at Area 51 without being told what they were paying for. D'Amato was provided the appropriate security clearances and sent to investigate.

D'Amato confirmed the alien projects but was not able to penetrate them. He told Steven Greer, *"Senator Byrd and some others have asked me to look into these things, and we've gotten close enough to know that these projects do exist. But I'm telling you that with a Top-Secret clearance and subpoena power from the Senate Appropriations Committee, I cannot penetrate those projects. You're dealing with the varsity team of all-black projects, so watch out, and good luck."*[24]

Marcel stated that he and D'Amato met around a huge conference room table. On the table was a novel that had been written by Whitley Strieber called *Majestic*. The book is about the Roswell crash and the MJ-12 control group that was established to deal with the extraterrestrial appearance on earth. D'Amato said, *"I want to tell you something. This (pointing to the book) is not fiction."* Marcel asked, *"When are you doing to tell the public?"* D'Amato replied, *"If it were up to me, I'd have done it yesterday, but it is not up to me. I am just here to investigate the cost of keeping it secret. In reality, there is a black government. They have control of the debris. They answer to no one, and they are not elected. They have unlimited money to spend. They are the ones who have control over it."*

The second new piece of evidence came from an unlikely source, Dr. John Alexander. John was a Colonel in the US Army and had been interested in the UFO mystery since a young boy in 1947. He also had done work on 'esoteric projects,' specifically in the intelligence community with psycho-kinesis. Alexander wrote a book on his UFO investigations called *UFOs: Myths, Conspiracies, and Realities*. In the book, Alexander pointed out that although UFOs are real, they are of no interest to the American government. Therefore, there is no cover-up of the facts by American officials. Alexander is also well known in the UFO community for hosting a Top Secret - Special Access series of meetings in the mid-1980s to look at the UFO problem for a possible new government look at the problem. The group was called the Advanced Theoretical Physics Group and, interestingly, had the same "Top Secret Restricted" classification as the MJ-12 document.

In a June 15, 2013, interview with radio show host Nancy Du Tertre, Alexander suddenly announced that the MJ-12 group had existed.[25] This sudden disclosure was strange. That is because the MJ-12 controversy is central to the whole government cover-up theory believed by most in the UFO community. Yet Alexander did not talk about the MJ-12 idea in his book, which had as its basic premise that no government control group deals with the UFO mystery. This is the transcript of the interaction.

Alexander: *"I think that there actually was a group, and they created something known as COG, continuity of government, and it was to prevent nuclear decapitation of the United States. It was really super, super sensitive."*

Nancy Du Tertre: Well, let me ask you this. Does MJ-12, as far as you know, exist today?

Alexander: *"I don't think so. I had someone whisper to me that it had existed. I didn't think it had existed at all, but when I looked into it and asked if the names were correct, and they said yes, that should tell me what I need to know to figure it out. That's how we came up with this particular occupation because most of them were into nuclear warfare. That was one common thread of all the people on the list, and much more so certainly than with UFOs."*[26]

Even though Alexander's opinion of what the group might have differed from the UFO control group's interpretation, the significance of what Alexander said cannot be emphasized enough; MJ-12 existed. The names on the UFO document that appeared on a film in the mailbox of Jamie Shandera in 1984 were correct.

The Government Meets with the ETs

> "What would you think if I told you that there had been a landing of an alien craft at Holloman Air Force Base and it had been filmed?"
>
> --Security Manager at the Defense Audio Visual Agency at Norton Air Force Base talking to producers Robert Emenegger and Allen Sandler.

Most people know that *Close Encounters of the Third Kind* was a box-office blockbuster. The movie was released in 1977. It cost $20 million to produce and grossed almost $304 gross revenues. Most people don't know that the film was based partly on an event that occurred in May 1971. That is where Spielberg got the basic plot for the movie.

The story began to unfold in 1973. Allen Sandler had been approached to do a film project for the Department of Defense. He called up his partner Bob Emenegger with whom he had worked on previous projects. They headed for Norton Air Force Base in California. There they met with Paul Shartle, the Security Manager for the Defense Audio Video Agency at Norton, which held all the films from the various military units. They headed next to a 'clean room,' where the CIA filmed some of its training films. Shartle explained to the two men that the Department of Defense wanted them to produce several documentaries about the military to put it in a positive public light. They were told about programs where the Navy used dolphins, 3-D holography, and numerous other leading advanced project concepts.

Then Shartle dropped the bomb. He stated that the Defense Department would also like a film done on unidentified flying objects and would like the documentary to be hidden under the other documentaries. The statement wildly shook Emenegger as he had been telling his wife Marlene to quit reading all the UFO nonsense in the tabloids for years. Now he was being told it was true. Not only was it true, but Shartle stated that the Defense people were prepared to allow them to use the film of a landing of a flying saucer at Holloman Air Force Base, which occurred, they were told, in May 1971. It appeared that the military was preparing to disclose something to the public, and many newspapers and magazines were getting leaks hinting at a disclosure of some type.

> *"The government will release all its (UFO) information within the next three years."*
> **-The APRO UFO Organization, 1974.**

> *"The government is almost ready to release some of the information it has reportedly withheld from the public for 25 years concerning extraterrestrial life. This super cover-up concerning UFOs makes the White House's Watergate mess look like a high school affair."*
> **-National Examiner Dec 9, 1974.**

> *"We predict that by 1975 the government will release definite proof that extraterrestrials are watching us."*
> **-Authors Ralph and Judy Blum April 1974.**

> *"The government will tell us what's been going on in a series of television documentaries over a period of months...The entire story is slated to be disclosed by the 200th anniversary of Independence on July 4, 1976."*
> **-Robert Barry, head of the 20th Century UFO Bureau.**

The two men signed an agreement with Air Force Spokesman Bill Coleman to the Pentagon and began their documentary after a warning about classified material. Everyone in the government they requested interviews from agreed to talk. Emenegger was given free access to wander around the highly secure Holloman AFB. They were given access to UFO pictures and films from the Air Force and NASA. They had some indirect access to the Holloman alien landing film and were allowed to use 8 seconds of the film in the final documentary, *UFOs, Past, Present, and Future*. They still possess one Top Secret film showing two UFOs tracking a missile launch at Vandenburg AFB. This is despite Air Force assertions that there is no Top-Secret UFO material and that everything on the subject has been released to the public.

The strange part of the story was the Holloman alien landing, which they were allowed to present as *"Something that might have happened in the past or may happen in the future."* Unfortunately, the 16mm film was called back to the Pentagon just as Emenegger and Sandler were preparing to use it.

I asked Emenegger about it and how similar the Holloman landing story was to Spielberg's *Close Encounters of the Third Kind*, which came out two years after their documentary. I pointed out to Emenegger that Spielberg's story was the Holloman story with just a different location. Like Holloman was a story with a planned landing where officials greet aliens who come off the craft. *"I didn't tell you?"* Emenegger replied. *"Tell me what?"* I asked. *"We gave a copy of the documentary to Steven Spielberg when it came out,"* Emenegger said. *"I told you his sister Annie worked with us on some of our projects. She said Steven would like a copy of it, so we provided it for him. Later, Steven's mother even commented on it. She told me, 'I saw your version of the landing, and I saw Steven's version of the landing, and I like Steven's better.'"*

The Area 51 Story

This is a shortened version of the area 51 story. For those who need every detail, there is an extended account in the book *UFOs, Area 51, and Government Informants*.

The key to understanding the true Area 51 story is aviator John Lear. John was the son of the designer of the Lear Jet, which still flies most business executives around the country. John also made a name for himself in his own right. He had flown for the CIA and held many aircraft speed records and more Air Certificates for different planes than anyone else in the country. He ran for Nevada State Senator at one point. He had helped break the existence of the Stealth fighter and was very vocal about the UFO cover-up. When the Area 51 story first became public, Lear was a Lockheed L-1011 Captain until the company discovered he believed in UFOs. At that point, he was brought in and fired. He was told, *"We can't have someone flying passengers around who believes in UFOs."* John's strong interest in UFOs is a critical component of the Area 51 story.

When the Area 51 story broke worldwide in 1989, John was the Nevada State Director for the Mutual UFO Network. The national conference that year was in Nevada, and John played a key role in the planning. During his lecture, he gave a presentation titled, 'The UFO Cover-up, History and Current Situation.' Because of John's high profile, many people in Nevada and around the country listened closely to him. Lear was even invited to give a UFO speech to the Association of Former Intelligence Officers. The material he was putting out included the wildest UFO rumors and stories of the day, including underground battles with aliens.

The Government wanted the story out that they were back-engineering flying saucers and that there was a live alien at Area 51. It is only one of the dozens of reports they leaked in a plan of acclimatization since they claimed to have gotten out of the UFO investigation business in December 1969. The Air Force, however, needed to maintain the secrecy of the classified aspects of the program. So, they released the information under cover of false and unbelievable information. The plan also involved releasing it through Lear, who would get the information out, but whom people would not believe because of some of the other crazy stories he was telling. The idea of back-engineering and live aliens would make the rounds in the UFO community, but it would remain just a story put out by John Lear.

How do we know this? Firstly, Robert Lazar who was the whistle-blowing scientist who went public with what was going on at S-4, inside Area 51, clearly passed four lie detector tests given to him. Importantly, he ended up providing the leaked information to Lear, who he complained was unable to separate the wheat from the chaff when it came to UFOs. Secondly, George Knapp, the Las Vegas Emmy Award-winning KLAS-TV reporter who broke the story, had over two dozen other witnesses telling bits and pieces of the Lazar story. This included one key high-level witness he tracked down who confirmed the whole ET / S-4 story. Thirdly, in March 1989, Lazar could correctly predict twice, exactly to the minute, when a strange object would be tested on the base. Therefore, the story of saucers and aliens at S-4 was accurate. Fourthly, in the three interviews Lazar did with the Area 51 contractor EG&G in November 1988, the first question in the second interview was, *"What is your relationship to John Lear, and what do you think of him?"* The contractor, therefore, knew that Lazar and Lear knew each other before Lazar went to work at S-4. The contractor would have therefore known that Lazar represented a security risk. That he could tell Lear everything and that Lear would tell the world. The situation provided an opportunity to leak what was happening at the base and maintain the cover-up. With these facts in mind, everything that happened made complete sense.

In November 1988, Lazar (at Lear's suggestion) sent a resume to physicist Edward Teller, whom he had met earlier, asking for help in getting a job. Teller called shortly after and asked him if he wanted to work at the Radiation Lab in California or up at the Nevada test site. Lazar chose to work at the test site. Lazar got interviewed within weeks. Even more telling, he worked at S-4 within days of completing the final interview. This is telling because American officials described the flying saucer program to the Canadian government in 1950 as the most highly classified secret in the United States. It would, therefore, require the highest Top-Secret clearances, extensive background checks, and months to complete. Lazar reports that he was at the S-4 site working only days later. In a highly compartmentalized program like the back-engineering of flying saucers, a person would only be told what he needs to know to do his job. On the other hand, Lazar was given 125 documents to read when he started, which explained all sorts of information on the aliens and the saucer program. He was being set up to carry stories they wanted out to Lear, which is exactly what happened.

Within days of beginning his work in the flying saucer program, Lazar shows up at Lear's house and tells him that he has seen a saucer that belongs to the aliens. This transfer of information continues until March 1989, when Lear, Lazar, and others are caught watching a test of a saucer from the edge of the base. In the real security world, Lazar would have been arrested and put in jail for revealing Top Secret information to Lear and others who did not have clearance. None of this happens. Lazar is not arrested. He does not even lose his security clearance. It is only suspended. He is not even fired. Lazar is phoned later by his security handler Dennis Mariani and told to come to work. At that point, Lazar quits, fearing what might happen if he returns to the base.

Because Lazar passed the lie detector tests, it appears he was a pawn in a game to set up Lear. That game went well until May 1989, when George Knapp was short an interview for his evening TV spot at KLAS-TV in Las Vegas. He asked Lear to bring in that UFO guy he had been talking about who claimed to have worked back-engineering saucers until he was suspended for telling Lear and others when the saucer was being tested. At this moment, the whole plan went terribly for those in control of the leak. The story went viral, and as Knapp put it, *"Every network beat a path"* to Area 51 to do a story. People from Las Vegas and around the country went up into the mountains around Area 51 to look down on the primary Groom Lake Facility in hopes of seeing a flying saucer. The Soviet Union changed the orbit of one of its spy satellites so that it could look down on the base. The Senate Appropriations Committee, responsible for the federal budget, sent Dick D'Amato to Area 51 to find out if there was unauthorized flying saucer research going on at the base. Suddenly the security of everything happening at the base was compromised.

It was not until October 1993 that the Air Force was to get control of the story. The U.S. Air Force filed a notice in the Federal Register to withdraw 3,972 acres of land from the public on the eastern perimeter of Area 51, pushing sightseers back out of sight of the base. In later years the leaks would continue. During a 2013 award ceremony for Shirley MacLaine at the White House, President Obama joked that when he wanted to find out about Area 51, he had to phone MacLaine for information. He then joked about being the first President to talk about the formally non-existent Area 51 in public publicly. The media, who had published government denials about Area 51 for years, failed to mention the sudden reversal.

It appeared that the government also learned from the Area 51 leak disaster. In 2012, on the 65th anniversary of Roswell, Chase Brandon, formally the second most powerful person in the CIA to speak publicly on behalf of the CIA, gave a public interview in front of millions of radio listeners on *Coast to Coast AM*. In the interview, he stated the 1947 Roswell crash did happen, it was extraterrestrial, and there were bodies. The story, like the Area 51 story, took off. But, unlike the Area 51 story, once the CIA saw the reaction to the story, Brandon was told that it was time to *"pull back"* on the story. Brandon stopped doing interviews, and the story faded quickly into history. Attempts made to get details from the CIA went nowhere.

Evidence for Cover-Up

A key part of John Alexander's argument against a government cover-up is the fact that Alexander used his high-level government access to ask 'need to know' officials. This included the director or deputies in all the alphabet agencies asking whether or not a department within the government dealing with the UFO phenomena.

Alexander stated that he was told that although officials might have had personal experiences or interests, none of the officials indicated any knowledge of government involvement. This Alexander position came up again in the just concluded Dolan / Alexander debate on whether or not there is a government cover-up or a black program to deal with UFO technologies. Because of these inquiries by Alexander, many researchers and media people, recognizing Alexander's clearances, have conceded that maybe there is no government role in the UFO mystery.

Although Alexander probably tells the story as he experienced it, I have a problem with the no UFO cover-up based on my limited experience. I am a Canadian with no security clearances or access to high-level officials like Alexander. My limited encounters with high-level officials and the study of these officials have produced the opposite answers to what Alexander said he was given.

I have had only one personal encounter with a high-level official; in April 2001, I asked then Vice-President Dick Cheney about the UFO cover-up when he was a guest on the Diana Rehm show in Washington D.C. Assuming that Cheney would have the necessary 'need to know,' I asked, *"In all your jobs in government, have you ever been briefed on the subject of UFOs, and if so when was it and what were you told."* Cheney answered, *"If I had been briefed on that subject it would probably be classified, and I couldn't be talking about it."* That is a long way from Alexander's contention that there is no cover-up and that high-level officials openly conceded to him that they knew nothing. *"UFOs would probably be classified."* It sounds like some UFO material is being withheld from me. Suppose a nobody like me can get the only official encountered to concede that the UFO subject is classified (as opposed to the 'I know nothing' response that John Alexander got 100% of the time). In that case, it leaves open the possibility that Alexander talked to the wrong people or asked the wrong question.

A few years after I had this encounter with Cheney, my friend Dr. David Rudiak asked the same briefing question to General Wesley Clark after he made a statement while running for

President stating that he believed we could go faster than the speed of light and after I got an inside tip that Clark had been briefed on UFO crash recoveries. The conversation went like this;

Q: Gen. Clark, when you were running for President, you said you thought mankind would one day fly faster than light and visit the stars. My question is when you were in the military, were you ever briefed about UFOs? A: *I heard a bit. In fact, I'm going to be in Roswell, New Mexico, tonight.*

Q: So, you were briefed?

A: *There are things going on. But we will have to work out our own mathematics.*

Again, as opposed to Alexander getting the answer, 'I know nothing,' Clark indicated he heard a bit, and things are going on. Why did Alexander not get such an answer from all the people he asked?

The final example from my limited experience with high-level people came when I reviewed the personal papers of Senator Barry Goldwater. Goldwater wrote several letters on UFOs in the documents, which he was very interested in. In many, he described how he attempted to get into the Blue Room at WPAFB (where all the Top-Secret UFO material was rumored to have been stored) but was denied access by General Curtis LeMay. Goldwater added in a 1975 letter about the LeMay incident, *"It is still classified above Top Secret."* Before 1981, Goldwater stated in his letters that beyond this Wright-Patterson incident, he didn't know anything more than the man on the street.

In 1981, after Goldwater became Chairman of the Senate Intelligence Committee, the tone of the letters changed. He no longer stated that he knew no more than the man on the street. After 1981 Goldwater began to speak of a cover-up of UFO information by the government. Speaking to a fellow ham radio operator Goldwater made this statement indicating that he had obtained some secret inside knowledge on Roswell, *"Relative to your question about the accuracy of the details in the 'Roswell*

Incident,' they are partially true, but not completely. I can't give you any other answer than that, so please don't push it."

In addition, unlike Alexander's contacts, who claimed total ignorance, Goldwater indicated in another post-1981 letter that despite the USAF position that all the files were released in 1969, there was information covered up. It would not be coming out any time soon, *"I have been interested in this subject for a long time, and I do know that whatever the Air Force has on the subject is going to remain highly classified."* Note that Goldwater says, *"I do know"* instead of " I think " or " I would guess. Finally, in an interview with Larry King, Goldwater stated, *"I think some highly secret government UFO investigations are going on that we don't know about and probably never will unless the Air Force discloses them."* Is there a cover-up of UFO information by the government? My brief interaction with high-level officials shows the answer is a resounding yes.

The CIA Confirmation of Roswell

Coast to Coast AM is the biggest overnight talk show in America, with an audience of millions. UFOs are a common topic of conversation. On June 23 and then July 12, Chase Brandon, a 43-year veteran of the CIA, was a guest. The appearances occurred just before and after the 65th anniversary of the infamous 1947 Roswell UFO crash. The science fiction book that Brandon was promoting was timely as it dealt with the CIA's handling of the Roswell crash. Brandon was a key member of the CIA. He had spent 25 years as a covert agent around the world. Then from 1995-2005, he held the job of the chief CIA liaison to Hollywood. Brandon stated that that job made him the second most powerful official (after the director) inside the CIA to make public statements on behalf of the agency. His job involved helping the Hollywood people get the right impression of the CIA when it came up as a subject in a movie. Brandon indirectly confirmed that he is still under contract with the

Alien Bedtime Stories

CIA, telling the *Coast to Coast AM* audience that no one ever retires from the CIA. Everyone likes to help out.

The story Brandon told the audience that evening was that while he was at CIA headquarters, he was waiting for a film crew to do some filming in the Collections area. Although Brandon stated that no one is allowed in the area without an escort, he was wandering around looking at the archives boxes when he saw one that had Roswell written on the label. He stated that he pulled the box down and looked inside. What he saw was a collection of materials that he would not specify. He said that at no time would he ever spell out what was in the box, but that what he saw confirmed to him that the 1947 Roswell UFO crash had been an extraterrestrial event and that it involved cadavers. Brandon did not specify whether or not the material in his Roswell science fiction book had come from material he had seen in the box, but he did hint that the book was much more than fiction. He stated that if readers read the book, they would get an interesting read, but if they read between the lines, they would learn something.

In terms of Obama, the important question is, why would company man Brandon throw the CIA under the extraterrestrial Roswell bus after the CIA has gone 65 years covering up any involvement they might have had in the 1947 crash? The simple explanation for all these seemingly contradictory stories is that the CIA approved Brandon's Roswell disclosure that it was an extraterrestrial event. Brandon was just doing what he was told and broke no security laws in how he put the story out. In his half-dozen interviews about the Roswell box with Brandon, The CIA is contracted to provide intelligence and only does what they are told to do. They are answerable to the President, who is responsible for their actions as they work for him. Thus, Obama would have been very aware and would have to have green-lighted the Roswell Box disclosure to the American people, as he would have been held responsible if the story had backfired with serious questions asked by opponents of the President in an election year. Instead, Obama *was* behind the story, which seemed to be set up as a 'Happy 65th Birthday Roswell' message to the public.

1973-1975: An Age of Awakening

The 1975 Carman Manitoba sightings came at the time of a great awakening in the UFO world. It was in Carman where I saw my first UFO in early May 1975.

In 1973-1975 a series of events set the stage for almost every idea that makes up the modern UFO paradigm. These beliefs include CE-5 contact with extraterrestrials, abduction by the grey aliens, peaceful contact with human-type Pleiadian aliens, the UFO nuclear connection, and the channeling of alien messages. Before 1973, researchers had little idea of what was happening other than strange objects. It was almost as if the force behind the UFO phenomena chose this time in history to awaken researchers to what was going on.

Before 1973 there had only been a few reports of well-known abduction cases. In the 12 years before 1973, there were only a few famous incidents, such as the Betty and Barney Hill encounter in 1961 and the cases of Nebraska Police Officer Herbert Schirmer and Betty Andreasson in South Ashburnham, Massachusetts, in 1967. In 1973 all that changed with the highly publicized shipyard co-workers 42-year-old Charles Hickson and 19-year-old Calvin Parker's dramatic abduction late in the year. The case would become widely known in the media and the UFO community. Less than a month later, on November 2, another abduction report was in Goffstown, NH. In 1973, the pattern developed where abduction and humanoid reports began to rise dramatically. An unrepeated to this day mass wave of humanoid reports took place throughout France and some parts of Italy in 1973, and a considerable number of UFO sightings were reported worldwide. By the time the late 1970s had arrived, reports of humanoids in and around ships started to decline to the point that humanoid sightings are rarely reported anymore.

The abduction reports continued to rise, and they are the main form of alien contact being reported today. It was in 1973 that Dr. Steven Greer had his famous encounter with grey aliens that taught him the CE-5 protocols for contacting extraterrestrials. Greer became the leading spokesman for attempts at interactive encounters with extraterrestrials and the modern UFO disclosure movement. Also, in 1973, Canadian-born Darryl Anka had two close-up UFO sightings during the day in Los Angeles, separated by a week. These experiences set him on the road to becoming the most prominent UFO channeler in history, channeling the entity Bashar. He continues to appear in front of large crowds today.

In July of 1974, contactee Charles A. Silva repeatedly met face to face an extraterrestrial human woman, who said he could call her 'Rama.' She and other witnesses associated with her came here from their home planet in the Pleiades. The movement known as Mission RAMA continues today. According to Dr. Joe Burkes, its mission is *"The creation of a worldwide network of contactees who are promoting interplanetary solidarity and peace."*

The second half of 1974 also brought the bizarre abduction of Carl Higdon while he was elk hunting in Wyoming. The encounter describes one of the first accounts of aliens using their minds to fly the craft. Other 1974 abduction reports came from Utica, Cincinnati, Ohio; Hinesville, Georgia; Cordova, Alaska; Mount Vernon, Indiana; Denver, Colorado; Los Angeles, California; Valley Washington, Council Bluffs, Iowa; Brooksville, Maine; Metcalf, Illinois, Hobbs New Mexico, Gila Bend, Arizona, Chile, two in Brazil, Ireland, Egypt, Wales, Senora Mexico, Sweden, Norway, Australia, Quebec Canada, Morocco, and three in England.

Mike Clelland had two encounters in Michigan in 1974, including a close-up UFO sighting with missing time that was probably an abduction experience. Mike goes on to be the critical person doing interviews with UFO abductees. He is also the foremost authority in the field dealing with birds (primarily owls) and the connection of synchronicity in the UFO phenomena.

The most famous abduction researcher in history, Bud Hopkins, began his research into alien abductions in 1975. He will discover the concept of missing time and the idea that egg and sperm samples are being taken in a hybrid program.

The most famous and infamous modern contactee, Eduard 'Billy' Meier, appeared on the UFO scene in January 1975. He reports his contacts with the Pleiadeans just like the Peruvian RAMA group. He produces a series of very clear photos of UFOs, still the subject of much debate inside the UFO community.

Also, in 1975, there were three widely publicized abductions. The first was on August 13, when Air Force Sergeant Charles L. Moody reported being abducted in New Mexico. Then, less than two weeks later, just south of the Carman, Manitoba sightings, near two Minuteman 111 missile silos at Buffalo, North Dakota, Sandy Larson is abducted with her boyfriend and daughter. The final abduction in 1975 that put the abduction subject on the map took place in front of five witnesses when Travis Walton was abducted for five days in Arizona.

At the same time these abductions were in the news, a movie, *The UFO Incident,* was released on NBC to millions telling the story of the most famous UFO abduction of all time, the 1961 Betty and Barney Hill story. "Abduction" becomes a household word. Starting eight days after *The UFO Incident* aired, as part of a huge flap of sightings along the Canadian-US border, UFOs began visiting the nuclear weapon storage areas at numerous Strategic Air Command (SAC) bases in the northern tier states forcing a high-priority (Security Option 3) alert. These incursions continued at various bases (Loring, Wurtsmith, Minot, and Maelstrom) until a week after the Walton abduction on November 5, 1975. The incidents drew the attention of the CIA, the Joint Chiefs of Staff, and the Secretary of Defense. The Air Force informed the public and the press that individual sightings were isolated incidents. However, an Air Force document says, "Security Option III was implemented, and *security measures were coordinated with fifteen Air Force bases from Guam to Newfoundland."*

Alien Bedtime Stories

The period of intense activity, which started in 1972, also brought intense research into paranormal phenomena by intelligence agencies. The work on remote viewing was begun at the Stanford Research Institute, and Uri Geller and Peter Hurkos were brought to America by Andrija Puharich. Geller and the psychic Ingo Swann are tested at length in various government laboratories to assess their mental abilities.

Puharich, who was working for the CIA in the early through to mid-1970, gathered a group of what is now referred to as 'Star-seeds,' or 'Space Kids.' Puharich worked with a couple of hundred young people between the ages of 9 and 21 or 22. They were identified by their abilities to bend metal as Uri Geller was doing. Puharich regressed these young people back to their previous lives, and the children reported coming to Earth for a reason. The story they told was the same story told above about a plan to help in the awakening of the world. Puharich explained:

> *The ones who had these spontaneously given powers would remember that they had lived somewhere else in the Universe. That was the basics, and they would actually go there and describe it. It would turn up that there were actually 24 civilizations that they came from that are now somehow connected to Earth...some civilizations are here for healing, some for pure science, and some for the political aspects. They are all kind of specialized. But the story was always the same. These youngsters I investigated were asked by the leaders of their civilizations to come to Earth because Earth is heading for a lot of trouble. They were asked to incarnate, and grudgingly they said, 'Okay, I'll volunteer.' None of them were happy about this assignment, like being sent to the slums. The youngsters, who are here as representatives, are souls from those civilizations who came here to carry out those roles. They are always connected and are being fed information; they also know that there is going to*

be some kind of cataclysmic crisis for humanity. They are here because that crisis is arriving.

I spoke to one of the Space Kids in Puharich's program, and she said she knew most of the kids involved. She named two:

> Puharich spoke to me of two of his earliest space kids, the first one being Charles Tart, the mathematician. The second one he spoke about kindly was Michael Philips, the producer of 'Close Encounters of the Third Kind.' In his Faraday cage sessions, Michael found out his 'mission' was to produce a movie about extraterrestrials, which he did. And I got to congratulate Michael after the premier (opening night) in NYC of 'Close Encounters of the Third Kind.' I saw him standing in the lobby watching people coming out of the movie, shook his hand, and complimented him on, 'completing his mission.'

The period of 1973-1975 also brought hundreds of reports of bizarre and mysterious cattle mutilations across America and, to a lesser extent, in Canada. However, these mutilations started in 1967 and continued into the century, when they seemed to diminish in number.

Finally, it is important to add to these 1973-75 patterns that the crop circle phenomena started in the UK in 1976 with a message given to Joyce Bowles and Ted Pratt that designs would start appearing in wheat fields. Colin Andrews, who coined the phrase 'crop circle,' spoke of the significance,

> Pat Delgado lived just 6 miles away from this event and was the first person, apart from the police, to visit the spot and investigate this pivotal event. I lived 14 miles away and was on my way to a meeting and witnessed the very first crop circle 'cross design' to appear, as indicated to Joyce Bowles and Ted Pratt. This location was within sight of the Bowles incident. I believe that my overwhelming inner sense of

significance ascribed to 'the cross' was primed in my psyche by two strange events that happened to me while in bed at my home near Stonehenge when I was five years old (1951). As you might know, I was regressed by Dr. James Harder, who had heard about my experiences. Harder had also regressed Betty Hill and Travis Walton. During my 45-minute regression, I revealed details about the future climate and other details noted on file. Topographical details not known to me where the UFO arrived were checked out after the regression and were found to be 100% accurate. My parents and my brother had a very close encounter with a UFO also when I was in my early teens; this happened just a few miles away. It's a long story but a very bizarre one.[27]

Years later, Travis, Betty, and I would come together to share details. And so not only was the new stage set for the crop circle subject, but thanks to the choreography from an unknown selective process, a new chapter in the journey for humanity was also prepared. The tip of a large transition seemed to be taking place. All of these mid-70s events form a strong pattern of events that indicate something beyond our individual conscious minds is building our belief system and awareness slowly through carefully designed events.

Like to Talk to an Alien?

Did the US Navy begin efforts in 1998 to prepare for a world where extraterrestrials exist and are living among the human population? This bizarre story arose with a 2002 article written by C. Austin Fitts, a former Assistant Secretary of Housing and Urban Development in the Bush administration, called '*The $64 Question:*

What's Up with the Black Budget.'[28] Her claim was that in 1998 after she had left the Bush administration, she had been approached and brought onto the board of the Arlington Institute, a futuristic think tank in the Washington, D.C. area. The President of the Arlington Institute, who offered Fitts the position, was a man by the name of John Petersen. Also on the institute's board was former Clinton CIA Director James Woolsey. Petersen arranged for the Starlight Director, Dr. Steven Greer, to attend a private dinner party at his home in Arlington, Virginia. He would spend three hours talking to Woolsey about the UFO situation in December 1993 while Woolsey was still the sitting Director. *"At the time, I was the target of an intense smear campaign that would lead the normal person to assume that I would be in jail shortly or worse."* Fitts recalled: *"John explained that the Navy understood that it was all politics; they did not care. I met with a group of high-level people in the military in the process, including the Undersecretary of the Navy (Jerry MacArthur Hultin)."* Part of the reason she had been brought on board was to help with a project set up *"to help the Navy adjust their operations for a world in which it was commonly known that aliens exist and live among us. When John explained this purpose to me,"* Fitts wrote in her original article:

> *I explained that I did not know that aliens existed and lived among us. John asked me if I would like to meet some aliens. For the only time in my life, I declined an opportunity to learn about something important. I was concerned that my efforts with Arlington could boomerang and be connected with the smear campaign and the effects that I was managing. I regret that decision. At John's suggestion, I started to read books on the topic and read about 25 books over the next year on the alien question, the black budget, and alien technology.*

The idea that a Washington think tank would indicate some aliens lived among us is big news, especially when a former CIA Director is sitting on the board of directors. Petersen denied the

Fitts story when he learned I might put it on my website. He and Woolsey are also on record denying that the 1993 meeting with Woolsey was anything but a dinner party where Greer carried on about things no one really asked for. Months later, I sent the denial to Fitts for her comment, and she replied in length that she stood behind her story on every point.

Fitts has tried to stay out of the dispute over the years but did enter it again after researcher Dr. Michael Salla got involved in 2008. Salla interviewed Petersen, who again denied the story. Salla also talked to board member Joe Firmage, who also denied Fitts' version of events. After Salla made his inquiries public, Fitts contacted him and made public notes from an Arlington Institute board meeting that backed up her story that extraterrestrials had been discussed. The notes from March 26, 2006, board meeting read:

> *Mr. Petersen then reported that the Institute had been approached to determine if it was interested in publishing a study by Pickford and Lindemann on the subject of life outside of the earth. After discussion, there was general agreement that publication of the study would be a good idea and would be consistent with the work otherwise being done by the Institute with respect to wild cards.*

Although nothing is on record of what Pickford and Lindemann produced for the Arlington Institute, they are on record as having done work related to the discovery of extraterrestrial intelligence. (ETI) Professor Allen Tough, futurist, scientist, and author, talked about an ETI workshop he attended sponsored by Pickford and Lindemann:

> *I experienced one useful model for such a workshop just two weeks before the Hawaii seminar. Called the second 'Contact Planning' meeting and held in Denver, Colorado, this workshop was sponsored by the International Space Sciences Organization and*

organized by Kyle Pickford and Michael Lindemann. For me, there were three personal highlights:

(1) The 23 participants were a fascinating mix of backgrounds and beliefs and competencies, but all became enthusiastically involved in the effort to anticipate just what might happen during the hours and days after contact with ETI. Quite an experience to spend 48 hours immersed in contact!

(2) We spent one afternoon in five groups: business, religion, science, government, and media/public. Each group role-played its behavior for each of the eight scenarios. Although I have read lots of literature on post-contact behavior, this was the first time that I deeply grasped just how people in each of those categories may actually behave right after contact. Very sobering.

(3) What can we do now to prepare? We spent the last few hours of the meeting generating and clustering various strategic planning possibilities. A large number of these ideas clearly fit into two clusters that I find very encouraging: (a) Tell the general public the truth right away and (b) Prepare to communicate and negotiate with ETI in a friendly and cooperative manner, even if its behavior seems unfriendly.[29]

CHAPTER 4

CONSCIOUSNESS AND UFOS

"I regard consciousness as fundamental. Everything that we talk about, everything that we regard as existing, postulates consciousness."
- Max Planck, Nobel Prize recipient. The father of Quantum Physics.

"The laws of quantum mechanics itself cannot be formulated...without recourse to the concept of consciousness."
- Eugene Wigner, Nobel Prize recipient.

"The universe does not exist 'out there,' independent of us. We are inescapably involved in bringing about that which appears to be happening. We are not only observers. We are participators. In some strange sense, this is a participatory universe."
-Nobel Prize recipient John Wheeler

"I believe that the discovery of the important connection of consciousness to the UFO phenomena will go down as important as quantum physics and general relativity were to science in the 20th century."
-Nikola Tesla

A comparison between a human being and any of the many aliens that have been reported since 1947 would show almost no differences. Aliens, after all, fly in metal spaceships with doors and windows, benches, and tables. The aliens have two arms, two legs, feet and hands, an upright torso, and a head with two eyes, two ears, a nose, and a mouth.

So, what is different? The main and maybe only difference between aliens and humans is that aliens have complete control of telepathy. Humans can get a noise-free signal when in the presence of the alien but are fairly poor with telepathy when the alien is no longer around.

This would indicate that humans have telepathic abilities, but the alien must assist. Telepathy is an attribute of consciousness. The high-level ability to perform telepathy shows that the aliens have a great understanding and mastery of consciousness.

Cleaning House

"A human being is a part of the whole called by us 'Universe,' a part limited in time and space. He experiences himself, his thoughts, and feelings as something separated from the rest, a kind of optical delusion of his consciousness."
--Albert Einstein.

The UFO phenomenon has been an elusive mystery to the UFO research community. It has not been very repeatable. It is almost impossible to measure and doesn't seem to follow any laws of nature. The problem may be that we have started on the wrong foot. Most of what we have done in research has tried to fit into the scientific materialistic paradigm. In that worldview, the universe starts with a big bang. This scientific materialistic paradigm would have us believe that the universe's matter, all energy, and all the laws that came with the universe, such as gravity, the laws of motion, and electromagnetic force, sprang from nothing in a single moment for no reason.

Psychonaut, lecturer, and writer Terence McKenna talked of this big bang materialistic paradigm:

That is the limit case for credulity. Do you know what I mean by that? I mean, if you can believe that you can believe anything. That is the most improbable proposition the human mind can conceive of. Modern science is based on the principle: 'Give us one free miracle, and we'll explain the rest.'

Understanding the UFO mystery may help start off on the right foot with a consciousness-based model of the universe. In this model, all we know for sure is that we are conscious and aware. That is it. Everything else, because it passes through and is interpreted by the mind, is a subjective experience. In such a model, the mind is the builder, and everything is not quite what it appears to be. Take matter, for example, the basis for the materialistic worldview. In a consciousness model, most of what we think is matter is space. The solid nature of matter is a subjective interpretation. The remaining space makes up 99.9999999999999% of the volume of what we think is matter. To put into perspective how much space there is, we could take all 7+ billion human beings on the Earth and remove all the space between their atomic material structure, and we would be left with a pile of matter about the size of a grain of rice. The material structure of matter is actually created by the electromagnetic forces that hold the matter in place and by the chemical bonding forces. These are two elements that materialistic science requires to have appeared from nothing and for no reason as part of the big bang miracle. They are laws that are required on 'big bang day one,' and not elements that evolved.

Working from a consciousness understanding, the UFO world starts to be easier to explain. Stories such as people moving through walls and closed windows no longer seem unbelievable. Both the body and the wall are almost all space, and the task is not that difficult once the rules are understood. It would be simple as the aliens say, who know the rules. Moving one seemingly solid object through another seemingly solid object is not that big a task.

Modern physics and biology have begun to move towards the consciousness model of the universe. Consider the following experiments.

<u>The Entangled particle experiment</u>, which Einstein called "spooky action at a distance," shows that two particles can become entangled so that they retain a non-local connection that has been estimated to be almost instantaneous (10,000 times the speed of light) even when separated over long distances. Time and space are not factors, as expected in a physical-based world. The experiment repeatedly shows that if you influence one particle, such as an electron, by changing its spin, its entangled partner, no matter how far away, will change its spin. It is, therefore, aware of what you did to its buddy. Now look up the definition of consciousness, and you will see it is to be aware. You are aware and therefore conclude that you are conscious. More importantly, the experiment shows that the smallest particles, like photons and electrons, are conscious because they are aware. If this experiment is valid, then the idea that UFOs must obey physical laws as we presently define them goes out the window. It would also predict that if we detonated trillions of particles in a July 1945 atomic bomb explosion, civilizations who fully grasp the laws of an entangled universe would know what we had done and would show up in large numbers as UFOs have done since 1945 to monitor the situation.

<u>The Double-slit experiment</u>[30] repeatedly showed that observation of the experiment affected the result. The experiment showed that our consciousness creates our reality rather than being an observer of concrete physical events. Therefore, UFO events are not necessarily unchanging physical events but may be co-creators with the observer's mind. Once it is accepted that the mind creates reality, anything is possible.

<u>Morphogenetic Field experiments</u>. There are many which illustrate this effect, but the main one, referenced by Rupert

Sheldrake, who came up with the idea of morphogenetic fields, was an experiment conducted at Harvard University starting in 1920.[31] In the experiment, rats were trained over 21 generations and 15 years to move through a water maze to obtain food. The succeeding generations of rats made fewer and fewer mistakes, indicating some genetic memory being passed from generation to generation, helping the rats get their food. Later, however, in an identical experiment run in Australia, the same type of rats, but not genetically related to the Harvard rats, ran the maze even better right from the start, indicating the learning was not genetic but being tapped by the rats from some sort of field. Experiments with other animals confirmed a non-local morphic field where minds were loading information and other minds could later tap from while loading their own information. This universal mind concept is central to information provided by people who have encountered so-called aliens. It is almost a standard message. The idea presented is that the aliens can access information and operate in a 3-D holographic universe. This 3-D universe is inside us *"since the 'reality' of everything external to you (i.e., the Universe) is ultimately transmitted to you (to your mind) via your five senses. The Universe or your Universe is therefore only perceived and interpreted by and within your mind."*[32] At this point, the physical-based understanding of the universe, saying that extraterrestrial visitation is impossible, is dead.

    Mind machine experiments or symbiotic machines. The idea that the mind can interact and control the physical environment is shown dramatically in an experiment done a decade ago with a neural network of 25,000 neurons from a rat's brain in a petri dish attached to electrodes. The neurons slowly adapted to the point where the neurons started to communicate with the other neurons, as opposed to dying as the physical worldview would predict. This mass of neurons eventually learned to fly an F-22 jet fighter simulator which is hard for the best-trained pilots. The primitive rat brain learned to control the pitch and roll of the aircraft. After a while, it produced a nice straight and level trajectory, even after the worst weather conditions possible were loaded into the simulator.[33] This experiment backs up many stories told by contactees, that similarly, the aliens fly the flying saucer using their minds. Many contactees have reported that they have been trained on how to do this and used their minds to fly the ships. This experiment shows the power of the mind to control reality. The aliens simply understand how consciousness works and employ its potential.

When we use the consciousness model for the world, it is easier to see what the government may have figured out about UFOs. For example, in the Top-Secret Canadian memo that detailed what the American officials had shared about the flying saucer mystery, the statement that 'mental phenomena' might be involved. This clearly shows that the consciousness model to explain the mystery was in play.

Similarly, the former President of the Ivy League, Penn State University, cut off an interview on UFOs to state, *"Unless you understand ESP and how it works, you will not be taken on. Very few understand it."*

The most significant statement that indicates the consciousness model as the Rosetta stone to understanding the UFO problem came from Ben Rich, president of Lockheed Skunk Works. Lockheed is and was a top black budget technology company that works on the leading edge of technology. Much of its direction came from the Defense Advanced Projects Research Agency (DARPA), whose role was to *"maintain the technological superiority of the U.S. military and prevent technological surprise from harming our national security by sponsoring revolutionary, high-payoff research bridging the gap between fundamental discoveries and their military use."*

Rich first hinted that Skunk Works was working on the UFO problem during a speech at WPAFB in 1991, where he showed a slide with a flying saucer. Then during a speech to the UCLA engineering Alumni at UCLA in 1993, Rich confirmed that the UFO problem had been solved, saying they had discovered the mistake in the equation and that we now have the technology to take ET home. Most importantly, Rich spelled out the consciousness connection, *"Anything you can imagine we can already do."* This closely ties into statements that have been made about the power of the mind, such as Napoleon Hill, who said, *"Whatever the mind can conceive and believe, it can achieve,"* or Jesus, who stated, *"If you have faith as small as a mustard seed, you can say to this mountain, 'Move from here to there,' and it will move. Nothing will be impossible for you."* Jan Harzan, one of the attendees of the Rich lecture, questioned Rich after the lecture, asking what UFOs use for propulsion. Rich's reply went straight to the mind as opposed to some new physical propulsion system. He asked Harzan, *"What do you know about ESP?"* Taken aback at being asked a question, Harzan replied, *"That means that all things in time and space are connected."* Rich confirmed the consciousness basis of the alien technology, saying, *"That's how it works."*

As a final observation, consider one common element in the UFO story that has rarely been discussed in UFO literature. There are many complaints that there are very few common elements in describing UFOs or the aliens who fly them. At the same time, the argument is made that the universe's physical laws clearly show that extraterrestrials can't get here from there. There is one description given by almost every contactee, which shows the non-local and non-physical nature of the beings we are dealing with.

Almost without exception, contactees state that the aliens are telepathic. We are not. We are still in the Stone Age on the issue, and that is what separates their ability to travel the universe and our disbelief that it can be done. The aliens understand the power of consciousness which is exhibited by their ability to employ telepathy without any noise in the signal. Whether you call it telepathy, consciousness, or the mind, as Ben Rich and Dr. Eric Walker said: "That is how it works." Some elements of the UFO community have adopted the consciousness model of the universe to help explain how UFOs do what they appear to do. The military black budget world also seems to understand the consciousness connection and has developed alien technology. Physicist Jack Sarfatti stated that he had been told that the military had known about the conscious connection since Roswell.

The key to building a practical, cost-effective, 'UFO-like advanced propulsion system may be a better understanding of the fundamental meaning of quantum mechanics and its relation to consciousness. If the photos of the Roswell crash are not bogus, then the panels with handprints provide a significant clue that the craft is controlled by consciousness. The late Brendan O'Regan, who worked with Astronaut Edgar Mitchell and the IONS Noetic Institute, told me in 1973 that he had classified information that such was the case.[34] Once secular stream science drops some of its religious views of the reality of the material universe; we will be off to the races on building a new and improved world.

Consciousness and the Flying Saucer

When I first received the idea that high-level sources such as the Canadian government, Dr. Eric Walker, and Ben Rich had all volunteered the information that mental phenomena were a key element in understanding UFOs, I gave a speech on consciousness at the 2013 International UFO Congress in Phoenix, Arizona.

I thought that I had just invented the wheel and that everyone should know how important consciousness was to UFOs. Following my presentation, I was sitting at my book table and faced a series of people giving me their books or research on the consciousness connection. It then appeared I had just woken up after 35 years instead of being the wheel's inventor.

As a part of this flood of people wanting to talk consciousness with me, there was an older lady in Phoenix. Stacey, the director of Phoenix MUFON, asked me if I was still willing to talk to this woman. Thinking that I must have agreed at some point I said yes.

On the next Monday, the woman showed up at the house where I was staying and said, *"What did Stacey tell you about me?"* Stacey had just said we should talk. That's good the woman said, and the conversation began. She told me about doing remote viewing work for an agency and her lifelong experiences with UFOs. As a researcher for almost 40 years, I have heard many such stories and calmly listened. Then she dropped the bomb. She mentioned that she had flown the craft. Completely shocked, I asked, *"You flew the craft? Are you saying you flew the flying saucer?"* "Yes," she said. *"I have flown three different ones."* I had heard many weird UFO stories, but never in all my years had I heard such a thing. The thought that the woman might be crazy crossed my mind. *"So, how do you do that?"* I asked. *"You do it with your mind,"* she replied. Suddenly I knew why the woman wanted to talk to me, and it had been done in secrecy. I also got the impression that I again had been asleep to what was going on for decades.

Synchronicities often follow the world of UFOs. This situation was no different. Once I knew that people were flying crafts, the cases were popping up everywhere. Within a year, I had two dozen cases. Most of the cases involved women. I saw this as an essential point, as in Saudi Arabia, it is illegal to drive a car if you are a woman. Yet here, it appeared that if they abducted a Saudi woman, she would be allowed to fly the craft and wouldn't even need a license or insurance.

The idea of people flying ships was also important for two other reasons:

1. In every case where someone hinted that they had flown a craft, I would immediately cut them off and ask, *"How do you do it?"* In 100% of the cases, the reply would be, *"With my mind."* Not a single one would mention a steering wheel. Instead, they all seemed to describe what legendary songwriter Cat Stevens wrote about in his song, ' Freezing Steel,' which told about his alien abduction: "*I was on the ship with no guiding wheel."*

2. The fact that people were being taught to fly the ship seemed to go completely against the popular 'evil alien'

hypothesis. Why would evil aliens be teaching people to fly the ship?

I discovered something else I didn't know as I gathered the cases. First, people reported being in classes as children and being taught to levitate things. Then came the MILAB stories that many researchers consider to be the evil run-away government re-abducting abductees to find out things from them about their experience. Finally, I came across a couple of cases where these reported evil military people were involved in experiments where they seemed to be teaching abductees to levitate things. It led me to guess that the evil aliens and government units were much less evil than I had first thought.

These MILAB and alien abduction stories did go a long way to confirm that consciousness and ESP were important keys to the UFO mystery, as Rich, Walker, and the Canadian government had pointed out decades ago.

The Story of the Modern-Day Computer: An Inspired Download

Many would think that modern technological advances were advanced by brilliant scientists using their education and talent to develop big inventions. They would be wrong, especially regarding the big inventions of the 20th century. The most significant innovations of the century were the television and the computer. Both came in sudden visionary downloads. As with most inventions, both visions came to engineers and not scientists. As with many inventions, both inventors and engineers were basically ignored as others took over the idea and made money.

Television has been credited to RCA, but it was invented in America in 1924 by Philo T. Farnsworth at 14. He had a vision of producing a television image while plowing a potato field in Utah. He saw in the furrow lines he was making a way of transmitting electrons, one line at a time, using a magnetically deflected beam of electrons. Six years later, at 21, he demonstrated his first postage stamp television image.

Twenty-five years later, engineer Douglas Engelbart became the man who single-handedly conceived the modern interactive communications computer. The event was not a rationally calculated invention but rather an inspired download of the concept, which occurred in December 1950. The computer download came at a time when Engelbart realized that he had achieved all the goals in life that he had set for himself. *"My God, this is ridiculous; no goals,"* he said. On the night of the vision, he was trying to come up with something to contribute to the world. The field of medicine, the Peace Corps, sociology, and economics were considered but rejected. Then in one hour, he reported being struck with a series of connected flashes of insight into a vision of how people could cope with the challenges of complexity and urgency. His insight was a product that would help humans deal with those challenges.

Here is how Engelbart described the inspirational download of what would become the modern computer:

> *It unfolded rapidly. I think it was just within an hour that I had the image of sitting at a big CRT screen with all kinds of symbols, not restricted to our old ones. The computer would be manipulated, and you could be operating all kinds of things to drive the computer. You could harness any kind of lever or knob or button, or switch you wanted to, and the computer would sense them and do something with them. I really also got a clear picture that one's colleagues would be sitting in other rooms with similar workstations, tied to the same computer complex, and could be sharing and working and collaborating very closely. And also, the assumption that there'd be lots of new skills, and new ways of thinking would evolve. Within a matter of hours, that image came, and I just said, 'AHA!' I rarely*

made decisions in such a definite way. That one just unfolded and went 'Bam!' and I just said, 'Boy, that's it. That just fills all kinds of different needs.'[36]

Douglas Engelbart began to envision *"people sitting in front of displays, 'flying around' in an information space where they could formulate and organize their ideas with incredible speed and flexibility."* Then, in 1961 in a research proposal to SRI, he spoke of a vision of a symbiotic *"integrated man-machine working relationships, where close, continuous interaction with a computer avails the human of radically changed information handling and portrayal skills."*

With funding from the Defense Department and later from DARPA, Engelbart invented networking computers, the computer mouse, the video conference, email, the word processor, and the hyperlink. The first public demonstration of his 1950 computer vision came on December 9, 1968, to an audience at the ACM/IEEE-Computer Society Fall Joint Computer Conference in San Francisco. It would be dubbed *"The mother of all demos."* The Engelbart Institute described the event:

> *It was the world debut of personal and interactive computing; for the first time, the public saw a computer mouse used to demonstrate a networked computer system that featured hypertext linking and composing with real-time text editing, multiple windows with flexible view control, knowledge management, shared-screen teleconferencing, and more.*[37]

Engelbart would also be a key player in the ARPANET in 1969 as his computer was one of the first two nodes in the Network Information System that was the system's backbone. Engelbart later used LSD to help 'bootstrap' or drive the inventive process. While at SRI, Engelbart was part of a group of engineers that would have invention sessions using LSD (this was before the *Look Magazine* article describing what they were doing and the government shutting them down).

Engelbart seemed sensitive to the compound, so he was only given a 1/2 dose in the second invention session, even though he tried to get a full dose. During that session, he invented the 'Tinkle Toy.' In the book, *What the Dormouse Said,* the following account is given of the invention:

> Engelbart's contribution to the creativity session was a toy he conceived under the influence of LSD. He called it a 'tinkle toy,' and it was a little waterwheel that would float in a toilet bowl and spin when water or urine was run over it. It would serve as a potty-training teaching aid for a little boy, offering him an incentive to pee in the toilet.

The Engelbart computer vision was only the first of a series of inspirational downloads that would lead to the computer and internet age we know and take for granted. Near the end of his life, Steve Jobs at Apple Computers would come forward to describe where his inspiration for the Apple iPad, iPhone, and other Apple products had come from. The creativity had come from meditation and his use of LSD, which he described as *"One of the two or three most important things"* he had done in his life. He also stated:

> It reinforced my sense of what was important: creating great things instead of making money, putting things back into the stream of history and of human consciousness as much as I could.[38]

Mark Pesce, who co-invented the Virtual Reality coding language VRML, also gave credit to LSD for the inspiration behind his invention. He stated, *"To a man and a woman, the people behind (virtual reality) were acidheads."*[39] Then, there was Bob Wallace, who invented the concept of computer shareware. Wallace was the ninth employee of Microsoft. He now runs *Mind Books*, devoted to psychedelic and alternative consciousness. Wallace was the creator of the word processing program PC-Write and the founder of the software company *Quicksoft*. His conception of shareware as a formal business application was psychedelically inspired.

Then finally, there was Larry Page, who stated that the invention of Google had come from a 1996 dream. During a commencement address at the University of Michigan, he stated:

> When I suddenly woke up, I was thinking, what if we could download the whole web and just keep the links, I grabbed a pen and started writing! Sometimes it is important to wake up and stop dreaming. I spent the middle of that night scribbling out the details and convincing myself it would work. Soon after, I told my advisor, Terry Winograd, it would take a couple of weeks to download the web. He nodded knowingly; fully aware it would take much longer but wise enough to not tell me.[40]

Were the ideas of computers, computer software, and the internet presented in some cosmic downloads to help us advance? The history of computer and internet development indicates that it is a possibility.

The Intergalactic Computer Network

> *"The human mind operates by association. With one item in its grasp, it snaps instantly to the next thing that is suggested by the association of thoughts, in accordance with some intricate web of trails carried by the cells of the brain. Man cannot hope fully to duplicate this mental process artificially, but he certainly ought to be able to learn from it."*
> **--Vannevar Bush, 1945.**

As many will know, in 1950, the Canadian government produced a Top-Secret memo detailing what had been learned about flying saucers from the questions asked by American officials. The Canadians were told flying saucers existed, that it was considered significant, and was the most highly classified subject in the United States. More importantly, they were told that other things might be associated with the saucers, such as 'mental phenomena.'

In 1973, documentary producer Robert Emenegger told a story of a tour through the military labs at DARPA, which indicated the military was involved in the race to link the mind to a machine. In one lab, the scientist refused to describe what he was doing until he was told by the official conducting the tour that he could explain what was going on. The man stated that he would sit on one side of the room, and a computer would sit on the other. The man would think of a word, and the computer would repeat the word without a physical interface. They were at the point that the computer could pick up almost ten words.

In 1990 during an interview with the former President of Penn State University and former Defense official Dr. Eric Walker, he seemed to confirm that consciousness was associated with the saucers. In the middle of one interview, he cut off the conversation by asking, *"What do you know about ESP?"* When he didn't get an answer, he stated, *"Unless you know about it and how to use it, you will not be taken in. Only a few know about it."*

Then in 1993, another high-level person again seemed to hint that a consciousness *and* machine symbiosis was the key. During a lecture to the UCLA engineering alumni, Ben Rich, who headed up the key black world projects at Lockheed Skunk Works, stated that we now have the technology to take ET home and that *"We"* have found the mistake in the equation. Two attendees approached Rich after the lecture to see what he had meant. They posed the question of how UFO propulsion worked. Rich repeated what Dr. Walker had asked two years earlier, *"Let me ask you a question.*

How does ESP work?" The questioner responded with, *"All points in time and space are connected?"* Rich then said, *"That's how it works!"*

The theory of consciousness proposed by biologist Rupert Sheldrake and others suggests that consciousness is a field outside the brain and that the brain is nothing more than a radio/TV receiver or computer that taps into the consciousness field. This leads to an exciting parallel connected to the origins of the internet. Like the Sheldrake consciousness field concept, internet information is stored away from the computer. Like the consciousness field idea, all computers simply log on and access all the information. The internet concept has even gone a step further with cloud computing. Everyone on the globe is interconnected and accessing programs and data at any site, from anywhere. It sounds very similar to the idea of the holographic universe, commonly referred to by consciousness researchers like Edgar Mitchell.

The statements made by the Canadian government, Walker, and Rich all seemed to indicate that the military may have figured out consciousness and have been able to develop UFO-type technology using what they had learned. What may be significant is that the internet was developed by the US military, supposedly as an idea where the information would not be stored in one place and therefore could not be taken out by a Soviet nuclear attack. It was developed by the Advanced Research Projects Agency (ARPA), which later became DARPA which does leading-edge research for the black budget world. The original system was called the ARPANET, which the Department of Defense used to link its projects at universities, and research laboratories in the U.S.[41] Had the US military used what they had learned about UFOs and mental phenomena to come up with the idea of a secure information cloud that computers could link into? A look back at the key designer of the ARPANET makes this look even more possible.

The origin of the internet idea actually goes back to the same man who was given the job of investigating flying saucers in 1947,

Vannevar Bush. In 1933, in a paper called The Inscrutable Thirties, Bush proposed a way to use and make technical information more available through a mechanization process to *"support innovation in knowledge transfer and storage."* Starting in 1939, he proposed the 'Memex,' which he envisioned as a work desk with viewing screens, a keyboard, buttons, and levers. Within the desk were mechanisms capable of storing information through microphotography. The material would be stored using microfilm, dry photography, or a keyboard. Bush wanted the Memex to operate like the brain does, assimilating information with the association. It would use associative trials, analogous to the mental association trail of the human brain. In 1945 he updated his computer concepts in an article called, *'As We May Think'*, which foretold many kinds of future technology such as hypertext, personal computers, the Internet, the World Wide Web, speech recognition, and online encyclopedias. Whether or not Bush's ideas came from his direction of the program dealing with extraterrestrial technology is not possible to determine at present, but *'As We May Think'* inspired people who read it, like Douglas Engelbart to, *"Envision people sitting in front of displays, 'flying around' in an information space where they could formulate and organize their ideas with incredible speed and flexibility."* In 1961 in a research proposal to SRI, he spoke of a vision of a symbiotic, *"Integrated man-machine working relationships, where close, continuous interaction with a computer avails the human of radically changed information-handling and portrayal skills."*

With funding from the Defense Department and later from DARPA, Engelbart invented networking computers, the computer mouse, the video conference, email, the word processor, and the hyperlink. Engelbart would also be a key first player in the ARPANET in 1969 as his computer was one of the first two nodes in the Network Information System that was the system's backbone. In August 1962, the work of Joseph Licklider, who was Director of Behavioral Sciences Command & Control Research at ARPA, moved the internet closer to what we know today. In 1962, Licklider proposed the idea of a network in which he believed everybody could use computers anywhere and get data anywhere in the world and the idea of cloud computing. The name Licklider gave to his idea makes one wonder if he had any insight into the work being done related to UFOs and mental phenomena. That is because he called his idea, *'The Intergalactic Computer Network'* and addressed his colleagues as *"Members and Affiliates of the Intergalactic Computer Network."*[42]

The internet we know today was initially called the *Intergalactic Computer Network*. One more thing links Licklider into the world of the flying saucer/mental phenomena connection that was first spelled out in the Canadian Top-Secret memo. This relates to reports by contactees who claim to have direct knowledge of flying saucer propulsion and a paper that Licklider wrote in 1960 called *'Man-Computer Symbiosis.'*[43] In this paper, Licklider proposed:

> *The development of man-computer symbiosis by analyzing some problems of interaction between men and computing machines, calling attention to applicable principles of man-machine engineering, and pointing out a few questions to which research answers are needed. The hope is that, in not too many years, human brains and computing machines will be coupled together very tightly and that the resulting partnership will think as no human brain has ever thought and process data in a way not approached by the information-handling machines we know today.*

Compare this human-computer symbiosis idea proposed by Licklider to the many accounts that exist where contactees, who have been on the ship, talk about a symbiotic relationship between the mind of the person piloting the ship and the ship itself. For example, in February 2013, I met a woman in Phoenix who first mentioned this, saying she had flown several different crafts. When I asked how, she stated, *"I do it with my mind."*

From a case discussed in Helmut Lammer's book, *MILABS*, *"The being was telepathically instructing her how to maneuver around objects while navigating. The Gray told her that the craft could 'sense' objects and maneuver around them."* From researcher Melinda Leslie, *"I willed the ship with thought. The ship is alive; you just think it. The ship did what I thought. I did it with feeling like it was alive."*

One contactee Allen Drake told me, *"One of the communications I received from the visitors indicated the craft are controlled by their minds."* Another contactee named Ron in Utah said to me of his experience, *"I asked him, 'what am I supposed to do?' He told me that it's already inside of me and all I have to do is think about what I want to do, and the ship will respond to my thoughts."*

In reply to a question to Australian researcher Mary Rodwell, who has over 2000 cases of experiencers, as to whether she has encountered cases of people claiming to have flown the craft, she replied, *"Yes, many have said they are 'taught' to fly the craft, even as children."* The children-related cases I encountered involved children being taught to levitate different colored balls.

Rebecca Hardcastle Wright wrote about her contact experience in her book *Exoconsciousness: Your 21st Century Mind:*

> As they escorted me out of the room, I ran up into my favorite place in the craft, the cupola. In the cupola, I was privileged to navigate the craft. As I stood up at the helm, my mind drifted off into a relaxed glide, my small hands one with the craft. I navigated the craft through space. Star maps were stored in my conscious mind. I navigated easily among the star system. I intuitively knew how to navigate as well as launch and receive crafts. The cupola was my home. My consciousness fits the craft. We were one.

Niara Isley was a security officer at Nellis Air Force Base. Her recollection is stunningly similar to Licklider's human-computer symbiotic idea. She stated:

> You would sit in a chair in this craft, and it was like a neural interface. You could fly it as easily as moving one of your arms and legs because it would slip right into your neurology. You could think that you wanted to go here, and basically, all you had to do is think it. The computer on the ship was extremely sophisticated beyond anything that we had. It would take that desire that you had generated in your thought, and it would translate it into something that would create a donut-shaped electromagnetic field. I called them donuts. They served the same purpose as an electromagnetic coil. It would cause a field that would propel it off the surface of the earth and then move it in a direction that you wanted it to go.

Besides people who claim to have flown the craft, there are claims that the Roswell craft used symbiotic technology. For example, Philip Corso claimed that the Roswell aliens were part of the craft. Another claim of this Roswell alien ship symbiosis is from William McDonald.[44] In the 1993 lecture referenced above, Ben Rich stated, *"Nearly all 'biomorphic' aerospace designs were inspired by the Roswell spacecraft, from Kelly's SR-71 Blackbird, onward to today's drones, UCAVs, and aerospace craft."* Finally, there is the story of David Adair, who claimed that he was shown a symbiotic flying saucer engine during a tour of Area 51. Adair was basically written off as some sort of deluded fraud, but in light of all the other material above, maybe his claims should be re-examined.

UFOs and Fear

This bedtime story is one of those stories that might just keep you awake. It has remained in my mind after all these years because it appears to describe an aspect of the UFO phenomena that is rarely investigated, the fear factor.

Alien Bedtime Stories

It goes back to a story I heard just after my UFO sightings in 1975 and 1976. It involved a hunter in Manitoba who was out in the remote bush country when he came across an object that had landed in a bush clearing. The story happened at night. The man moved in to investigate what the object was, but the closer he got to the object, the more he felt fear that was becoming more and more pronounced. There did not appear to be anything that was causing the fear. The man pushed on, getting closer and closer, but the fear became so overwhelming that he could go no further. He turned and left, walking away from the landed object. After a few minutes of walking, the man's curiosity got the better of him, and he turned around and headed back towards the light, thinking that he had just imagined the fear. However, as he got closer, the fear began to increase as it had the first time, and like the first go-around, he got to a point where he could go no further. He left, and that is the end of the story.

After many decades of research, I have come to find out that others have repeated this man's story. Even I had a similar experience which was not just fear associated with some accident, unexpected event, or anticipation. People who have experienced this fear describe it as beyond words. It is usually described as the most fearful moment of their life. This is unusual because the event that caused the fear does not, from the outside, look all that scary.

In many cases, the person is not seeing anything. They simply describe a fear that comes over them for some unknown reason. Often a UFO event occurs shortly after the fear begins. This may have implications for the government's disclosure of the UFO story. Will this fear be experienced by most people who come in contact with the extraterrestrials when they start walking the street? Logic would say no. People who have experienced the fear would say, *"Yes, there is a good chance that might happen."*

My experience with the fear came in April of 1976, just south of Brunkild, Manitoba. I had been investigating a series of UFO sightings that had plagued the area for over a year. I had seen many UFOs, and no fear was associated with any of those sightings. The feeling before this particular event was excitement and awe. We often chased it across the country in the car because the UFO was moving so slowly. However, the sighting along Highway 20, south of Brunkild, would be different. I have always described it as the scariest moment of my life and a fear that cannot be put into words or be compared to any other scary situation, I have been in. In my case, the fear made sense. In the twelve months previously, we had chased the object around because it moved very slowly and low to the ground. I was the hunter. Now I was the hunted.

There are, however, cases where people see UFOs that are not hunting them. Instead, the UFOs appear to be simply flying around. One such case occurred in Erie County, Pa, on May 1, 2013, when a witness described a ten-second sighting of a fluttering rectangular-shaped object just flying in the sky. Although the object did not appear to do anything to the man, he became overcome with fear. He stated:

> *My feeling when I saw this was complete fear. I couldn't even watch to see how long I could see this object until it was out of view. I grabbed my tea and ran inside and tried to catch my breath. I became sick. I was shaky, and my head felt weird.*[45]

Chris Bledsoe described two encounters with fear. The first was on January 8, 2007, when he had a 5.5-hour missing time and abduction experience. The incident began minutes after leaving for a walk while fishing with a group of men and his son along the Cape Fear River in North Carolina. Minutes after beginning his walk, the fear began:

> *As I am walking along, I hear this noise, and it is following me. As I am walking, it is moving. I stopped it stopped. I started, and it started. It's loud, and it's noisy. There were no birds chirping and no wind blowing; it was really getting on my nerves whatever was tracking me in these bushes. I get down on my knees and look through the bushes. I used to be a big hunter, I shot one*

of the biggest bears in North Carolina, standing on its hind legs six feet away, but this was different. I don't know what it was, but something put fear in me. It was unlike any fear I had experienced before. I froze in my tracks. In fact, I froze so badly that I squatted down and tried to use what was left of the hill in front of me to hide from these things. As soon as I squatted down, I thought, 'Oh my gosh, oh my gosh.' It hit me that bad. I knew at that moment that they had seen me. There was no telling me that it didn't see me and that it reacted to my thoughts. I felt the chills in my toes. I crawled down thinking that I was hiding on the side of the road In fishing pole-type reeds. I take off running back to the fire.

Bledsoe's second incident occurred a couple of nights later when a bright object appeared to land in a clearing in a field of evergreens behind his house. He took his gun and crawled under the low-hanging trees toward the light. He could not get to the object, and at a certain point, he became overwhelmed by an uncontrollable, unexplained fear. He had to reverse his direction and crawl back out of the trees towards his house.

One good explanation that might explain what might cause the fear is frequencies. The idea is that the aliens and their ships are resonating at a much different frequency than human beings. We just cannot see it, like radio or TV waves. It is this differential that causes fear. As it is invisible to the human eye, the effects are felt even when the being and craft are not visible. This idea has even been proposed to explain why people are so fearful during a reported alien abduction. The idea is that the aliens are vibrating at a much higher frequency that causes great fear when it interacts with the fearful human vibrating at a much lower rate.

Another theory concerns the filters we must view the world. Everyone has emotional energy that they push through their bodies when events happen. When a person has positive filters to see the world, that person will view a positive situation. However, a second person may take the same emotional energy, put it through negative filters, and see a very negative, fearful situation even though it might be the same event.

That is why some see life as a positive experience, and 37,000 Americans see the same life as so negative that they take their lives each year. It is the same life experience and two different assessments of it.

A Nobel Prize for Woo-Woo?

> *"I have data that could mute the Great Randi challenge. I know that is quite a statement, but I do."*
> **--Dr. Diane Hennacy Powell.**

> *"We are all one with the one who is all."*
> **--Reply of aliens to question about God by abductee Bret Oldham.**

In a fair and just world, if confirmed, the research experiments just conducted by Dr. Diane Powell would be a contender for a Nobel Prize. The keywords are, of course, 'fair and just.' Dr. Powell is a practicing psychiatrist, a John Hopkins-trained neuroscientist, a former faculty member at Harvard Medical School, and a contributor to the Institute of Noetic Sciences. She is also the author of the book, *The ESP Enigma.*

Dr. Powell's interest in ESP was sparked in part by one encounter with a female patient in a hospital ward who indicated she was receiving psychic information about Dr. Powell that she should hear. What the woman said in terms of information was 98% accurate. It was a life-altering event for Powell. The scientific investigation work that Powell has just completed in the field of ESP was described accurately as data that could mute the great Amazing Randy challenge. This is a challenge for a one-million-dollar prize to anyone who can show, under proper observing conditions, evidence of any paranormal, supernatural, or occult power or event.

What does Powell have that is so good that Randi will possibly have to eat crow and payout the prize? What is such a major discovery that it might deserve a Nobel Prize? The research has to do with non-verbal autistic children. In her newsletter Powell described her research:

> Another source of evidence might come from mute autistic children whose caregivers frequently report that their children can read their minds. If true, that suggests telepathy might be an alternative or default means of communication for those with language impairment. Parents of the autistic savants I evaluated in India all reported telepathic experiences, in addition to other abilities.
>
> Then, shortly after my return to the USA, I read an article about an allegedly telepathic, autistic girl named Nandana. When possible, I hope to investigate her abilities. Her mother described her daughter's process of communication as follows: 'I taught her how to use the keyboard. Now, if I ask her to write what I'm thinking, she can do it. Sometimes spelling errors happen, and she still does not understand well the concepts of punctuation. If I say 'space' (between the words) in my mind, she types the word 'space' instead of typing the separation between terms.'
>
> Next month I'll be filming experiments with another ten-year-old autistic girl who was referred to me by my colleague Darold Treffert, the psychiatrist famous for his fifty-plus years of work on savants. Her parents were initially strong skeptics, so they were startled when they witnessed her ability to read her therapist's mind. Recognizing the profound significance this may have for our understanding of consciousness, they reached out

to aid science, while requesting that their identity be hidden. The family first thought their daughter was a mathematical savant because she could provide answers to multiplication and division problems involving numbers over six digits, even though she couldn't do much simpler multiplication. Then her answers switched from an ordinary numerical format to an exponential one. Immediately after, the therapist began calculating a device that displayed in exponential notation. This prompted the therapist to ask the girl how she knew the answer. The girl typed, 'I see the numerators and denominators in your head.' The therapist then tested her with pictures and sentences that were hidden from the girl's view. She was able to type accurate answers, even if the sentences were in a foreign language. These sessions were videotaped by the family and sent to me and Dr. Treffert. They are very intriguing and show 100% accuracy.

Are these reports of telepathy real? Stay tuned. A couple of nights ago, the results of the filmed scientific testing started to leak out. The results are absolutely staggering, hinting that severely autistic children who exhibit ESP abilities may, in fact, be receiving a pure signal and be 100% accurate on the given targets. The 100% accuracy has already been seen with autistic prodigious savants. Whatever their talent is, they are usually 100% accurate. Therefore if you give them two five-digit numbers to multiply together, they will be accurate on the first try, or if they do calendar calculations, they will be able on the first try to tell you the days of the week for any date in the past or future you can give them even though they often can't multiply 7 x 4 or think there are 10 minutes in an hour and 10 seconds in a minute.

Were the non-verbal autistic children accurate? This is what Dr. Powell stated in an interview on June 12th:

Believe it or not, I have data that could mute the Great Randi challenge. I know that is quite a statement, but I do. To meet that challenge, you have to have it reviewed scientifically, and they want a recommendation from some science journal. They want to see it in print somewhere. This is fresh. I just did these experiments last month. That's how fresh this information is. I have digit sequences that are 18 and 19 numbers long and have 100% accuracy. The stats on that are incredible. I even had this one sequence where it's a series of random numbers given one after another that added up to 162 digits where there were only seven mistakes, and when told, 'that is the wrong number,' this autistic child got it right on the second go. The stats on that are just staggering. That's why I am saying it is well beyond the great Amazing Randi challenge.

This evidence was filed and, if repeatable, will be conclusive evidence that there is a consciousness element independent of the brain which can make a non-local connection with other consciousnesses. It will be the final nail in the coffin of the idea that the brain produces consciousness and disappears at death. If confirmed, there would be few discoveries in the history of science that would rival its importance.

A simplistic model of what might be going on has to do with the right/left brain and its connection to a non-local mind that is part of the holographic universe. This idea has been proposed by many people, such as Dr. Edgar Mitchell, the sixth man to walk on the moon. He pointed out that as soon as science develops a generalized theory of information, non-locality, the Zero-Point Energy field, and the Quantum Hologram, we will begin to develop an accurate understanding of consciousness, *"I theorize that there is a spectrum of consciousness available to human beings,"* said Mitchell. *"At one end is material consciousness. At the other end is what we call 'field' consciousness, where a person is at one with the universe, perceiving the universe."*

The revelation of this new worldview of consciousness began in 1935 with the Einstein, Podolsky, and Rosen experiment, challenging an idea that had arisen out of the mathematical calculation of the time that there was a non-local quantum interconnectedness to the universe. The idea was that entangled photons appeared to be conscious of the other at a distance, and any action placed on one would be instantly balanced by the other independent of time and space. Physicist John Steward Bell provided mathematical proof of this non-local interconnectedness in 1964, and the experimental proof was delivered in several experiments around the world in the early 1980s. It became a fact that our space-time reality is non-local. At the same time, work done on rat brains in the 1950s by biologist Karl Lashley showed that trained rats could still run a maze with huge brain sections removed, indicating that memory was not stored in any particular part of the brain. Lashley declared that there was no memory center in the brain.

In the 1960s, Dr. Karl Pribram noticed that when brain-injured patients had large sections of their brain removed, their memories became hazy, but they also did not suffer a loss of any specific memories. He also importantly pointed out that the brain used 'Fourier transform mathematics' (converting images into waveforms and back again). About the same time, the hologram was discovered in 1964 by Dr. Dennis Gabor, and he described the same two factors:

1. Like the brain that lost no memory when parts were cut out, no information was lost when a hologram was cut into pieces. Instead, each piece contained the information of the whole hologram, but like human memories, the image would become hazier as the pieces got smaller.

2. The hologram image, like the human brain, used 'Fourier transform mathematics' and indicated a key common characteristic between the two systems.

In 1977 Pribram proposed that memories are not localized in any specific brain cells; instead, memory seemed to be distributed throughout the whole brain, just like the hologram. He described a holonomic model for the brain. Next, in 1992 Dr. Walter Schempp, a mathematician at the University of Siegen in Germany, discovered the quantum hologram while studying functional Magnetic Resonance Imaging. The quantum hologram stated:

> *The event history of all macro-scale matter is continuously broadcast non-locally and is received by and interacts with other matter in its environment through a process of exchange of quantum information. This is an extension of the known process of quantum emission/absorption.*[46]

The discovery placed the storage of all information in the zero-point energy field. According to Dr. Edgar Mitchell, it elevates information in physics to the same level of importance as energy itself:

> *Information, if we define it broadly as patterns of energy, so the particular mathematical formalism that goes with the quantum holography is a group study. It also tells us that this information or energy is non-local, which means that it is carried in the zero-point energy field. We can then start to say we have heard the mystical tradition, for example, of the akashic record. Well, this seems to be the mechanism of that allows the akashic record to take place. It is a natural memory system. I have written a paper called the 'Quantum Hologram, Nature's Mind' to suggest this ubiquitous application. It is a mechanism to carry the history of everything, and it carries it out throughout nature, and the point is that it is recoverable through resonance. Resonance is exactly how we get information." The mind, therefore, is a hologram enfolded in a holographic universe, or as Dr. Mitchell's Quantrek*

> *group describes it, "The totality of our physical and subjective experience can be thought of as a multimedia hologram resonant with ourselves and the zero-point field.*

Like a piece cut from a hologram, our minds contain all the information in the universal hologram. However, the quality of that information depends on how much noise and interference there is from the left of the brain. In the normal brain, the left side is the dominant part of the brain responsible for language, hearing, and processing most of the tasks of speaking. It's also in charge of carrying out logic and exact mathematical computations. The brain of the physical world acts as a reducer and regulator, producing only the consciousness necessary to survive in the physical world and blocking out the rest. The right side is the creative side that handles spatial abilities, visual imagery, face recognition, and music processing. Most artists and musicians have dominant right brains. Dr. Roger Lear, famous for performing alien implant removals, lived and worked in Hollywood. He maintained that the only common characteristic of people claiming the abduction experience is that they were all right-brained. The other analogy that can be used is the signal-to-noise ratio. The left brain is noise, and the right brain is signal. This can be seen when people are trying to meditate. People will complain that they cannot do it. Whenever they try to find that quiet place, thoughts keep coming into their minds that they cannot stop. Those thoughts are the left rational brain creating noise in the experience that prevents a right-brain inspirational experience.

In the same way, abductees report that their experiences appear to have made them more psychic. This may be explainable by the fact they have interacted with strongly telepathic aliens (the key difference between aliens and humans is that aliens are telepathic). In addition, abductees report that when the alien talks to them telepathically, the signal is clear with no noise. They know exactly what the alien is saying. Therefore, the aliens may be teaching the abductee or altering their brain to receive the signal with the right side and block the noise from the left hemisphere.

Autistic people have damage to the left brain. Because of this, the normally dominant left brain cannot produce the noise into the signal as it usually does. The more severe the damage, the less noise there is. Consequently, the less noise there is, the better the signal is. That may be why Powell's non-verbal autistic subjects have almost pure telepathy. The left brain is severely damaged, as evidenced by the inability to speak, and nothing is preventing the mind's connection to the information stored in the zero-point field. This idea of brain damage creating a clear signal is also supported by some of the most fantastic psychics of the last century who reported related brain injuries. Peter Hurkos, considered by some as the most remarkable psychic ever, received his psychic abilities after falling off a ladder in 1941 and sustaining a head injury. Edgar Cayce, considered the best psychic in America, received his excellent abilities after being hit in the head with a baseball (and he claimed that the psychic material he was providing was coming from the akashic field). Joe McMoneagle, the top remote viewer for the CIA work being done at the Stanford Research Institute, suffered from brain seizures while in the army.

The results being reported by Powell of perfect telepathic hits on 18- and 19-digit numbers or the complete hit on a 162-digit number would indicate that a condition exists where the brain is receiving all signals and no noise. The left brain has gone on a permanent coffee break. In one interview, Powell described that the child was being taught to develop some verbal communication, and she wondered if this would affect the ability to do psi down the road. This is a valid consideration because activating and training the damaged left brain should, in theory, create noise in the signal. Therefore, if the child was successfully brought back to full normal capability, theoretically, the psi ability should disappear. The non-verbal autistic savants are, consequently, the perfect candidates to demonstrate this telepathic ability that we all theoretically have but cannot prove because of noise and interference from the left hemisphere dominance. The savants are also the perfect candidates because they are compulsive and very good at what they do. They will not be rattled in an experimental setting because they live in their performance world and have the rest of the world on mute. Because of this, they do not suffer from stage fright.

We are getting close to confirming that the physical universe is only a small part of overall reality. Of course, material reductionist scientists will fight the idea to the bitter end, but it appears that it may already be all over except for the crying. The evidence is gathering quickly that we all have telepathic abilities, but we cannot pick up the signal because of our brain's wiring. This idea is supported by the fact that experiencers report pure telepathy during their alien encounters but not in daily life.

The accumulating evidence in quantum physics, along with work done with autistics by Powell, points to the idea that the brain is simply a computer interface between the quantum hologram and the physical world we perceive with our senses. The research done in the past years with savants has helped to develop the idea of left brain/noise and right brain/signal. This new understanding of the brain has even allowed some scientists to perform supporting experiments in the laboratory. Dr. Allan Snyder at the University of Sydney's Center of Mind has done successful experiments that show that the damaged savant brain may actually provide signals and important new ideas about reality. He refers to the fact that *"less is sometimes more"* when it comes to the compromised left hemisphere of the savant. What Snyder did in his lab was inhibit the high-level functioning left hemisphere. He sent a series of electromagnetic pulses (transcranial magnetic stimulation) into the left frontal lobe. In 40% of test subjects, this produced a strange savant-like intelligence in drawing, proofreading, and mathematics. The savant-like abilities were caused by shutting part of the brain down, just like brain damage does in the savants.[47] *"We all have that information,"* Snyder said, *"but our brains are deliberately wired not to see it."*[48]

The days are coming when the general realization will come, *"Wow, I guess consciousness is not all in the brain."* At that point, the really exciting job of understanding the true nature of reality and the consciousness that underlies it will begin.

Amazing Right Brain Telepathy Tales

"We must postulate a cosmic order of nature beyond our control to which both the outward material objects and the inward images are subject."
--Wolfgang Pauli, Nobel Laureate quantum theorist.

"Yes, I think telepathy exists, and I think quantum physics will help us understand its basic properties."
--Dr. Brian Josephson, Nobel Laureate.

"As a man who has devoted his whole life to the most clear-headed science, to the study of matter, I can tell you as a result of my research about atoms this much: There is no matter as such. All matter originates and exists only by virtue of a force that brings the particle of an atom to vibration and holds this most minute solar system of the atom together. We must assume behind this force the existence of a conscious and intelligent mind. This mind is the matrix of all matter."
--Max Planck, Nobel Laureate.

There are countless stories of savants who can do unbelievable calculations and instantaneous counting in their heads, faster than computers. How they did this was a total mystery in the past, but that is changing. Now many non-verbal autistic people can communicate using computer keyboards and stencils. We are learning that the savant is not using a left-brain function to calculate or count. The answer appears in the savant's mind, indicating some right-brained telepathic process. This new understanding coincides with the physical diagnosis that most savants suffer from some left-brain impairment, implying no ability to calculate. The observation further supports that those who exhibit the best savant telepathic abilities seem to be the non-verbal subjects with the left brain most severely shown by left-brain speech damage. Therefore, the shutting down of the left brain, which helps us operate in the physical world, would allow the right brain to become dominant and access information from some non-local matrix.

Daniel Tammet is one of the calculating savants who can describe what goes on in his head when he calculates. He confirmed that the process does not involve calculation but rather waiting for the answer to appear as an image in his head. In his book, *Born on a Blue Day*, Tammet described what goes on in his head when he multiplies. Tammet has synesthesia, seeing color, shape, texture, and taste when he experiences numbers. He gave an example of how he multiplies two complex numbers and how the answer downloads into his mind. When he sees the numbers 53 and 131, he sees distinct shapes associated with the numbers. As soon as he multiplies them, a third shape appears, which fits neatly between the two other shapes like a piece in a jigsaw puzzle. That shape has a number associated with it, '6943', which Tammet recognizes. It is the answer.

Tammet is quite clear about what happens in his head. The answers to the complex math he is asked to do pop into his head like a right-brain telepathic download. He does not do any left-brain calculating. Another critical aspect of the Tammet story is his connection to prime numbers (numbers divisible only by one and the number itself), which many savants are fascinated with. The Sacks Twins, for example, (described below) could go back and forth between themselves and identify 6- and 7-digit prime numbers in sequence even though there is no real way to calculate prime numbers. In Tammet's experience with primes, he sees a prime number as having a pebbly appearance when it appears in

Alien Bedtime Stories

his head. This would confirm it is not some calculated left-brain operation but some right-brained download or the ability to tap into a field where all the prime numbers are stored.

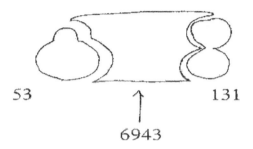

53   ↑   131
     6943

Another savant who adds to this telepathic story is Zacharias Dase. Dase was a 19th-century mathematical savant who had epilepsy from early childhood. He had an almost legendary ability to do complex calculations involving 100-digit numbers. He multiplied and divided large numbers in his head, but when the numbers were huge, he required considerable time. Schumacher once gave him the numbers 79532853 and 93758479 to be multiplied. From the moment they were given to when he had written down the answer, which he had reckoned out in his head, there elapsed 54 seconds. He multiplied mentally two numbers, each of 20 figures in 6 minutes; 40 figures in 40 minutes; and 100 figures in 83/4 hours, which last calculation must have made his exhibitions somewhat tiresome to the onlookers. He mentally extracted the square roots of a number of 100 figures in 52 minutes.[49] One of the fantastic abilities Dase had was the ability to count items almost instantaneously. He had one ability not present to such a degree in other ready reckoners. He could distinguish some thirty objects of a similar nature in a single moment as quickly as other people can recognize three or four. The rapidity with which he would name the number of sheep in a herd, books in a bookcase, and windowpanes in a large house was even more remarkable than the accuracy of his mental calculations. Once again, this ability appears not to have been a logical left-brained function but rather a right-brained telepathic ability, as illustrated by another story told about Dase counting peas. Dase would instantly call out, '183' or '79' if a pile of peas was poured out and indicate as best, he could that he was also a dullard, that he did not count the peas but just (mentally) saw their number, as a whole, in a flash.[50]

The very same ability to count instantly was seen in the Sacks Twins. John and Michael were savant twins that psychiatrist Oliver Sacks met and studied in 1966 in a state hospital (A video of them in action can be seen at[1]

Although they could not do logical left-brain mathematics like 7 x 4, or 10 – 3, they could exhibit right-brained telepathic type abilities such as giving the day of the week for any date in history and instantly counting. This instantaneous counting became part of the movie *Rain Man* where the autistic savant Raymond instantly counts 246 toothpicks that fall from a toothpick box in a restaurant. The true story that the movie story was based on occurred by the twins in the presence of Dr. Sacks, and he described it as follows:

> *A box of matches on their table fell and discharged its contents on the floor: '111,' they both cried simultaneously; and then, in a murmur, John said '37.' Michael repeated this; John said it a third time and stopped. I counted the matches - it took me some time - and there were 111. 'How could you count the matches so quickly?' I asked. 'We didn't count,' they said. 'We saw the 111.' 'And why did you murmur, '37,' and repeat it three times?' I asked the twins. They said in unison, '37, 37, 37, 111.' And this, if possible, I found*

---

[1] https://www.youtube.com/watch?v=YuhTFsiEcMU.

even more puzzling. That they should see 111 – '111-ness' in a flash was extraordinary...But they had then gone on to 'factor' the number 111 - without having any method, without even 'knowing' (in an ordinary way) what factors meant. Had I not already observed that they were incapable of the simplest calculations and didn't 'understand' (or seem to understand) what multiplication or division was? Yet now, spontaneously, they had divided a compound number into three equal parts. 'How did you work that out?' I said rather hotly. They indicated, as best they could, in poor, insufficient terms, but perhaps there are no words to correspond to such things - that they did not 'work it out' but just 'saw' it in a flash. John made a gesture with two outstretched fingers and his thumb, which seemed to suggest that they had spontaneously trisected the number or that it 'came apart' of its own accord, into these three equal parts, by a sort of spontaneous, numerical 'fission.' They seemed surprised at my surprise, as if I were somehow blind, and John's gesture conveyed an extraordinary sense of immediate, felt reality. Is it possible, I said to myself, that they could somehow 'see' the properties, not in a conceptual, abstract way, but as qualities, felt, sensuous, in some immediate, concrete way? And not simply isolated qualities, like '111-ness' but qualities of relationship?[51]

The final example of this telepathic ability comes from a non-verbal autistic girl named Haley, a test subject for psychiatrist/neuroscientist Dr. Diane Powell. The fact that Haley's left brain non-verbal centers were not operational provides strong evidence of the telepathic ability being accessed by the right brain. A series of young children worldwide have been identified with this pure telepathic ability. During the 2014 testing that Powell administered to Haley, where a series of random numbers Haley was asked to read from the mind of one of Haley's therapy workers.

The therapist was behind a divider out of view of Haley, looking at the telepathic targets. In a series of target numbers that totaled 162 digits given to Haley, she was able to correctly read all the numbers from the therapist's mind on the second try. Haley could also correctly telepathically pick up sentences, images, made-up words, and foreign languages in the therapist's mind. In another series, Haley was asked to read complex mathematical questions from the therapist's mind telepathically. One formula she was given and gave back with complete accuracy was: $1513347 / 35 = 43238.4857$.

The theory of what is going on appears to be the ability of the savant to telepathically tap into some non-local morphic field and obtain the answer to the equation, the calendar date, or the instant count of items without having to count. The idea of morphic fields and their ability to provide non-local information comes from the research of former Cambridge professor Dr. Rupert Sheldrake. To explain how this information might be obtained from the morphic field, Sheldrake referred to experiments such as those conducted on rats starting in 1920 by William McDougall at Harvard that illustrate the concept of morphic fields, which *"organize the form, structure and patterned interactions of systems under their influence."* The experiments were set up to study the possibility of Lamarckian inheritance. McDougall used carefully inbred Wistar rats that were trained to run a water maze, and the number of errors made by a rat before it learned to leave the tank indicated the learning rate. The tests continued for 32 generations and 15 years. Each generation was bred only after being tested to prevent any possibility of conscious or unconscious selection in favor of quicker-learning rats. The Lamarckian theory seemed to be confirmed as each generation appeared to learn faster, making fewer and fewer mistakes before learning to run the maze. Even though McDougall's techniques to prevent bias as with much new scientific research, skeptics arose, such as F.A.E. Crew of Edinburgh University (later also W. E. Agar and his colleagues at Melbourne University), who years later repeated McDougall's experiment with rats derived from the same inbred strain but unrelated to the Harvard rats. What Crew discovered is that the untrained rats made the same number of mistakes as the Harvard rats in their first attempts after 30 generations. A considerable number went through the maze without making a similar mistake.[52] The results showed that the unrelated rats had somehow picked up the knowledge that the Harvard rats had accumulated. As they were unrelated, the information was not from a hereditary factor.

The morphic field idea, however, may be an idea that, like the abolition of slavery, women's right to vote, African Americans using white bathrooms, smoking in public, uncontrolled toxic dumping into public rivers, and gay rights, maybe a few years off.

Those in control of science are not about to take their failed ideas quietly into the night. In a flashback to the burning at the stake of Giordano Bruno in 1600 for his views, described as heresy, that the universe was infinite and that stars were distant suns with their planets and extraterrestrial beings, John Maddox, the long-time editor of Nature, is on record as having called Sheldrake's views, 'heresy' that *"deserved to be condemned."* But, he added about Sheldrake's 1981 book, A New Science of Life, *"while it's wrong that books should be burned, in practice, if book burning were allowed, this book would be a candidate...I think it's dangerous that people should be allowed by our liberal societies to put that kind of nonsense into currency."*[53] Fortunately for Sheldrake, Maddox did not call for Sheldrake to be burned at stake.

The day will come when morphic fields and ESP become accepted ideas in science. Maddox will be wrong as he was when in 1983, he wrote that there was *"No Need for Panic about AIDS"* He wrote that *"for strictly prophylactic purposes, male homosexuals should be persuaded to change their ways...The pathetic promiscuity of male homosexuals is the most obvious threat to public health. Still, it is probably no more serious now than it was before homosexuality ceased to be illegal."* He described AIDS as a *"perhaps non-existent condition."*[54]

CHAPTER 5

PRESIDENTS TALES

President Roosevelt and the Battle of Los Angeles

Roosevelt was the first United States president we know of who had to deal with the UFO situation. That happened on February 25, 1942, in a Los Angeles incident. As it was only weeks after the attack at Pearl Harbor, the country was on alert to stop another surprise attack.

Just before 2:30 in the morning, the unidentified object was spotted. Air raid sirens sounded, and a blackout ensued. The 37th Coast Artillery Brigade began firing anti-aircraft shells at the object and continued to do so for an hour as the slow-moving object drifted in from the west. Unfortunately, what goes up must come down, and the falling shells killed three people. Three more died of heart attacks. Numerous houses and businesses were also badly damaged by the falling ordinance.

The same day General George Marshall, Roosevelt's Chief of Staff, wrote a secret memo to President Roosevelt about the unidentified objects over Los Angeles. He reported to the president that *"Unidentified airplanes other than American Army or Navy planes"* were over Los Angeles early that morning and that 1430 rounds of ammunition were shot at, what he estimated could have been as many as 15 planes moving from *"very slow to as much as 200 mph."* He further reported that no bombs were dropped, no troops were injured, and nothing was shot down. He concluded, *"Investigation continuing. It seems reasonable to conclude that if unidentified airplanes were involved, they might have been from commercial sources, operated by enemy agents, for the purpose of spreading alarm, disclosing the location of anti-aircraft positions, and slowing projection through a blackout."*

Roosevelt wrote his Secretary of War Stimson asking, *"Can anyone other than an authorized official of the United States order an air alarm?"* Roosevelt did not write Marshall, the chief of staff, and Frank Knox, the Secretary of the Navy. He came under attack from California newspapers, hinting that the details of what happened were being covered up. The Long Beach Independent wrote, *"There is a mysterious reticence about the whole affair, and it appears some form of censorship is trying to halt discussion of the matter."*

Indeed, leaked documents and testimonials would later claim that the Army had shot down an extraterrestrial craft. Still, the secrecy clampdown seemed to be in, and proof of the claim would remain elusive. If they recovered a craft and bodies, the next story might tell the story of where they ended up.

Roosevelt and the First UFO Crash

The Roswell UFO crash is generally considered the first UFO crash inside the UFO community. There is evidence of one that occurred much earlier, and the evidence is relatively strong, coming from two sisters who were in their 80s when they first contacted the Center of UFO Studies in December 1999. The two women, Lucille Andrew and Allene Holt Gramly, were daughters of the late Reverend Turner Hamilton Holt. Reverend Holt was the minister at the Shenandoah Christian Church in Greenwich, Ohio. He was also a community leader and the author of *Life's Convictions*.

In April 2009, I traveled to Ashland, Ohio, to interview the two sisters. They told me that in 1948, they were separately told an amazing story about creatures in Washington. Lucille stated that she had been told the story as a teenager and was too young to realize the significance of what she heard. Allene knows that the date she was told was 1948 because her father talked to her while she was playing in the backyard with her two-year-old daughter Eloise. Her father started the conversation by stating, *"Now that the next generation is here, I have a story I would like to share with you."* According to Allene, this conversation was unusual because she and her father did not talk often. He was usually busy working in his upstairs office. He insisted that the story not be told until he and his cousin[55] Cordell Hull, President Roosevelt's Secretary of State from 1933 to 1944, were dead. Although Reverend Holt did not give a date for the event, it had to have occurred no later than 1944, when Hull left office due to ill health, or three years before the Roswell crash.

The story told by Reverend Holt is that while attending a conference in Washington, his cousin Cordell took him to a sub-basement in the U.S. Capitol building and showed him an amazing sight. After being sworn to secrecy, their father reported being shown four 'creatures' in the fluid inside large glass jars sitting on stands. He figured they were about 4' tall. Holt described, *"They were like people, but they weren't."* Holt was asked to lift a wrecked, round metallic object near the bodies. He reported that it was very light in its size. Cordell stated that what Holt had seen had to remain secret as the public would panic if told. As far as the daughters can remember, Cordell didn't explain exactly what they were looking at. Holt's daughters had nothing more to add to the story. Each had been told the same story about some creatures that the United States government was secretly holding in Washington.

Later research showed a sub-basement under the Capitol building where legislators write up the laws of the land.

Researchers talked to U.S. Capitol building curator Barbara A. Wolanin who chuckled a bit after being told the story. She told the Ohio researchers she had never heard about these creatures being stored at the Capitol, but she confirmed that a sub-basement was divided into storage rooms back then.[56]

Harry Truman and the Roswell Crash

On July 8, 1947, newspapers across the country reported that the Army Air Force had released a press release stating that they had recovered a crashed flying disc. The release was quickly corrected by a second release stating the event was nothing but a weather balloon. President Truman was the President at the time. Although there are no documents describing his involvement in the Roswell event, there are many players around the President whose actions showed the President was very much in charge. The actions taken by these men showed that they knew exactly how to cover up the situation, and the silence they created about what they found remains almost seven decades later.

The next day after the Air Force had reported they had recovered a disc, the United Press reported on the Roswell crash, *"Reports of flying saucers whizzing through the sky fell off sharply today as the Army and Navy began a concentrated campaign to stop the rumors."* The idea of shutting down the story made perfect sense if the crash was of an extraterrestrial craft with advanced technology hundreds or thousands of years beyond our own. It would have also made sense if one of the aliens who had been recovered was alive because reports were that the alien was telepathic, and the military would have highly valued the discovery of this.

Much of this reason for the cover-up of the recovery details were spelled out to the Canadians through a military liaison working through the Canadian Embassy in Washington. The

Alien Bedtime Stories

Canadian were told that *"flying saucers exist,"* *"It is the most highly classified subject in the United States,"* and that it was believed that 'mental phenomena,' was associated with the saucers.

Logically, the information being gathered at the crash site had made it up to the President. The President, after all, would have been constitutionally responsible for all aspects of an extraterrestrial crash. If the crash involved extraterrestrials, the only person in the United States that can constitutionally make deals or arrangements with them is the head of State, the President. The whole recovery was conducted by the Army Air Force, which means that they would report their results to the civilian commander of the military as spelled out by the Constitution, the President. All the intelligence agencies that would have been involved in the Roswell crash would have reported directly to the President, as the only role of U.S. intelligence agencies is to provide intelligence for the President, his executive office, and the intelligence chairs of the House and Senate. Any government agencies would also have been reporting to the President as he is the chief executive officer of the U.S. government.

During the time of the Truman administration, few questions were asked of the President regarding UFOs, and when asked, they were the wrong question. Such was the case two days after the Roswell crash announcement by Truman, but the question was not about the Roswell crash but what Truman knew about the flying saucers making headlines every day in the newspapers across America. Truman easily walked around the question, stating that he only knew what he was reading in the paper. No reported followed up, and no UFO question would be asked of the President five years later. The true story is he knew more. In one video interview done at the time of the UFO over-flights above the White House, Truman stated that he had discussed the subject of UFOs at 'every meeting he had had with the military.'

More importantly, in an oral history interview given to the Truman Library in 1974 by his Air Force Advisor General Robert

Landry, Landry stated that one of the jobs he had been given in February 1948, when he got his White House job, was to gather material from the CIA and then brief Truman orally on the subject of flying saucers every three months. This would have implied 16 or more briefings before Truman left office in January 1953.

Some officials would confirm that Truman was in the loop in interviews they did later in their life. For example, General Arthur Exon told researcher Whitley Strieber that everybody *"from Truman on down"* had known about the Roswell incident from the day it happened and that it was known to be an alien spacecraft *"almost as soon as we got on the scene."* Exon also testified that General Clements McMullin had instructed General Ramey that, according to Exon, they were to concoct a *"cover story"* to *"get the press off our back."* At the time, McMullin was Deputy Commander of Strategic Air Command, and Roswell was a SAC base.

Then there was Ben Games, the pilot for Major General L. C. Craigie, who initiated the first investigation into flying saucers in December 1947, six months after the Roswell crash. In that study, he requested the Air Force *"collect, collate, evaluate and distribute to interested government agencies and contractors all information concerning sightings and phenomena in the atmosphere which can be construed to be of concern to the national security."* Games stated that he had flown Craigie to Roswell in early 1947 for a visit that only lasted for hours. Games said that Craigie never disclosed what he discovered as he had promised Truman that he wouldn't talk about what he had found.

Then there was General Hoyt Vandenberg, the acting Army Air Force Chief of Staff at the time of the crash. His name appeared on the memo that General Roger Ramey was seen holding the day after the crash announcement at 8th Air Force Headquarters. On that same day in Washington, Vandenberg also attended a hastily schedule 2½ hour meeting of the Research and Development Board (in charge of all military weapons technology) that replaced a previously scheduled appointment. Just before the meeting took place of the JRDB, Vandenberg was briefed about the conference by Gen. Curtis LeMay, then vice-chief of staff of the AAF for Joint Research and Development (one Roswell photographer recalled being told that he might encounter LeMay at the body crash site). One of the people at this JRDB meeting was General Craigie, who later flew into Roswell and was then sworn to secrecy by Truman. The day after the big meeting at the JRDB, Vandenberg, after many discussions with AAF Secretary Stuart Symington, gathered all the most potent military people advising Truman.

More potentially important meetings occurred on July 9, including several more with Symington. First, Vandenberg and Symington conferred with Lt. Gen. James 'Jimmy' Doolittle in the morning (Doolittle was often rumored to have headed up investigations into the WW2 foo-fighters and the Scandinavian ghost rockets). Then, the three men went to an hour-and-a-half meeting with Army Chief of Staff Eisenhower. Also at this meeting was Gen. Lauris Norstad, AAF Director of Plans and Operations. During this meeting, Vandenberg talked with Truman on the phone.

The Washington Post reported that Vandenberg was very interested in the crash; *"Army Air Force officials here were as flabbergasted as the rest of the world (about the Roswell base press release) but under the personal direction of Lieut. Gen. Hoyt Vandenberg, acting AAF chief, who dropped into the Washington AAF public information headquarters in the midst of the excitement, they burned up the wires to Texas and New Mexico."*

Craigie was not the only one who was sworn to secrecy by Truman. When Jim Carey and Don Schmidt published their second book on Roswell, they reported that witnesses had been sworn to secrecy. I wrote them, noting that Truman had not been to New Mexico, so how could this happen? Carey wrote back, stating that a secret service agent for Truman had been there and was swearing people to secrecy on behalf of the President. I asked for the name and was given two names, including Gerald McCann. Having worked with the *Truman Library* and seen how their records worked, I checked them, and sure enough, the stories were confirmed. Gerald McCann had been a Secret Service agent for Truman for almost his whole presidency.

Even General Landry hinted to his family that he had been let in on the true story of what occurred at Roswell as the President's aide. He promised his family that before he died, he would tell his family the truth. Unfortunately, he died before he could keep his promise, but he did drop one hint to his grandson. He told him, *"If I told you what really happened back at Roswell, you would never see life in the same way again."*

Eisenhower and the Alien Meeting

I have conducted radio interviews on the Presidents and UFOs, and the number one question asked by a long shot is, *"What is the true story on Eisenhower and the aliens?"* The Eisenhower Library also is asked the same question a lot. *"We've had so many requests on that subject,"* Eisenhower archivist Jim Leyerzapf stated, *"that we have a person who specializes in this."*

The short version of the story states that there was a rumored meeting with live aliens and Eisenhower that took place at Edwards Air Force Base (then known as Muroc Field) while the President and his wife were 110 miles away on a winter holiday at Palms Springs, California on February 20, 1954. The facts are clear: the President disappeared from his business friend Paul Helms's ranch, where he was staying. The reporters had somehow picked up on it, and James Hagerty, the White House press secretary, had to be called back from a barbeque he was attending on the other side of town to deal with the press. The *Associated Press* had already gone on the wire with the story that the President had suffered a heart attack and was dead. Minutes later, they withdrew the story.[57] Haggerty told the press that the President had damaged a tooth while eating fried chicken at dinner and had gone to the dentist to fix the problem. The White House Press core accepted the explanation, and the whole story disappeared when Eisenhower

Alien Bedtime Stories

appeared the following day publicly at the local Community Church, despite the fact he didn't like to go to church.[58]

Although the press dropped their interest in the disappearance, the UFO community never dropped the story, and it has become a crucial part of UFO lore. The story told, however, has changed over the years. One of the key versions is a fear-based conspiracy story in which Eisenhower signed a treaty with grey aliens, allowing them to abduct people in exchange for advanced alien technology. This story is nonsense for the following reasons.

The idea is accurate that the only person who can sign a treaty on behalf of the United States is the President, the head of state. However, the treaty idea is stupid. How do you enforce such a thing? Do you take the aliens to court if they violate the terms? The Greys don't need a treaty. Anyone who knows about the Greys knows they do whatever they want. The Greys were not around in 1954. They did not make themselves known until the 1960s. Why would the aliens provide the United States military with advanced weapons with which the military would then turn around and try and shoot down the alien crafts?

That is the 'evil alien' version of the story. Now here is the good alien story version. If the alien encounter occurred at Edwards in 1954; it most probably happened with human-looking aliens, the predominant aliens who had encounters with people in the 1950s. That was what was contained in the original leak on the story that was put out a couple of weeks after the event. It is a significant release, as there would be no story about Eisenhower meeting aliens without it. The original story came from Gerald Light, the head of a Southern California metaphysical organization. In May 1954, he wrote a letter to Meade Layne, the then-director of Borderland Sciences Research Associates. In the letter, Light actually claimed to have been at Edwards, where he saw Ike, the saucers, and the aliens. Light wrote:

> *I have just returned from Muroc (Edwards Air Force Base). The report is true. Devastatingly true! I made the journey in company with Franklin Allen of the Hearst*

> *papers and Edwin Nourse of Brookings Institute (Truman's erstwhile financial advisor), and Bishop McIntyre of L.A. (confidential names for the present, please).[59] When we were allowed to enter the restricted section (after about six hours in which we were checked on every possible item, event, incident, and aspect of our personal and public lives), I had the distinct feeling that the world had come to an end with fantastic realism. I have never seen so many human beings in a state of complete collapse and confusion as they realized that their own world had indeed ended with such finality as to beggar description. The reality of the 'other plane' aero-forms is now and forever removed from the realms of speculation and made a rather painful part of the consciousness of every responsible scientific and political group. During my two days visit, I saw five separate and distinct types of aircraft being studied and handled by our Air Force officials with the assistance and permission of the Ephesians![60]*

Another report given about the meeting came from the son of a former Navy Commander who claimed that his father had been present at the Eisenhower event. According to Charles L. Suggs, a retired Sgt from the US Marine Corps, his father, Charles L. Suggs (1909-1987), was a former Commander with the US Navy who attended the event. In a 1991 interview, Suggs stated that according to the father, he accompanied President Ike along with others on Feb. 20th. They met and spoke with two white-haired Nordics with pale blue eyes and colorless lips. The spokesman stood several feet from Ike and would not let him approach any closer. They posed detailed questions about our nuclear testing.

If there were a meeting between aliens and Eisenhower, this scenario would make much more sense as:

1. The description that was given in the 1950s of aliens was not greys but human-type aliens

Alien Bedtime Stories

2. The main message being reported by contactees in the 1950s almost always contained a message about stopping nuclear testing and construction.

Another fact that fits a possible nuclear connection to any meeting that Eisenhower may have had with the alien's centers on timing. The February 20/21 rumored meeting occurred only days before a key event dealing with nuclear weapons testing. It was a test that would go very bad and remains the most significant accidental radioactive contamination ever caused by the United States.

The test was called *'Castle Bravo.'* It was part of a series of six Operation Castle atmospheric blasts testing thermonuclear weapons small enough to be carried and dropped by aircraft. The test took place on February 28, 1954, at Bikini Atoll in the Marshall Islands. It involved the first test of a dry-fuel thermonuclear hydrogen bomb. Added to this test was a layered flask containing two chemicals, tritium (heavy water) and lithium-6-deuteride. It was the first test of the 'Teller-Ulam configuration,' intended to hold the bomb together for an extra hundred millionth of a second, thus allowing fusion to take place within the tritium and lithium-6-deuteride.[61]

The test went totally out of control, being 250% more powerful than expected and resulting in a bomb 1,000 times the power of the bomb dropped in Hiroshima. The crew in charge of the detonation had to be rescued from a nearby island twenty miles away when radiation detectors told them something serious had gone wrong, and their lives were now at risk. Like giant ghosts at Halloween, they covered themselves with bedsheets, with holes cut out so they could see, to protect themselves from the radioactive fallout. They ran to a nearby landing pad where helicopters from the command ship rescued them. The test ended up causing the most significant radiological contamination accident ever caused by the United States government. The original projection of the test size was 4-6 megatons, but the calculations were completely off. The test ended up being 15 megatons. A total of 7,000 sq. miles were contaminated, and two islands (Rongelap and Utirik atolls) had to be evacuated because hundreds of residents were sick from the radioactive fallout. Those evacuated have never returned. There was suddenly a change in the world's view of nuclear tests, and there was an international call for the end of atmospheric nuclear testing. Did the aliens know this, and was the meeting with Eisenhower a warning? We will probably never know.

President Johnson and the Official UFO Study

Dr. James McDonald confessed that his chosen examples excluded a large amount of UFO phenomena that experience taught him to omit from any brief discussion. He believed that it was simply too baffling to lay before unprepared audiences like the President.
-From the Frank Rand Manuscript on the UFO study for the President.

Many people in the UFO community believe that the president is cut out of the UFO story. The idea is that he is only there for a couple of years and, therefore, has no need to know. None of this is probably true. Consider:
- All secrecy is granted and organized not by law but by executive order. Therefore, it all comes from the Executive Office of the President. The president is in charge of secrecy and security classifications. He, himself, does not have a security clearance. He can see whatever he wants, and those reporting to him will "move mountains" to ensure he

gets what he demands. He can declassify anything he wants.
- The issue of dealing with aliens constitutionally would be the role of the president. He is the head of state, meaning no one else can negotiate or sign treaties.
- The president is the CEO of the government, so if that is where the cover-up is, he is in charge. He appoints the people who head the various departments. They are his people, and if he does not trust them, he fires them and puts someone else in.
- The president is in charge of the two and half intelligence agencies. Their job is to gather intelligence for the President and the executive branch. The president again appoints the heads of all these agencies.
- The president is the Commander-in-Chief of the Military. They must salute and obey his orders. Hiding anything would be insubordination which would go against what people are trained for in their military careers.

So it is that most people would believe that President Johnson had no clue about UFOs and that all the people he appointed were hiding stuff and lying to him.

A couple of years back, I was contacted by a researcher whose friend was the daughter of a man named Frank Rand. Rand was an assistant to President Johnson. Her father had died, and he had left a manuscript dealing with a UFO study done for the President in 1976.

We know the time was 1967 because a schoolteacher from the Westall School in Australia reported being interviewed by Dr. James McDonald (a University of Arizona professor researching UFOs), who was working on the study. The teacher had been part of hundreds of schoolchildren who saw a UFO land in the schoolyard and then fly away.

The Johnson UFO study was the idea of Dr. McDonald. He had demanded a study from his friend Lyndon Johnson. Finally, Johnson gave in just to shut McDonald's down.

The study was done secretly, and the report to the president was eyes-only, meaning that the documents were destroyed once they were read.

We know about the study because Rand's daughter contacted Jamie Burress. She did not know what to do with a manuscript her father had not completed when he died. The manuscript told the whole story of who conducted it, how long it ran, the conclusion arrived at, and what Johnson did with the information he received.

In what looked like a proposal for the book Rand wrote:

> *My book carefully summarizes our Eyes-Only investigation of the UFO phenomena we undertook at the request of President Johnson.*
>
> *That unclassified UFO investigation uniquely portrays the type of activity that I was engaged in while working in the White House as an assistant to the president. Initially, we did not set out to prove UFOs were real or that there were interplanetary or extraterrestrial visitors. However, based on our in-depth physical analysis of Nuclear Fusion & our investigation of our Solar System and surrounding universe, we did suggest UFOs are technically feasible. We further attempted (if they are real) to answer the question of how & why they might elect to visit the Earth.*

The president authorized the investigation under pressure from McDonald's. Rand wrote that he had been told, "Contact him (McDonald) and get that bastard off my neck. Take your time but tell McDonald that you are looking into my problem." According to Rand, the resulting study of nine months involved eight investigators. They were called by Rand the "Special Team." Five were government, and three were outside the government.

The group "had known each other for years and often worked on programs and special committees for the Defense Department or intelligence community."

Rand was given a need to know "inside the highly classified projects of the CIA, NSA, AEC, and other Air Force, Navy, or Army programs of the Defense Department."

Interestingly the names of the people investigating paralleled the names of the tea, of people who had joined To The Stars Academy of Arts and Science headed by rocker Tom DeLonge who was given a whole list of government insiders on what was supposed to be some big UFO disclosure by insiders.

1. One of the vital government people Rand used to help with the study was Arthur Lundahl, who had analyzed the UFO photos for the Robertson Panel with his Navy photographic lab. After the Robertson Panel, the CIA offered him the job of running the National Photographic Interpretation Lab at the CIA, which would handle all the U-2 photos and later the SR-71 and satellite photos.

   Rand stated that he had known Lundahl for thirty years and was always interested in UFOs. His interest had gotten Rand interested.

2. Kelly Johnson (Pres. Lockheed Skunkworks) was a key member. Skunkworks is the contractor most often associated with UFO back-engineering efforts. He had his own UFO sighting early in his career and had made it public.

3. Dr. Brockway McMillan is Under the Secretary of the Air Force and NRO Director. The NRO was in charge of space reconnaissance and was not public until the early

1990s. McMillan was, therefore, in a deep dark spot in the intelligence world in 1967 when the study was run.

4. Lee Brocking (renamed top University of California physicist). We do not know who this is.
5. Dr. Walter Bleakley (Princeton nuclear physicist) was on the committee. He was an associate of Blue Book's Edward Condon at the same University.
6. Dr. Doc Losh was a female astronomy professor at the University of Michigan.
7. General James T. Stewart was a 4-star General at Wright Patterson Air Force Base.
8. Frank Rand was an assistant to the President and the head of the study.
9. We know that Dr. James McDonald contributed to the study as the Australian reported him to be questioning people in 1967 about the Westall School UFO sighting in which hundreds of children were involved.

Johnson Study Investigators	TTSA officials and scientists
Arthur Lundahl (CIA)	Jim Semivan (CIA)
General James T. Steward (4-Star WPAFB)	General Neil McCasland (2-star WPAFB)
Kelly Johnson (Pres. Lockheed Skunkworks)	Robert Weiss (Pres. Lockheed Skunkworks)
Dr. Brockway McMillan Under Secretary of the Air Force, NRO Director	NRO General – name unknown

Alien Bedtime Stories

Lee Brocking (renamed top University of California physicist)	Hal Puthoff (physicist Inst. For Advanced Studies)
Dr. Walter Bleakley (Princeton nuclear physicist)	Dr. Adele Gilpin and Dr. Paul Rapp
Dr. Doc Losh – Astronomer	Dr. Eric Davis (astrophysicist)

Like the Advanced Aerospace Threat Identification Program, the special team focused on military sightings around Air Force Bases. However, they also looked at particular times and noticed a noticeable flap of sightings worldwide in 1952 and 1953.

The report's conclusion to the President was long-running and had many pages. It may become a subject of an extraordinary book. Here are the first conclusions listed in the report that summarizes much of what was discovered. The basic conclusion is exactly what Lue Elizondo, Kit Green, Jacques Vallée, and Barack Obama stated. There is a UFO phenomenon. There is solid evidence, but no one has a clue about the origin of the phenomena of the intelligence behind it.

1) There is abundant evidence that suggests:
- The Unidentified Flying Objects (UFOs) or crafts are real
- They have intelligence.
- They are often observed with highly reflective metal-looking outer skin surfaces.

2) At night they have been observed with high intensity, multi-colored lights beaming up as well as down towards the ground beneath the hovering UFOs.

3) Some UFOs have been observed as they closed and then have flown along in formation with both military and commercial aircraft. Some were observed while flying in close formation for extended periods by both military and civilian crews and passengers aboard these aircraft.

There have always been conspiracy theories that McDonald was killed for this report or for other discoveries he might have made. However, this does not hold up when the facts are reviewed—a couple of examples:
- I reviewed McDonald's MASSIVE UFO collection of UFO files. There was no indication he had any inside knowledge. There were no indications of anything beyond sightings. There was some correspondence with Arthur Lundahl, who claimed to do the UFO briefings for the president. That correspondence showed both men were curious and interested but swimming in a sea of ignorance.
- McDonald did not commit suicide till five years after this report was given to the president.

Recommendations

The panel recommended that the "President set up 1) a Special nominating Committee and 2) a standby Scientific team consisting of a Team Chairman supported by a team of scientists and engineers. Both groups should be elected to serve for one year."
As far as I can determine from the report, the president did nothing.

Nixon and the Alien Bodies

Over the years I have done a number of interviews on the Presidents and their involvement with UFOs. The story of Nixon showing dead alien bodies is the second most asked question. Did it really happen?

In February 1973, President Richard Nixon took a trip to Florida. On February 19, according to White House Records, the President met on the 18th green at the Inverness Golf and Country Club with Jackie Gleason. He had come to help open a charity golf tournament run by Gleason. If some rumors are to be believed, Nixon also came to Florida in 1973 to show Jackie Gleason some bodies that were not from this planet. Gleason was considered one of the foremost television comedians of the 20th century producing the Jackie Gleason Show for almost 20 years and playing the character of Ralph Kramden on the top-rated Honeymooners TV show in the mid-1950s. He appeared in 21 movies and produced 20 music albums from 1953 to 1969.

Jackie Gleason and President Nixon had several things in common and became good friends. Gleason was a strong supporter of the Republican Party. Gleason lived in Florida, and Nixon had a compound on Biscayne Bay only miles away. In addition to being avid golfers, both had high regard for the FBI. Nixon had, in April 1937, applied to become an agent with the FBI, and Gleason worked for the FBI as an official 'contact' for the Special Agent in Charge (SAC) in Miami, where he lived for the last twenty years of his life. According to Gleason, one of the other things they had in common was a large collection of UFO books. Both were fascinated by the subject.

Gleason had long been a fan of UFOs. He was a subscriber to the newsletter of the group *Just Cause* (Citizens Against UFO Secrecy). Gleason had 1700 books on parapsychology, UFOs, and the unknown. These were donated to the University of Miami by his third wife when he passed away in 1987. Gleason had even built a house in Peekskill, N.Y., which he called "The Mother ship."

Gleason had architects build everything around like a flying saucer. Most of his furniture was round, and the garage, called the 'Scout Ship,' was also round, like a flying saucer.

Biographer William A. Henry, in his book, *The Life and Legend of Jackie Gleason,* described his view of Jackie Gleason's interest in the unknown:

> *Jackie Gleason had a lifelong fascination with the supernatural. Everything that Shirley MacLean was to explore in her exotic life and the best-selling book had already been explored by Gleason. He would spend small fortunes on everything from financing psychic research to buying a sealed box said to contain actual ectoplasm, the spirit of life itself. He would contact everyone from back-alley charlatans to serious researchers like J.B. Rhine of Duke University and, disdaining the elitism of the scholarly apparatus, would treat them all much the same way. Gleason was a frequent insomniac. He would stay up all night reading (or re-reading) some of the hundreds of (UFO and paranormal phenomena) volumes in his library.*

Gleason did not see a UFO until later in his life when he was living in Florida. In 1955 at the height of his popularity with the American people, he stated during a magazine interview, *"I have never seen a flying saucer anywhere personally but have read published flying saucer literature. Most of this literature is ridiculous, but amongst the trash, there are some undeniable points that cannot be refuted even by the United States Government."*

Gleason let the public know that he was interested in UFOs, but he was very secretive about how strong his belief was. While living in New York, he invited Sheila MacRae for a visit to his saucer-shaped home in Peekskill. MacRae replaced Audrey Meadows as the 'Honeymooners' Alice Kramden when Jackie Gleason moved his TV shows to Florida in the sixties. He showed her his massive collection of books on spiritualism, the occult, and UFOs. *"I'm kind of a nut on the subject,"* he told Sheila. *"Hey, maybe 'nut' isn't the right word, eh? Think of the fun the columnists and the writers for TV Guide would have if they got a load of all this, huh?"*

There were a few people whom Jackie trusted with whom he would discuss the subject. One of these people was Bob Considine. In his book, *How Sweet It Is: The Jackie Gleason Story*, Jackie Gleason's publicist James Bacon described how Gleason was always arguing about UFOs with Bob Considine, a columnist for the New York Journal-American. These UFO debates took place in Gleason's favorite watering hole, 'Toots Shor's Restaurant and Bar in New York City. Gleason would tell Considine how both sides had seen small UFOs during World War 2 and that four Presidents of the United States had told him about these UFOs. Considine didn't believe Gleason until General Rosie O'Donnell, then head of the Strategic Air Force, overheard the two arguing. He came up and said to Considine, *"Jackie's right."*

According to Gleason's second wife, Beverly McKittrick, Gleason had done more than talk and golf with his friend Richard Nixon while in Florida. McKittrick stated that one-night, Gleason had returned home very shaken. It was during Nixon's February 1973 visit to Florida. She related that President Nixon had taken Jackie to a heavily secured area at Homestead Air Force Base, where he had viewed the remains of small aliens in a top-secret repository. McKittrick related this story in an unpublished manuscript of Gleason called, *'The Great One.'*

Larry Bryant, the editor of Just Cause, the newsletter Gleason, had a subscription and filed a Freedom of Information Act Request with Homestead Air Force Base. Bryant requested documentation on the top-secret repository and Gleason's visit to see the alien bodies. The Air Force Base replied that no such records existed. Bryant also sent an advertisement to the Homestead Air Force Base Newspaper soliciting information from anyone on the base which could provide information about the alien bodies or Jackie Gleason's visit to see them. The public affairs officer at Homestead denounced the Bryant advertisement and forbade its publication. At the same time, Bryant wrote Gleason, providing him with a draft affidavit. He asked Gleason to execute the affidavit so it could be used as part of a growing accumulation of evidence Bryant collected in preparation for taking the government to court to release all information on alien crash retrievals. Gleason did not reply. About the same time as Bryant was approaching Gleason to provide an affidavit about his experience at Homestead, Gleason was approached by the film industry about the rumored story. Bryant recounted, *"Though I never did hear from Gleason,"* said Bryant, *"I did learn that a third party in the film industry had contacted him."* At this confrontation, Gleason chose to neither confirm nor deny the story, saying that he would prefer not to discuss it:

> *The way I see it, Gleason easily could have set the record straight in reply to my proposal or in an explanation to the inquisitive film-industry representative. If the story was a fabrication or misinterpretation on the part of his wife, he now had every opportunity to say so. That he chose not to merely deepens the mystery.*

Shortly before his death in 1987, one story says Gleason finally confirmed the story about seeing the bodies at Homestead. The person Jackie Gleason told the story to was Larry Warren, a member of the Air Force Security Police at RAF Bentwaters. Bentwaters was one of two bases in England where in late December 1980, three days of bizarre UFO incidents took place. Many US airmen stationed at the base were involved in sightings, radar tracking, pictures, and videos. Larry Warren had been involved in events on the second night of sightings. He saw an object land in a forest clearing and, along with several other airmen, saw three beings come out of the craft. The case became known as the 'Rendlesham Forest Case,' and was considered by many to be the most significant UFO incident in the history of Great Britain.

Larry Warren's encounter with Jackie Gleason occurred in May 1986, shortly before Gleason's death in June 1987. CNN and HBO

Alien Bedtime Stories

had been running stories on the 1980 Rendlesham Forest case. *"Through mutual friends who knew members of his family,"* recounted Warren, *"I was told that Gleason would like to talk to me privately in his home in Westchester County, and so the meeting was set for a Saturday when we would both have time to relax."* Timothy Green Beckley, a New York City author, produced an excellent account of the meeting between the two men; *"After being formally introduced, the two men ventured into Gleason's recreation room complete with pool table and full-size bar. There were hundreds of UFO books all over the place, but Jackie was quick to tell me that this was only a tiny portion of his entire collection, which was housed in his home in Florida."* For the rest of the day, the UFO researcher and UFO witness exchanged information. *"Gleason seemed to be very well informed on the subject,"* Larry says, *"as he knew the smallest detail about most cases and showed me copies of the book 'Clear Intent' that had just been published, as well as a copy of 'Sky Crash,' a British book about Bentwaters that was published before all the details of this case, was made public. I remember Gleason telling me about his own sightings of several discs in Florida and how he thought there were undersea UFOs bases out in the Bermuda Triangle."*

But it wasn't until after Warren had downed a few beers and Gleason had had several drinks, his favorite, 'Rob Roy,' that conversation got down to brass tacks. *"At some point, Gleason turned to me and said, 'I want to tell you something very amazing that will probably come out someday anyway. We've got 'em!' 'Got what?' I wanted to know. 'Aliens!' Gleason sputtered, catching his breath.* According to Warren, Jackie told him the intriguing set of circumstances that led him to the stunning conclusion that extraterrestrials have arrived on our cosmic shores. *"It was back when Nixon was in office that something truly amazing happened to me,"* Gleason explained. *"We were close golfing buddies and had been out on the golf course all day when somewhere around the 15th hole, the subject of UFOs came up. Not many people know this,"* Gleason told Warren, *"but the President shares my interest in this matter and has a large collection of books in his home on UFOs just like I do. For some reason, however, he never really took me into his confidence about what he personally knew to be true. One of the reasons being that he was usually surrounded by so many aids and advisers."* Later that night, matters changed radically when Richard Nixon showed up at Gleason's house around midnight. *"He was all alone for a change. There were no secret service agents with him or anyone else. I said, 'Mr. President, what are you doing here?' and he said he wanted to take me someplace and show me something."* Gleason got into the President's private car, and they sped off into the darkness, their destination being Homestead Air Force Base. *"I remember we got to the gate and this young MP came up to the car to look to see inside, and his jaw seemed to drop afoot when he saw who was behind the wheel. He just sort of pointed, and we headed off."* Warren says that later Gleason found out that the secret service was going absolutely crazy trying to find out where Nixon was. *"We drove to the very far end of the base in a segregated area,"* Gleason went on, *"finally stopping near a well-guarded building. The security police saw us coming, and just sort of moved back as we passed them and entered the structure. There were a number of labs we passed through first before we entered a section where Nixon pointed out what he said was the wreckage from a flying saucer, enclosed in several large cases."*

Gleason noted his initial reaction was that this was all a joke brought on by their earlier conversation on the golf course. But it wasn't, as Gleason soon learned. *"Next, we went into an inner chamber, and there were six or eight of what looked like glass-topped Coke freezers. Inside them were the mangled remains of what I took to be children. Then, upon closer examination, I saw that some of the other figures looked quite old. Most of them were terribly mangled as if they had been in an accident."*

According to Larry Warren's testimony (regarding Gleason's lengthy conversation about UFOs and space visitors), *"I forget whether he said they had three or four fingers on each hand, but they definitely were not human. Of this, he was most certain!"*

For three weeks following his trip with Nixon to Homestead Air Force Base, the world-famous entertainer couldn't sleep and couldn't eat. *"Jackie told me that he was very traumatized by all of this. He just couldn't understand why our government wouldn't tell the public all they knew about UFOs and space visitors. He said he even drank more heavily than usual until he could regain some of his composure and come back down to everyday reality."* Larry Warren is convinced that Gleason wasn't lying to him. *"You could tell that he was very sincere, he took the whole affair very seriously, and I could tell that he wanted to get the matter off his chest, and this was why he was telling me all of this."* And as far as Larry Warren was concerned, the Great One's personal testimony only added extra credibility to his own firsthand experience with aliens while he was in the service. *"Jackie felt just like I do that the government needs to 'come clean' and tell us all it knows about space visitors. It's time they stopped lying to the public and released all the evidence they have. When they do, then we'll all be able to see the same things the late Jackie Gleason did!"*

The obvious question that has been asked about this incident is how Nixon, the most protected man in the world, was able to get away from his secret service detail, get a car, and head off to Homestead with Jackie Gleason. The story seems at first totally impossible. The Director of the Secret Service under President Clinton, Lewis Merletti, claimed that the idea of a President escaping his secret service agents only happens in the movies. In response to a question by reporter Joan London about the possibility of the President escaping his protection to go out and secretly do something, Merletti claimed, *"That's all Hollywood; there's no sneaking out. It has never happened."*

However, Marty Venker, a Secret Service agent who worked with Merletti under Presidents Ford and Carter, tells a different story. In his book *Confessions of an Ex-Secret Service Agent,* he says that not only can the President disappear, but it has also happened.

Venker stated that in the same year of the Homestead incident with Gleason 1973, Nixon had tried to cut his secret service protection. Venker also noted that it was not uncommon for Nixon to try to elude his secret service detail. However, the agents working on the Nixon Presidential detail had been warned about it. Venker even recounted one occasion when Nixon was able to ditch his secret service guards while at his California compound:

> *Nixon always felt that he was overprotected. He felt he couldn't pick his nose without some agent taking notes. In 1973, he tried to cut his detail by a third. 'I don't like it, and my family doesn't like it!' he said. I'd be warned of the lengths Nixon would go to elude us. One time he snuck out of the San Clemente compound. His valet, Manolo Sanchez, drove past the agents in a car with Nixon stretched out in the back seat under a blanket. Nixon just wanted to go to a restaurant. But some reporters saw him and phoned the house. They wanted to know was Nixon was up to. The secret service told them he's not at any restaurant; he's here at home. But then the agents found he was gone, and they chased him down.*

Nixon was very familiar with Homestead Air Force Base, which was only minutes from his Biscayne Bay compound. Every time Nixon flew south to his 'Southern White House,' Air Force One would land at Homestead. In Nixon's first term as President, he traveled to his Key Biscayne compound 55 times and spent 118 nights there. On the other hand, Gleason lived in nearby Miami and owned his golf course, the Inverrary Country Club, nearby in Fort Lauderdale, Florida.

This author wrote about Gleason's third wife when Jackie Gleason died to ask for her assistance in clarifying the story.

She wrote back one simple hand-written line, *"So sorry we cannot be of any help to you."*

There is no proof that Nixon escorted Jackie Gleason to view alien bodies at Homestead, but everything checked out indicates it could have happened. It would have been very easy in terms of distance for the Gleason/Nixon alien event to have occurred.

The Jimmy Carter UFO Sighting

Many internet sites display a UFO sighting report related to President Carter's 1969 UFO sighting. The NICAP report is only a retyped version of the original report filed with the International UFO Bureau in Oklahoma City, Oklahoma. Below you will find the original handwritten report by Georgia Governor Jimmy Carter in 1973. This copy was found at the Carter presidential library in Atlanta.

The Carter ET and UFO Studies

"Knowledge will forever govern ignorance, and a people who mean to be their own governors must arm themselves with the power which knowledge gives."
--President James Madison. Inscribed on the Madison Building in Washington D.C., where Daniel Sheehan claimed he was allowed to view classified sections of the USAF *Project Blue Book* in 1977 and where he discovered the picture of a crashed flying saucer.

"It's always difficult to strike a balance between the public's right to know and NASA's need for candor."
--Marcia Smith, Space policy, senior analyst at the Congressional Research Service in Washington, D.C.

Shortly after President Carter came to power in January 1977, Daniel Sheehan, then General Counsel to the United States Jesuit National Headquarters, National Office of Social Ministry in Washington, D.C., was reportedly approached by Marcia S. Smith, Director of the Library of Congress's Science and Technology Division of the Congressional Research Service from 1984-1985. The Congressional Research Service of the Library of Congress is a research group of more than 400 people researching for Congress and the White House. Over the years, they have played more than a passing interest in the UFO problem. Every one of these UFO research efforts has been led by Marcia Smith.

Sheehan reported that Smith asked him to participate in a highly classified significant evaluation of the UFO phenomena and extraterrestrial intelligence. The person who made the offer was Marcia Smith. She made Sheehan a special consultant to the Congressional Research Service. Marcia had, in turn, learned of Sheehan from her friend Rosemary Chalk, who was the Secretary to the National Science Foundation at the time. Chalk and Sheehan attended the same church in Washington. During one conversation between the two, Sheehan had told Chalk that he had wanted to be an astronaut as a young man but that the appointments he had sought to attain this goal had been given away as political prizes to others. He told Chalk that his goal had been *"To become an astronaut and to go out into outer space and meet other civilizations."* When Sheehan was finished telling his story about how he ended up becoming a lawyer, Chalk was surprised. She said, *"Wow, I never imagined that was true, but I know someone that you have to talk to."* The person who called was Marcia Smith.

A part of this contact with Marcia Smith and the CRS involved Sheehan being asked to use his position inside the Jesuit community to obtain the UFO documents held in the Vatican library. Sheehan approached his contact at the Vatican. *"She called,"* recalled Sheehan, *"and asked me if, as Legal Counsel for the Jesuit Headquarters, I could get access to the Library of Congress from the Vatican library. The Vatican library has a fairly large section concerning the issue of extraterrestrial intelligence and UFOs. I undertook to contact the Jesuit who actually runs the Vatican library, and much to my shock, they said we couldn't have access to it. I related this to Marcia Smith."*

After the discussion with Marcia and Father Bill Davis, who was the Director of the National Office, Sheehan made a second approach to the Vatican library. *"I sent back a second letter to the*

Jesuit who was the head of the Vatican library and explained to him that this was an official request that had come from the Congressional Research Service of the Library of Congress. That it had come from the Congress of the United States and that the President himself had wanted to get this information. So, I thought that would get us the information, but I received a second response from the Vatican Library saying no, the Jesuit National Headquarters would not be provided with this information. So, I had to regretfully report that back to Marcia Smith, letting her know that I was not able to get it."

Sheehan recalled the encounter with Marcia, where she related to him the reasons behind the study. *"Marcia informed me that she had been contacted by the Chairman of the Science & Technology Committee of the House of Representatives (Congressman Olin Earl Teague), who in turn had received a directive from the President of the United States, informing the Committee that he, (Carter) in fact had personally seen a UFO while he was in Georgia."* Marcia further informed Sheehan that Carter had approached the House of Representatives Science and Technology Committee based on information he had obtained from former CIA director George Bush. Marcia Smith stated that Carter had approached Bush and stated, *"I want to have the information that we have on UFOs and extraterrestrial intelligence. I want to know about this as President."* George Bush, according to Smith, said, *"No. That he wasn't going to give this to him, that this was information that only existed on a need-to-know basis. Simple curiosity on the part of the President wasn't adequate."*

This Carter-Bush UFO question, referred to by Smith, was probably asked during the first 45 minutes of a multi-hour briefing on November 19, 1976. This was the only time that Bush and Carter met while Carter was President-elect. Bush was replaced as DCI once Carter became President, so there was never a meeting between the two after Carter entered the White House. The 45-minute segment of the briefing given to the President-elect was described by the CIA as a briefing on certain exotic weapons and very closely held items relating to sources and methods. The then Director of Central Intelligence (DCI) for President Ford, George Bush, and his assistant Jennifer Fitzgerald took Carter and Walter Mondale to the Carter living room to provide the selected sensitive information. The other six senior agents weren't cleared for this part of the briefing. They remained to wait in the Carter study until this key part of the briefing was completed.

No matter where the Bush/Carter encounter occurred, the fact remained that Carter was refused the requested UFO information from the CIA Director. Once Carter had been denied the requested information on UFOs, he decided to follow Bush's suggestion for getting the information that Carter wanted on UFOs. *"If he was going to do this, he would have to follow a different procedure,"* stated Sheehan, *"that was going to involve all the different branches of government in authorizing this information because they were afraid that President Carter was going to somehow publicly reveal this. Bush told him that he was going have to go to the Science and Technology Committee of the House of Representatives, in the legislative branch, and have them ask the Congressional Research Service to issue a request to have certain documents declassified so that this process could go on."* *"They were,"* said Sheehan, *"trying to stall this thing. That was going to take a long time, the NSA, the CIA; all these groups were going to hold back documents. So, the President, much chagrined, decided that rather than having a major confrontation with Mr. Bush, he would follow this process."* Carter contacted the Science and Technology Committee of the House of Representatives. They, in turn, contacted the Library of Congress Research Service, and they undertook two major investigations:

1. To determine whether extraterrestrial intelligence existed in our galaxy.
2. To determine the relationship of this UFO phenomenon might be to extraterrestrial intelligence.

Marcia Smith was, at the time, an Analyst in Science and Technology at Science Research Division at the Congressional Research Service. She was not ignorant about the field of UFOs and classified research. Records show that she had been involved in at least five UFO or SETI-related investigations by the Congressional Research Service. In 1975 and then in a 1978 update, Marcia Smith joined with Dr. George Gatewood, Director of the Allegheny Observatory and the NASA Ames research center SETI Program office, to write a report for the Congressional Research Service called *Life Beyond Earth.* This paper (later turned into a book), was not about UFOs. *"The paper is,"* wrote Smith, *"instead, a synthesis of past and current thought on the possibility that there is extraterrestrial life in the universe, together with discussions of the possible impacts of making contact with it."* In 1976, just before Carter won the Presidential election, Smith wrote, 'Extraterrestrial Intelligence and Unidentified Flying Objects: A Selected, Annotated Bibliography,' for the Library of Congress Congressional Research Service.

In 1976 Smith also co-authored a report called, 'The UFO Enigma,' which was produced for the Congressional Research Service. The report was an overview of the U.S. government's involvement in solving the UFO puzzle and information that had been released under the Freedom of Information. In 1983, Smith produced an updated report by the same name, updating the report with events that had occurred between 1976 and 1983. The CRS UFO-related reports were fundamental UFO reports with nothing of a controversial or classified nature. Part of this is that the reports were publicly published, and UFOs were not a popular subject to write about inside the government.

James Oberg, a former NASA consultant, worked in the 1970s with Marcia on Congressional research reports. Both had an interest in UFOs, but they also shared an interest in Oberg's specialty, the Soviet space program. *Aviation Week & Space Technology* magazine eventually came to refer to Marcia Smith as 'The Congressional Research Service Russian space guru.' Oberg recalled Smith's reluctance to write reports on UFOs. *"Back in the late 1970s,"* Oberg told this writer, *"We briefly discussed the overview of 'The UFO Enigma' (written the year before Carter became President), and she expressed exasperation at having to put something like that together, but basically the CRS researches what Congress asks them to do."*

When the story broke that Smith had done two reports for President Carter in 1977, Oberg contacted this author and provided him with Marcia Smith's email so I could obtain her comment. Smith did not respond to the email, but she and Oberg did discuss the two reports. In a second email, Oberg wrote, *"She is talking to me. Is she talking to you?"* Asked what Smith had told him about the ETI and UFO studies, reportedly done by Smith in 1977, Oberg refused to say anything. A researcher out of Washington, D.C., wrote Oberg asking for Smith's phone number, but this request was also ignored. Oberg, always ready with an opinion about anything and everything, was forced into complete silence. The reason for this silence was that anything Oberg would say, pro or con, would simply increase the pressure on Marcia Smith to confirm or deny the Sheehan recollections. Smith had no intention of talking, and Oberg planned to do what he could to help his long-time friend.

Besides the high school level UFO-related reports listed by the CRS, as being authored by Marcia Smith, there were two that won't be found listed in a CRS directory. Those two reports were the 1977 reports requested by President Carter on extraterrestrial intelligence and UFOs. These two reports, according to Sheehan, were also written by Marcia Smith. Sheehan's description of the reports showed that these two were not high school-level reports. Sheehan had known of the writing of the two reports due to his role as a special consultant for the CRS. Sheehan reported that he even was able to read the two reports before they were sent off to the Science and Technology Committee of the House of Representatives.

Sheehan's role for the CRS was to help obtain the Vatican UFO files and a second, more dramatic role in reviewing classified UFO files from the former USAF *Project Blue Book,* which was closed in 1969. This incident occurred in a vaulted room in the basement of the Library of Congress Madison Building in downtown Washington, D.C. The new Carter administration had reinstated funding for the *Search for Extraterrestrial Intelligence*. Marcia had phoned Sheehan asking him to speak to the scientists at the Jet Propulsion Laboratory in the SETI program. The topic of the presentation would be the theological and religious implications of potential contact with extraterrestrial civilizations. Sheehan qualified for this because of his degree in religion. Sheehan reported that he told Smith, *"Look, if I am going to be doing this, which I am totally delighted to do, I would like to be able to get access to some of the data that you might have available in the course of your doing this investigation for the Science and Technology Committee in Congress."* Asked what data he would like, Sheehan stated he wanted to see the classified sections of *Project Blue Book*. Marcia, according to Sheehan, stated she didn't know if she could get the Air Force and Defense Department to release those files but agreed to try. *"She contacted them,"* recalled Sheehan, *"and shortly thereafter, she called me, and she said, much to her surprise, 'They have agreed to do this.' She gave me a particular date and time and told me that I should go over to the new building at the Library of Congress."* Sheehan stated, *"This building had not even been opened yet. There were no people in it. She told me they were going to bring the files down to the new building. They had this big vault room downstairs."*

Sheehan continued to tell what has now become a very controversial series of events that occurred two hours into the search. It is a story he told Marcia Smith just after it occurred and a story he has told dozens of times since:

> *There was a room and these two security officers there at the door, and there was actually a third, plain clothed, sitting at a desk to the right of them. As I came in there, I showed them all my identification, and they checked some documentation that they had and said,*

Alien Bedtime Stories

yes, I was supposed to be here. As I started to go in, the man sitting at the desk told me I had to leave my briefcase there. I wouldn't be allowed to take any notes. It turned out I had a yellow pad under my arm, so I set the briefcase down, gave it to him, and I went into the room. I was there for some time. There were a bunch of documents there. There was actually a film machine. It was like a little reel-to-reel kind of a film machine there. I don't know if it was 35mm, or whatever those things were. So, there were actually some little films there. I looked at some of the films, and they were like the classic films that you have seen, sort of far-distant shots of strange moving vehicles. So, I decided I wasn't making much headway on this, so I began to look into these little boxes that had these canisters there. There was one of these overhead filmstrip machines that were in sitting in the room. I began to take these little canisters out, open them up, put the filmstrips in, and look through these things. I don't know how many I have gone through. I had gone through several, or at least a few, of these boxes when I hit upon this one canister that had film and pictures. I started going through, turning the little crank, and there it was. Again, I have told people about this a number of times. There were these photographs of an unmistakable, of a UFO sitting on the ground. It had crashed, apparently. It had hit into this field and had dug up, kind of plowed this kind of trough through this field. It was wedged into the side of this bank. There was snow all around the picture. The vehicle was wedged into the side of this mud-like embankment kind of up at an angle. There was Air Force personnel. As I cranked the little handle and looked at additional photos, I saw these Air Force people were taking pictures. In the photograph, they were taking photographs of this vehicle. One of the photos actually had the Air Force personnel with this big long tape measure measuring this thing. You could see that they had these parkas on, with little fur around their hoods. You could see that they had little name tags on their jacket. They were clearly U.S. Air Force personnel. I was kind of in this strange state saying, 'Here it is!' So, I turned the crank for more pictures, and I could see on the side of this craft these like little insignias, little symbols. So, I turned ahead a couple of pictures to see if there was a closer picture. Sure, enough, there was. One of the photos had kind of a close-up picture of these symbols.

So, what I did, was I got nervous. I looked around, and the guys weren't watching or anything. They were outside the room, so I took the yellow pad, flipped it open to the little grey cardboard backing, and flipped it under the screen. I shrank the size of the picture to the exact same size as the back of the yellow pad and traced the actual symbols out in detail, verbatim of what was there. Once I had actually seen these pictures and actually chosen to copy down and trace these symbols from this craft, I just decided that I should get out of there. So, I got up, closed the little pad, and put the film back in the canister. I put all the boxes back where they were, put the yellow pad under my arm, and just walked out. As I came through the door, I went over to get my briefcase up, and the man at the little desk that was sitting there pointed to the yellow pad under my arm, and he said, 'What's that you've got there?' I said, 'That's the yellow pad that I had with me.' He said, 'Let me see that.' He reached out, and I handed it to him. He flipped through the yellow pages, and never looked at the back, never looked at the inside cardboard backing, and handed it back to me. So, I just put it under my arm, got my briefcase, and walked out of there. I took this *with me, and I reported the details to Marcia. I also prepared my three-hour seminar for JPL.*

Marcia then drafted the two reports for the House Science and Technology Committee. I ended up getting copies of the two reports," said Sheehan, *"one on extraterrestrial intelligence and the other on the phenomena of Unidentified Flying Objects. The first report on extraterrestrial intelligence,"* recalled Sheehan, *"stated the Congressional Research Service of the official United States Congressional Library, in its official report to the President, through the House of Representatives Science and Technology Committee, concludes that there are from two to six highly intelligent, highly technologically developed civilizations in our own galaxy over and above our own. In the second report, they had drawings of different shapes of UFOs that have been sighted,"* continued Sheehan, *"They didn't cite any particular cases, but they said that they believed there was a significant number of instances where the official United States Air Force investigations were unable to discount the possibility that one or more of these vehicles were actually from one of these extraterrestrial civilizations. They put this together and sent it over to the President. I ended up seeing a copy of it.*

Sheehan's contact with the CRS went only to Marcia Smith. It did not extend to Smith's boss, Dr. Jack Gibbons. Sheehan told this writer that he was unaware of who Gibbons was. It is assumed that Gibbons knew and approved the UFO-related reports that Smith was writing. This would extend to the secret UFO report prepared for the House of Representatives, and President Carter, if the story Sheehan tells is true. This connection is meaningful because, following a long period as the head of the Office of Technological Assessment for the Congressional Research Service, Dr. Gibbons became Assistant to the President for Science and Technology in the Clinton White House. As science advisor to President Clinton, Gibbons dealt with the Rockefeller White House UFO initiated by Laurance Rockefeller. Despite his close relationship with the UFO investigations that Marcia Smith was conducting

According to 1,000 pages of UFO documents released by the Clinton Office for Science and Technology Policy, Gibbons quickly overcame his claimed UFO ignorance. He not only met with Rockefeller and his representatives about UFOs, but he headed up a White House initiative to declassify documents that it was hoped would reveal the true story of the events surrounding the crash of an object near Roswell, New Mexico, in July 1947.

Finally, a strange discovery was made in research to discover if Smith produced a secret UFO report for President Carter. As noted above, in 1976, Marcia Smith headed up a research report prepared by the Congressional Research Service titled, *'The UFO Enigma.'* Strangely, the very next year, 1977, a book using exactly the same title, *The UFO Enigma,* was published by Doubleday. The author was the arch-debunker of UFOs, Donald Menzel.

Alien Bedtime Stories

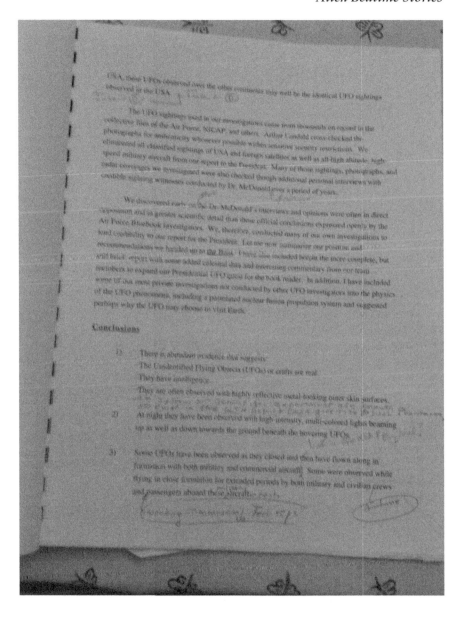

USA, these UFOs observed over the other countries may well be the identical UFO sightings observed in the USA.

The UFO sightings used in our investigations came from thousands on report in the collective files of the Air Force, NICAP, and others. Arthur Lundahl cross-checked the photographs for authenticity whenever possible within sensitive security restrictions. We eliminated all classified sightings of USA and foreign satellites as well as all high altitude, high speed military aircraft from our report to the President. Many of these sightings, photographs, and radar coverages we investigated were also checked through additional personal interviews with credible sighting witnesses conducted by Dr. McDonald over a period of years.

We discovered early on that Dr. McDonald's interviews and opinions were often in direct opposition and in greater scientific detail than those official conclusions expressed openly by the Air Force Bluebook investigators. We, therefore, conducted many of our own investigations to lend credibility to our report for the President. Let me now summarize our position and recommendations we handed up to the Boss. I have also included herein the more complete, but still brief, report with some added colossal data and interesting commentary from our team members to expand our Presidential UFO quest for the book reader. In addition, I have included some of our most private investigations not conducted by other UFO investigators into the physics of the UFO phenomena, including a postulated nuclear fusion propulsion system and suggested perhaps why the UFO may choose to visit Earth.

Conclusions

1) There is abundant evidence that suggests:
    The Unidentified Flying Objects (UFOs) or crafts are real.
    They have intelligence.
    They are often observed with highly reflective metal-looking outer skin surfaces.

2) At night they have been observed with high intensity, multi-colored lights beaming up as well as down towards the ground beneath the hovering UFOs.

3) Some UFOs have been observed as they closed and then have flown along in formation with both military and commercial aircraft. Some were observed while flying in close formation for extended periods by both military and civilian crews and passengers aboard these aircraft.

197

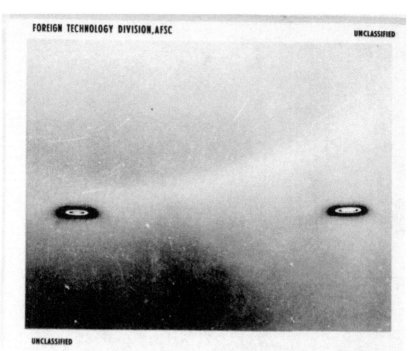

Figure 12 UFO near the President's Army 1 helicopter

Alien Bedtime Stories

Grant Cameron

Ronald Reagan Discloses ET Truth

For many years, people in the UFO community have talked about the day when the President of the United States finally stood up and said that UFOs are real. That is the day researchers believe when the cover-up will end, and the world will all learn the truth about this modern-day mystery. Energy will be cheap, and we can all drive big cars again. Well, the president has finally announced that UFOs (specifically, ETs) are real. Disclosure has finally taken place.

Dr. John Alexander was right when he wrote in his book, *Official disclosure has happened.* President Reagan stated, *"UFOs are real."* Yes, he did, Dr. Alexander. He certainly did. The problem is that the announcement was made on June 27, 1981, and no one paid attention. I doubt many more will after this book makes the rounds. Reagan had let the cat out of the bag before 1981. Reagan, as many know, had at least two UFO sightings. The first sighting occurred when he was invited to a party that actor William Holden was hosting in Hollywood. Several key personalities were invited. Two of those attending, comedian Steve Allen and actress Lucille Ball, both recounted the story of Reagan's UFO encounter. Reagan was missing when the party began, and the party was held up until he and Nancy arrived nearly an hour late. According to both Allen's and Ball's versions of events, Reagan was very excited. He said he and Nancy had seen a UFO while coming and stopped to watch the event.

In her account of the event, Lucy summed up her recollection of the event. It appeared in the biography, *Lucy in the Afternoon: An Intimate Memoir of Lucille Ball.* "After he was elected President," Ball said, *"I kept thinking about that event and wondered if he still would have won if he told everyone that he saw a flying saucer."* Left out of the Ball biography is the bombshell part of the story. Lucille Ball would later relate that part of the story to fellow Hollywood actress Shirley MacLaine. It would confirm a rumor related to the story that had circulated for years regarding this sighting, a contact experience. The only thing that varied in this storytelling was the party's location. Ball told MacLaine that it was at Helen and Armand Deutsch's house. Armand had been a Hollywood producer and later a member of Reagan's kitchen cabinet. Helen and Armand were considered one of Ron and Nancy Reagan's closest friends. According to Ball, Reagan told her that the UFO landed and an alien emerged. It told Reagan to *quit acting and take up politics*. This revelation appeared in a British newspaper quoting MacLaine.

The story of a United States president telling someone he had talked to and taken advice from an alien is a big story, so I began to check the story. It turned out not to be a British tabloid gone wild, but true. Shirley MacLaine had put most of the story[62] in her 2007 book, *Sage-ing While Age-ing;* I and everyone else had missed it, probably because the media picked up on the story told in the book that Ohio Congressman Dennis Kucinich had seen a UFO up close at Shirley's house. They asked him the famous *"Did you see a UFO"* question at the Philadelphia Presidential Democratic debate, and that ended his 2008 run for President.

MacLaine wrote the Ball account on page 142:

> *Reagan had seen a craft when he was an actor, as he and Nancy were driving on Mulholland Drive in Los Angeles. Apparently, the craft landed, and an occupant descended, who then spoke to him telepathically. He never told me directly, but he did tell a party of people who were waiting for him at Helen and Armand Deutsch's house. Lucille Ball told me he had arrived ashen and confused and told her the story. She told me because, as a Democrat, she wanted me to know that Ronnie must have been crazy.*

Now back to the official UFO/ET announcement. The location of the announcement was the White House Theatre on the evening of June 27, 1981. Those in attendance included Supreme Court Justice Sandra Day O'Conner, Astronauts Colonel Joseph Engle and Captain Richard Truly, NASA administrator James Beggs, former

Deputy Director of the CIA Vernon Walters, Chief of Staff James Baker, Deputy Chief of Staff Michael Weaver, Assistant for Political Affairs Alexander Morgan Mason, British Ambassador to the United States Sir John Nicolas Henderson, Journalist and Founder of the National Review Ralph de Toledano, journalist Allen Ryskind, Chairman of the 1984 Olympics Peter Ueberroth, journalist Martin Agronsky, journalist and screenwriter William Dodson Broyles, Undersecretary of State for Security James Buckley, Joseph Canzeri who was working for the first lady, Lane Calhoon, Kathleen Carey, Robert Gubitosi, Jerald Pasternak, and singer, Barbara Cook.

The event was a screening of the movie *ET: The Extraterrestrial*. The movie, produced and directed by Steven Spielberg, tells the story of an alien who gets stranded on earth after his UFO craft leaves him behind. He hides out with a young boy while the government hunts for him, and he tries to send a message to his home planet for rescue.

When the movie had ended, Spielberg recounted what Reagan said to the audience assembled to watch the movie; he just stood up and looked around the room, almost like he was doing a headcount, and he said, *"I wanted to thank you for bringing E.T. to the White House. We really enjoyed your movie."* Then he looked around the room and said, *"And there are a number of people in this room who know that everything on that screen is absolutely true."* And he said it without smiling! But he said that, and everybody laughed, by the way. The whole room laughed because he presented it as a joke, but he wasn't smiling as he said it.

This story[63] was like another story of an event that had occurred on the same evening. This story was told by another Hollywood producer Jamie Shandera, who had been working on a film project with Spielberg in Japan. Shandera stated that Spielberg had told him that Reagan had made an even more revealing statement just before the film ended. Reagan leaned over and told Spielberg, *"I bet there aren't six people in this whole room that know how true this whole thing is."*

Alien Bedtime Stories

A couple of years back, I was approached by Kina Merdinian, Co-Founder and Executive Director of Global Discoveries Network Foundation, who stated that in talking with a top Hollywood director (you would know if you heard the name), he had related being told the same story. I asked Kina if it was the same wording, of which she was unsure, so I sent her the *"There aren't six people in this whole room"* story from my website to show to the director to see if the story was the same. Sometime later, Kina replied that she had shown the story to the director, and yes, it was the same story that Spielberg had told him.

So, a United States president tells a fellow actress that he and his wife had contact with an alien and that the alien gave him direction in his life. Then he tells a room full of people that the whole ET thing is for real. What are we to make of this? Some will say it's true. Most media and skeptics will say that Reagan was crazy and shouldn't be believed. That is the sad part and the rub of the story. Everyone is waiting for the most influential and powerful person in the world, the President of the United States, to say, *"UFOs are for real."* When he does, he can still be written off as crazy, like the North Dakota farmer who claims he saw a strange light one night. Perhaps we need a new standard of what will cause disclosure if the words of the President don't seem to do it.

For 60+ years, there have been stories that disclosure was about to happen. One of the best rumors of imminent disclosure occurred in the late eighties, just before Ronald Reagan left office. The rumor was the combination of two rumors that swirled in the UFO community:

1. Reagan would disclose as the last act of his presidency
2. The United States government had an extraterrestrial guest (EBE3) stored in a safe house near the Washington Mall in Washington.

The rumor that many talked about was that as his last act as president, Reagan would appear on TV with the live alien. Now *that* would bring disclosure! The media would race to cover the story.

The scientists would admit their ignorance and arrogance and beg for forgiveness. Finally, the government would release all the files detailing their lies and misdeeds. Well, thinking it over, maybe not.

As an odd side note to this story, the showing of E.T. was the last event on June 27th. The very next event for the President was the next morning, June 28th. It was a meeting that included President Reagan, James A. Baker, Chief of Staff; Edwin Meese, Counselor; and Michael K. Deaver, Deputy Chief of Staff. They met in the Oval Office. From there, the four men went to the highly secure White House Situation Room where Barack Obama would thirty years later tell Jayden Smith, son of actor Will Smith, *"I can neither confirm nor deny the existence of extra-terrestrials, but I can tell you if there had been a top-secret meeting it would have taken place in this room."* It was there that the President participated in a briefing of the U.S. Space Program. Participants included six members of the National Security Council or National Security Affairs and no one from NASA.

Bill Clinton Talks UFOs

If you go on a trip to any presidential libraries looking for UFO material, you will be sadly disappointed. There may be a few letters to the president on UFOs demanding disclosure or providing information on the importance of the subject. You will not find any concrete discussion of the subject by the president or anyone in the executive branch. It is so little that a researcher could conclude, there is no such thing. The reason for this is simple. Like the discussion of research into fission-induced chain reactions that disappeared from scientific papers in the late 1930s, UFOs have military weapons capabilities, and it is a discussion that is left to the black-budget weapons people.

The president's positive words on UFOs could end the cover-up overnight. For that reason, UFOs, if they are the most highly classified subject in the United States, as American officials told the

Alien Bedtime Stories

Canadians in the late 1950s, would be the last subject the president would be talking about. Most presidents have played by these rules. Gerald Ford and Jimmy Carter would be prime examples. Even though both were adamant about there being openness on UFOs before becoming president, neither uttered the word UFO once in office.

For this reason, it is important that Bill Clinton went out of his way while in office to talk about UFOs and aliens. Although he did it often, he did it carefully, making each UFO or alien reference part of a joke so that no reporter gets the impression that the president was serious about UFO reality. This would lead to direct questions to the president and threaten the cover up. These are a collection of Bill Clinton UFO references that he worked into his speeches. Remember that many people carefully review every word in a presidential address. Because the president's word carries so much weight, nothing gets in a presidential speech that does not belong there.

> "They sort of try to turn you into a space alien...and now the Republicans are saying, 'Well, if your problems aren't all solved, it's just because the aliens have taken over Washington' (laughter). And while we have been working, they have been talking, blaming, dividing, turning us into aliens."
> **-Bill Clinton, October 3, 1994, remarks during a victory rally speech for Senator Robb.**

> "I got a letter from 13-year-old Ryan from Belfast. Now, Ryan, if you're out in the crowd tonight, here's the answer to your question. No, as far as I know, an alien spacecraft did not crash in Roswell, New Mexico, in 1947. And, Ryan, if the United States Air Force did recover alien bodies, they didn't tell me about it, either, and I want to know."
> **-Bill Clinton, November 1995 remarks in Belfast, Northern Ireland.**

"I don't know if any of you have seen this new movie, 'Independence Day,' (applause), but somebody said I was coming to Youngstown because this is the day the White House got blown away by space aliens (laughter). I hope it's there when I get back."
-**Bill Clinton, July 4, 1996, Youngstown, Ohio.**

"Yes, I think we'd fight them (the aliens) off. We find a way to win. That's what America does. We'd find a way to win if it happened."
-**Bill Clinton, July 15, 1996, interview with MSNBC's Tom Brokaw.**

"Very interesting, don't you think that this movie, 'Independence Day,' is becoming the most successful movie ever? Some say it's because they blew up the White House and Congress (laughter), and that may be. But, you know, you see story after story after story about how the movie audiences leap up and cheer at the end of the movie when we vanquish the alien invaders, right? I mean, what happened? The country was flat on its back, the rest of the world was threatened, and you see, all over the world, all these people have all of a sudden put aside the differences that seem so trivial once their existence was threatened, and they're working together all over the world to defeat a common adversary."
-**Bill Clinton, July 18, 1996, remarks at a ceremony for Boys and Girls Nation.**

"Sarah, there's a government inside the government, and I don't control it."
-**Bill Clinton, 1998, as quoted by senior White House reporter Sarah McClendon in reply to why Clinton wasn't doing anything about UFO disclosure.**

"You know, there was a recent poll which said that young people in the generation of the students here felt it was far more

likely that they would see a UFO than that they would draw Social Security...It's very important you understand this. Once you understand this, you realize this is not an episode from the X Files, and you're not more likely to see a UFO if you do certain specific things."

-Bill Clinton, February 9, 1998, remarks by the president, Georgetown University, D.C.

"Won't it be sad to have an internet connection to Mars if there are no Martians to write to or email us?"
-Bill Clinton, October 12, 1999 'Informatics Meets Genomics' evening at the White House.

"If we were being attacked by space aliens, we wouldn't be playing these kinds of games."
-Bill Clinton, November 7, 1999. In reaction to the veto of a new Republican bill.

"I get so angry at all these conflicts around the world and these expressions of hatred here at home based on race or religion or sexual orientation. If we were being attacked by space aliens, like in that movie, 'Independence Day,' we'd all be looking for a foxhole to get in together and a gun to pick up together. The absence of a threat sometimes causes us to lose our sense of focus, our center, our concentration...And what I'm saying is, you all laughed when I said this before; I referenced that movie, 'Independence Day,' but, you know, if we were being attacked by space aliens, we wouldn't be playing these kinds of games. These kinds of games are only possible because the economy is strong and the American people are self-confident."
-Bill Clinton, 1999, speaking to a school.

"They believe you have to drive people apart in order to win elections. And since they're wrong on the issues, they're right. In other words, people won't agree with them on the issues, so the

only way they could win is to convince them that we're the first cousins of space aliens (laughter). They've got this figured out now, we're right, and they're wrong on these big issues. So, the only way they can win is to convince people that we're space aliens."
-Bill Clinton, April 1, 2000, remarks at a fundraiser for Mrs. Clinton, Washington D.C.

"NASA even sent Chuck Berry's music on a space probe searching for intelligent life in outer space (laughter). Well, now, if they're out there, they're duck walking."
-Bill Clinton, December 3, 2000, Kennedy Center honors ceremony at White House.

"Well, I don't know if you all heard this, but there was actually when I was president in my second term, there was an anniversary observance of Roswell. Remember that? People came to Roswell, New Mexico, from all over the world. And there was also a site in Nevada where people were convinced that the government had buried a UFO and perhaps an alien deep underground because we wouldn't allow anybody to go there. And, um, I can say now because it's now been released into the public domain. This place in Nevada was really serious and there was an alien artifact there. So, I actually sent somebody there to figure it out. I did attempt to find out if there were any secret government documents that revealed things. If there were, they were concealed from me too. And if there were, well, I wouldn't be the first American president that underlings have lied to or that career bureaucrats have waited out. But there may be some career person sitting around somewhere, hiding these dark secrets, even from elected presidents. But if so, they successfully eluded me, and I'm almost embarrassed to tell you I did (chuckling) try to find out."
-Bill Clinton, September 2005, to CLSA group in Hong Kong.

Alien Bedtime Stories

"You know, I've always been really interested in this stuff. I'm going to read this."
-Bill Clinton, August 2007 to Hollywood producer Paul Davids when he was given the books *Witness to Roswell* and *The Roswell Legacy*, and a new affidavit that had been released following the death of Roswell witness Walter Haut.

"It's interesting that you said that because when we celebrated the anniversary of that event out in New Mexico, I actually got all the government documents and read them, and I'm convinced there wasn't a UFO there. On the other hand, you shouldn't give up hope because just a couple of months ago, our government astrophysicists spotted a planet revolving around a star that is one of the closest to our solar system that they believe has conditions close enough to earth that it might contain life. Unfortunately, it's 20 million light-years away, so unless you, your kids, and your grandkids, and maybe one more generation want to take a trip for us, we'll have to wait for them to come to us. And then we'll know the truth."
-Bill Clinton. February 6, 2008, answering the question: "When will we ever know the truth about UFOs?"

Hillary Clinton Talks UFOs

Hillary, like Bill Clinton was interested in UFOs and other paranormal subjects. As first lady, however, she was restricted in what she could say about UFOs because anything she would say would put her husband, the president, in a position where he would have to answer questions about what she had said. Hillary had learned her lesson on how talk of the paranormal could end a political career.

In June of 1996, the story broke that Hillary channeled dead people like Eleanor Roosevelt through her spiritual advisor Jean Houston. Hillary was forced to quickly state that there were no psychic or religious overtones to the sessions and that she had *"no spiritual advisers or any other alternatives to my deeply held Methodist faith and traditions upon which I have relied since childhood."* Therefore, like her husband Bill, it is significant that Hillary went to the effort to make references to UFOs and aliens. Like Bill, she shielded the comments by using them as part of a joke.

"That's part of the continuing saga of Whitewater. The never-ending fictional conspiracy that honest to goodness reminds me of some people's obsessions with UFOs and the Hale-Bopp comet."
--Hillary Clinton, April 10, 1997, on the Washington D.C. Diane Rehm Radio Talk Show attacking Republican Senator Dan Burton, who had asked for UFO files after a 1997 Congressional information session put on by Dr. Steven Greer.

"You look at the movies that have tried to predict what will happen in the future, and we often see a lot of death and destruction and environmental degradation. It's not just that people might live under domes on Mars, but they would have to live under domes here on this planet because of what we will have done to our environment. Or whether we will have to join together as human beings to stave off attacks from aliens in outer space, and then we'll have to put aside our really petty differences. Differences in our own country and differences among people around the world. To stand up for our common humanity."
--Hillary Clinton, January 14, 1999, Mars Millennium Project Kick-Off, National Air and Space Museum.

"In one of those popular movies I referred to that swept my country and apparently made a lot of money around the world, called 'Independence Day,' these movies always seem to start with an attack on Washington, D.C., which I don't really know how to take, the blowing up of the White House and Capitol, to begin with, the ending of it required all of us to cooperate to fend off an alien attack. And certainly, in the theater in which I saw it, there

Alien Bedtime Stories

were great cheers as people of all different races and backgrounds and societies around the globe came together as human beings to save ourselves. We certainly don't expect it to come to that."
--**Hillary Clinton, October 13, 1998, at Spanish Hall, Prague Castle.**

"Most of the movies about the future show aliens descending from outer space determined to blow up the world, and somehow, they always begin or end with Washington, D.C."
--**Hillary Clinton, January 25, 1999, White House, Fifth Millennium Evening.**

"In my own country, many of the movies in recent years express our innate fears about what awaits us. They are apocalyptic visions that leave only a few people on earth, whole cities surviving under domes because we have depleted our natural resources. And often in these movies, for reasons that I question, we have space aliens who are always blowing up Washington, D.C., and the White House."
--**Hillary Clinton, June 17, 1999, speaking in Paris, France.**

"Remember that movie Independence Day, where invaders were coming from outer space, and the whole world was united against the invasion? Why can't we be united on behalf of our planet? And that's what I want to do."
--**Hillary Clinton, Council Bluffs, Iowa, December 17, 2007.**

As Hillary Clinton makes a run to become the President of the United States, it might be important to look at her attitude towards UFOs and other events in the world of the non-local world. Ever since Tim Russert asked Dennis Kucinich the *"did you see a UFO"* question during the October 30, 2007, Democratic presidential debate, there has been a flurry of UFO questions to other White House hopefuls. Barack Obama, for example, was asked moments after Kucinich if he believed there was life in outer space. He carefully evaded by saying, "I believe there is life on Earth."

Bill Richardson, the governor of Roswell, has faced the UFO question many times during this Presidential campaign partly because a few years back, he wrote a forward to a book about an archeological dig done in New Mexico looking for evidence of the rumored 1947 flying saucer that crashed outside of Roswell, New Mexico. He has replied to all the UFO questions by saying that he doesn't believe in UFOs but thinks the government did not release all the material on the 1947 crash and is all in favor of the tourism that the UFO subject has brought to Roswell.

In reply to a question if he had ever seen one, John McCain said he'd never seen one, *"but I keep looking all the time."* Joe Biden told CNN's Chris Matthews, *"No, I don't think there are UFOs."* Republican Mitt Romney said, *"I'm afraid I do not believe in extraterrestrials visiting Earth."* Still, the one-time Republican front-runner Rudy Giuliani told an 8-year-old that if invaded by evil aliens, he said, *"We'll be prepared for anything that happens."*

Mike Gravel, the ex-Alaskan senator, said he was a believer, whereas Republican Mike Huckabee said he believed in *"G-O-D rather than U-F-O."* Even ex-president Jimmy Carter got dragged in when Dennis Kucinich defended his sighting, saying that Jimmy Carter had one prior to becoming President.

One of the few candidates that have not faced the UFO question is Democratic front-runner Hillary Clinton. This is even though her strategist Mark Penn complained that questions about outer space were easy compared to what poor Hillary was forced to answer during the October 30th debate. Secondly, it is strange that she is being avoided because Hillary has never hidden the fact that she once wanted to be an astronaut. In response to a letter she sent to NASA as a 12-year-old, she was told girls need not apply. Later, as First Lady, she played a key role in appointing the first woman, Eileen Collins, as a space shuttle commander.

Most importantly, it is strange that Hillary was not asked because Hillary is not exactly a stranger to the subject. As Herald

Tribune journalist Billy Cox put it, *"You had to wonder if Hillary Clinton's heart was fluttering just a little harder Tuesday night as Russert asked why her husband had written the National Archives requesting that their correspondences during his White House years remain sealed until 2012."* This might be because Hillary had to know that a good percentage of the FOIAs filed with the Clinton Library dealt with the Clintons' role in bringing openness and disclosure to UFOs during the Clinton White House years.

The fact that the Clintons, particularly Bill, had an interest in UFOs is no big secret in the UFO research community. After all, over 1,000 pages of documents from the office of Clinton's Science Advisor were released while Bill was still in office. These documents partly provided the names and dates for all the present FOIAs to the Clinton Library, which have yielded over 1,000 more documents.

In addition, Webster Hubbell, Bill Clinton's close friend and Associate Attorney General at the Justice Department, stated in his 1997 book *Friends in High Places* that Bill Clinton had asked him to look into two items.

1. Are there UFOs?
2. Who killed JFK?

Even a couple of months ago, Bill was openly interested in the subject. After receiving the latest Roswell book and other related items from Hollywood writer and director Paul Davids, Bill told Davids, *"You know, I've always been really interested in this stuff, and I'm going to read this."*

And so, what of Hillary? According to William LaParl, a UFO researcher and friend of former CIA agent Ronald Pandolfi (who got the request from Clinton's Science Advisor for a briefing on UFOs in 1993), Hillary *was* interested. *"It was known among the high CIA people and the people who had contact with these people that the Clintons were on the prowl for UFOs. She (Hillary) was almost an equal mover with him on this."* LaParl said. *"I would not give him any more weight at all on this UFO thing. If anything, she may have slightly been pushing it more than he was. That's the way I read the situation."*

Moreover, LaParl told me that *"Hillary even kind of tried to indirectly get me involved, as kind of like an outside researcher. She was putting out feelers that she needed help with and stuff like that. They were open to any kind of input along these lines."*

Later, UFO researcher Derrel Sims would tell me almost an identical story of a woman claiming to be a friend of Hillary's coming to him looking for material for Hillary and the President. He provided a series of UFO-related videos. Later the woman returned, stating Hillary and the President enjoyed the material and offered a way for Sims' work to receive funding. Simms turned down what was proposed by Hillary's friend. The documents obtained from the White House Office of President Clinton's Science Advisor also show Hillary's role in the effort to gather UFO material.

In a February 5, 1996, letter from Laurance Rockefeller to Clinton's Science Adviser, Dr. Gibbons, Rockefeller spoke of all the UFO-related letters that were going back and forth between Rockefeller and the White House. Rockefeller pointed out that all that back-and-forth correspondence would be going through the first lady's office. "You indicated," wrote Rockefeller, "that you will keep the First Lady's Office informed, and we shall as well."

This "Hillary as post office" was a way to keep the president informed but provide plausible deniability. Hillary was not a part of the government, yet she would be told everything that was happening. She could then talk to the president at night and provide instructions on proceeding without anyone knowing the president was involved.

Even more dramatic is a letter which was written by Rockefeller's lawyer Henry L. Diamond on November 1, 1995. Attached was a draft of a letter on "Lifting Security on Information About Extraterrestrial Intelligence as a Part of the Current Classification Review." This draft letter effectively demanded the president to disclose what he knew about the UFO subject. It was a UFO disclosure demand letter from one of the most influential people in the United States to the president. If Rockefeller were to send a final copy to the president, it would become news all over the country. This is a letter Gibbon and his staff did everything in their power to stop Rockefeller from sending.

Diamond was tying UFO disclosure into Executive Order 12958 on April 17, 1995, issued by Bill Clinton requiring his intelligence agencies to allow for the de facto declassification of papers 25 years or older, provided they did not compromise nuclear secrets, intelligence sources and methods and a host of other security concerns. Diamond writes, *"Attached is a draft of a letter to the President, which Laurance has been discussing with Mrs. Clinton and her staff."*

The stories are almost a unanimous opinion within the UFO community that Hillary Clinton sat down with Laurance Rockefeller in August of 1995 (while the Clintons vacationed at his Wyoming ranch) to listen to Rockefeller's pitch for disclosure. The question the present FOIAs will attempt to answer is, was the President also there? He was supposed to be there but received a letter from the Science Advisor days before hinting he should not meet with Rockefeller.

In a conversation with novelist and UFO researcher Whitley Strieber, Rockefeller stated that Bill Clinton did appear. Strieber spoke about Rockefeller's UFO discussion with Bill and Hillary:

> *He spoke of the time that he had spent with the President and Mrs. Clinton at the JY Ranch in the Grand Tetons in 1995, where he outlined for them the contents of the briefing that he had developed out of Project Starlight (mentioned in many of the first FOIAs coming from the Clinton Library), the 1993 Rockefeller funded program that developed into the Disclosure Project. He said that the Clintons had not commented on the information until the next morning, when, before the President appeared, Mrs. Clinton requested to Mr. Rockefeller that he not bring up the subject again.*

Why? During the 1992 presidential campaign, Hillary said, *"We'll have a woman President by 2010."* She may have realized she might be that President and should, therefore, watch which issue she hitches her wagon to.

Hillary and the UFO Book

Are We Alone? Philosophical Implications of the Discovery of Extraterrestrial Life. Professor Paul Davies wrote this book, currently at Arizona State University. The Amazon write-up of the book says:

> *The authentic discovery of extraterrestrial life would usher in a scientific revolution on par with Copernicus or Darwin, says Paul Davies. Just as these ideas sparked religious and philosophical controversy when they were first offered, so would proof of life arising away from Earth. With this brief book, Davies tries to get ahead of the curve and begin to sort out the metaphysical mess before it happens. Many science fiction writers have preceded him, of course, but here the matter is plainly put. This is a very good introduction to a compelling subject.*

The Hillary Book story was discovered after I filed 100 FOIA requests to the Clinton Library for information about the Clintons and people in their eight-year administration who had been involved in UFOs. The names of the people involved were known because, in 2001, the Clinton administration's Office of Science and Technology released 1,000 pages of UFO documents. Most of the 1,000 pages of UFO documents were related to the efforts by Laurance Rockefeller to get disclosure from the administration on UFOs. As a part of that effort, Rockefeller spoke to the Clintons about UFOs when they vacationed at the Wyoming Rockefeller ranch in August 1995. Therefore, many FOIA requests were made to get documents and photos from the Clinton files to provide details of the UFO meeting that had taken place at the ranch. One of the requests was for all photos taken of Hillary while there.

The FOIA was answered with a photocopy of a contact sheet of photos. I was forced to look at the images and guess which ones might be significant. I chose two and paid for 8 x 10 reproductions. One with what appeared to be when Hillary arrived at the ranch and walked across a small bridge with Laurance. Under her arm, she had a book where part of the back cover was visible.

A challenge was put out on the internet to answer two questions:
1. What two crosses were Hillary wearing?
2. What book was she carrying?

There was no success with the crosses. No one had an answer. The book was a different story. One researcher, Tonio Cousyn, took up the challenge of the book by looking at every book that had been published in the period just before the photo was taken. It took a while but eventually, he published the book: *Are We Alone? Philosophical Implications of the Discovery of Extraterrestrial Life.* It appeared that Rockefeller had given the book to Hillary on her arrival so she could read about the importance of the extraterrestrial issue. It also backed up the story that Rockefeller did sit down with Hillary and maybe the President and gave them a UFO briefing based on public material.

Hillary did not comment on the discovery of the book, and no media outlets brought it up. Paul Davies commented, saying he was happy that the First Lady had received his book as a gift.

Grant Cameron

Alien Bedtime Stories

Grant Cameron

Obama and the Mars Jump Program

One of the most bizarre stories in the world of UFOs is the story of the CIA Mars Jump Program and the part of the story that says that President Obama, as a 20-year- old was an active member of the program. The story goes on to say that because of the CIA's ability to time travel, they were able in 1980 to see that Obama would be elected President in 2009 and that CIA officials briefed Obama on the fact that he would one day be president.

Due to my work on consciousness and UFOs, I have spent less of my research efforts tracking presidential UFO stories. Secondly, the story has always been on the edge of believability, and it, therefore, seemed prudent to wait for the real story to shake out after an investigation by this skeptical researcher. This hesitation led to a critical attack article published in early 2013, which pointed out my lack of a position to the story. The fact remained that I had not attempted to check the story but had listened to many interviews and read many articles related to the Obama jump room aspect. Because I had done no serious personal investigation, I had nothing to add or say on the subject. Then there came a meeting in Milford, Pennsylvania, with five other researchers, where everything changed. I was about to be presented with material that was either one hell of a coincidence, a carefully controlled setup, or evidence that seemed to support the fact that there may have been a CIA Mars Jump Program.

The material was presented to me by a NASA scientist without involvement in the CIA program. He was interested in flying saucer materials research and believed that he now controlled 5 of his 35 patents inspired by the apparent crash recovery material he had owned. That story is his to tell on his timeline, and this article has nothing to say about that powerful story. The evidence the man showed me had been collected just as a byproduct of interest in the CIA jump story and a chance to visit the site in Los Angeles where jump room whistleblowers claimed had been used as a jump-off point. The material consisted of three videos. They were shown to at least one friend earlier in the year, and he had not considered it significant enough to tell me about it.

It was the first time I had ever met the man, and we were swapping stories of our research on the deck of a cabin. I told him about the UFO game I had been involved in, and he was mainly talking about the UFO hardware research he had done. Then there came the jump room video, which knocked me off my patio chair. He told me that the video had been taken in the building.

Obama Talks UFOs

"I will never hide the truth because it's uncomfortable. I will deal with Congress and the courts as co-equal branches of government. I will tell the American people what I know and don't know, and when I release something publicly or keep something secret, I will tell you why."
--President Barack Obama, National Archives, May 21, 2009.

Grant Cameron

> *"I ran for President promising transparency, and I meant what I said. That is why, whenever possible, we will make information available to the American people so that they can make informed judgments and hold us accountable. But I have never argued, and never will, that our most sensitive national security matters should be an open book."*
> **--Barack Obama.**

Obama first dealt with the UFO/ET question while running for the Democratic Nominee for President. A Chicago reporter from CBS asked, *"If you are elected, and you learned that the government knew that aliens had visited Earth and the public didn't know, would you make sure the public found out?"* Obama, like many politicians before him, used humor to deal with the UFO question, *"Well, it depends on what these aliens are like,"* replied Obama, *"and whether they are Democrats or Republicans."*

During a March 21, 2012, trip to Roswell, New Mexico, President Obama gave the following opening remarks to his speech. *"We had landed in Roswell. I announced to people when I landed that I had come in peace (laughter). Let me tell you; there are more nine and ten-year-old boys around the country; when I meet them, they ask me, 'Have you been to Roswell, and is it true what they say?' And I tell them, 'If I told you, I would have to kill you.' So, their eyes get all big, so we're going to keep our secrets here."* It appeared that Obama had just revealed the secret that an alien presence was being covered up. The message that the government would keep its secret on Roswell goes directly against the official Air Force investigations done in 1994 and 1997 that concluded there was no extraterrestrial crash at Roswell in 1947 and there was no cover-up of the facts. The statement about continuing to keep the Roswell secrets also went against an official statement put out in November 2011 from the Science advisor's office to the president, *'Searching for ET But No Evidence Yet.'* That

White House statement declared, *"The U.S. government has no evidence that any life exists outside our planet, or that an extraterrestrial presence has contacted or engaged any member of the human race. In addition, there is no credible information to suggest that any evidence is being hidden from the public's eye."* It did not appear that the statement was part of the official speech, indicating some tongue slip or a planned leak. What made the statement even more significant is that the President would do the same thing again.

A couple of weeks later, in May 2012, Obama again talked about aliens. This time he made the alien comment while on a tour of the White House with actor Will Smith and his family. Although this was a personal conversation, Obama would have known that the story would get repeated and eventually become public, which it did.

Jaden Smith, Will's 14-year-old son, wanted to ask President Obama about the existence of aliens. Will asked him not to do it. When the tour arrived in the Situation Room, a 5,000 square foot room in the basement of the White House run by the National Security Council for the President and his staff, Jaden prepared to ask his question.

Obama, however, somehow knew the alien question was coming. He looked at Jaden and said, *"Don't tell me, the aliens, right?"* Jaden confirmed that is what he wanted to know about. Obama answered the question with what is known as a Glomar response. It is usually used by officials who have been briefed on a classified program but who cannot even acknowledge the existence of the program because of the level of secrecy. *"I can neither confirm nor deny the existence of extraterrestrials,"* Obama told Jaden, *"But I can tell you if there had been a top-secret meeting, it would have taken place in this very room."* Speaking of his encounter with the president, Jaden stated, *"I talked to President Obama about extraterrestrials. He said he could neither confirm nor deny the existence of aliens, which means they're real.*

If people think we're the only people that live in this universe, then something is wrong with them."

Obama continued with his alien talk during an August 13, 2012, phone call to NASA. He was phoning to congratulate the agency on the successful landing of the *Curiosity* rover on Mars. But, instead of just simple congratulations, Obama strangely, as Bill Clinton had almost 20 years earlier, brought up the subject of Martians, *"Someone asked me the other day if you had already found Martians. I told them we have to give you a little bit of time. If, in fact, you do make contact with Martians, please let me know right away because I've got a lot of other things on my plate, but I suspect that will go to the top of the list, even if they're just microbes."* Fortunately for Obama, each comment was made with a tone of humor that kept the media asleep and helped avoid any serious questions on the subject.

Obama Denies ET Reality

In November 2011, the White House sent a reply through their Office of Science and Technology Policy Office in response to a petition asking to formally acknowledge an extraterrestrial presence engaging the human race (Disclosure), filed by UFO lobbyist Steven Bassett. The White House reply denied an ET Presence on earth. Also, it denied that the government had covered anything up, *"The U.S. government has no evidence that any life exists outside our planet, or that an extraterrestrial presence has contacted or engaged any member of the human race. In addition, there is no credible information to suggest that any evidence is being hidden from the public's eye."*

As the statement went against the general opinion of the American people, I filed seven Freedom of Information Act requests to try and determine what happened behind the scenes. As expected, the results were not encouraging. The FOIA documents released by the OSTP, totaling about 50 pages, can be summed up by one line written by the OSTP public relations officer Phil Larson who wrote the White House reply to the petition. In an email to David Weaver and Bob Jacobs at NASA, Larson stated, *"We got tagged with drumming up a ', please acknowledge the aliens' petition from 'We the People' feature on WhiteHouse.org."*

The first FOIA I filed with the OSTP asked what the OSTP office had used for research to produce their official government statement that there is *"no credible evidence"* that ETs have visited Earth. The answer, according to the FOIA, was nothing. They had no documents in the office concerning UFOs or extraterrestrials. Not a single piece of paper. The official conclusion of 'no credible evidence' by the White House was therefore not supported by any evidence itself, whether credible or not. The Obama White House had become like a student who writes a book report without reading the book. Even more unpardonable was that the FOIA exposed that the OSTP did not look for any evidence. The conclusion was the scientific arm of the White House was caught rigging the experiment to come to the required preordained conclusion.

Another of the FOIAs requested all the drafts of the ET petition response to determining who wrote it, which outside agencies had input on the wording, and what words were changed to arrive at a final draft. This FOIA investigation of the drafts was intended to get to the thinking that went into producing the official response. It has worked well in the past, such as in the case of the famous 'alien invasion' remark in the 1987 United Nations speech by Ronald Reagan. The drafts of that speech showed that the alien invasion remark had been pulled by speechwriters and was only put back in the speech when Reagan penned a note to put it back in. It was hoped that this FOIA would provide some similar insights.

The plan was thwarted by the constant use of the B5 FOIA exemption by the OSTP FOIA archivists, who reviewed and sanitized the documents. The use of this exemption to hide the facts was expected. This exemption, in short, says that any internal advice given is exempt because if it were not, people would be reluctant to give advice. The FOIA release showed that page after page was exempted from release, and none of the four that appeared to work on the ET reply had their advice or opinions made public. The OSTP simply used the B5 exemption to cover everything that happened behind the scene. One FOIA attempted to determine who tasked Larson to draft the official ET petition reply. That FOIA failed to produce a name. It failed because the ET petition reply was assigned to OSTP by Katelyn Sabochik, who runs the *We the People* site on the White House Website. As she does not work for OSTP, she and whoever she gets her orders from are exempt from the scope of the FOIA. The FOIA documents showed that NASA was the only outside agency contracted by the OSTP for comment and correction. The OSTP offices in previous administrations had contacted the CIA for information, but this did not happen this time.

At NASA, Bob Jacobs, the Deputy Assistant Administrator of Public Affairs, and David Weaver, Associate Administrator for the Office of Communications, had been sent a draft of the ET petition response. Both had nothing to add or change. This was no surprise considering that neither man is a working scientist with any expertise in UFOs but a senior administrator specializing in government, politics, media relations, and public policy. When the OSTP went public with their ET petition reply, Jacobs re-tweeted the news on his Twitter page but did not mention his involvement.

The most essential document in the FOIA release was the reply to the FOIA that asked for all documents that would show that President Obama, or someone representing him in the Oval Office, saw the petition that 12,000+ people thought was sent to him. The reply was, 'no records,' which means that, according to available OSTP records, Obama never saw the petition. The documents released also confirmed that the evidence for a possible ET presence on Earth is still unchallenged. It's not as if the White House did a study and found that UFO researchers are wrong or that their evidence is bad. The White House simply took a lazy political approach to the petition request. Their main goal was to stay clear of any controversy that properly dealing with the petition might have presented. The whole exercise of the *We the People* petition site was meant to make the American public think that the White House cared about their opinion by putting up a link on the White House website where they could sign their names on issues they cared about. The answer to the ET petition showed that, in reality that the, *We the People* site is a shallow political marketing effort, sort of like the appeal that Americans will be hearing many times in the next year, your vote counts.

The reality is the status quo. The White House is staffed by politicians, political advisors, and politically appointed staff interested in power and maintaining their jobs. They will continue to take the easy road as they have on other issues, such as the federal debt. They will continue to promote the idea that it is a government of the people by the people, when in fact, it is a game of what to say, what not to say, how to say it, and staying in power by making it sound like you give a damn when you really don't. The White House, its website, and the, *We the People* petition site will always take second place to political consultants who know the names of the 13,000 Washington lobbyists and the names of the people who pay up to $35,800 to attend political fundraising dinners. It is about votes and how to get elected and then re-elected. The 2012 election cost 6-7 billion. That money came from interest groups who will get their interests protected. They are being listened to, not those signing petitions on, *We the People*. The FOIAs to the OSTP on the ET petition have sadly confirmed these truths about how things are really in Washington. Hopefully, no one will be surprised.

The final irony of the White House's denial of ET and the cover-up is that it turned the whole petition into a joke of democracy. The *We the People* petition concept was established so the average citizen could get an answer from the White House on things of importance to the people on the street. Once the ET petition had been addressed, the number of signatures required to get an answer was raised to 25,000. Later a group got 25,000 signatures asking the White House about building a 'death star.' At that point, the number of signatures required was raised to 100,000. This means the government is answerable to the voters, provided you have 99,999 friends who will sign your petition to get an answer.

Trump and the ETS

"They may be anticipating some action; I have been waiting for President-Elect Trump to take office before taking more serious actions. He is very "pro-disclosure" and very anti "disinformation."

– **Ron Pandolfi**

They may be anticipating some action. I have been waiting for President-Elect Trump to take office before taking more serious actions. He is very "pro-disclosure" and very anti "disinformation." Dr. Ronald Pandolfi ran the UFO weird desk at the CIA.

Before the 2016 election, it appeared that Hillary Clinton was going to attempt to end UFO secrecy after she promised to get to the bottom of the UFO story.

As soon as Hillary lost, most researchers figured that we would return to the dark world of UFO denials by Washington officials. Then, just two weeks before Trump took office, there was a message posted on the Facebook page of Robert Collins, a former physicist at Wright-Patterson Air Force Base. Collins had been a long-time friend to Pandolfi and had gotten an interview at the CIA with Pandolfi's help.

He had received the message from Dr. Ronald Pandolfi, who was identified in the 1990s by one newspaper as the leading scientist in the CIA. More importantly, to the ufo community, Pandolfi was rumored to be the head of the weird desk at the CIA (a term he is not fond of). This desk was rumored to be the CIA unit in charge of UFOs and other paranormal phenomena.

More importantly, it was reported by Pandolfi's close friend Dan Smith that Pandolfi, former Clinton CIA director James

Alien Bedtime Stories

Woolsey and a China policy expert Mike Pillsbury were the UFO briefing team for the newly elected president.

Pandolfi hinted in the message that Collins posted that some sort of UFO disclosure might be planned under Trump, "They may be anticipating some action," wrote Pandolfi. "I have been waiting for President-Elect Trump to take office before taking more serious actions. He is very "pro-disclosure" and very anti "disinformation."

At the same time as all this was happening, a second disclosure initiative seemed to be forming. This movement centered around Blink 182 lead singer Tom DeLonge. He had been exposed in the leak of Hillary Clinton's campaign manager John Podesta's emails to WikiLeaks to be involved in some sort of official UFO disclosure effort.

When Trump won the election, many figured the DeLonge initiation was over. However, I checked and was told that the DeLonge imitative was still alive. I asked if the light was still green or if it had turned red. I was told it was still green and bigger than ever, with big names and big money behind it. This turned out to be true.

On October 11, 2017, DeLonge held a news conference to announce the To the Stars Academy of Arts and Sciences (TTSA). A number of former high-level government officials on stage with him claimed to be a part of this effort to bring UFO disclosure to the American people.

One of the officials on stage was Jim Semivan, a former high-level official in the CIA. In at least two conversations he had with researcher Melinda Leslie, Semivan confirmed that the TTSA effort was a constitutional process green-lighted by the Pentagon.

This strangely centered Pandolfi's view of TTSA and Semivan. He stated that "it is all fake. Just loons, Crooks, and Worse moving up the chain Believe, Fear, and Give."

When TTSA was announced, I put the question to someone in contact with Pandolfi, and strangely even though both men had worked at high levels in the CIA, Pandolfi claimed that he did not know who Semivan was. Later that story was changed to say he does exist, but his name is not Semivan.

 Ronald Pandolfi Alex Chionetti If Italian then perhaps forgiven for your ignorance of Techno Scammers Inc.. De Longe is just the front man for the Gang. He is the TTSA equivalent of Kenneth Shoulders of Jupiter Technologies and more than a dozen other Techno Scams. Always the same people make the big money. The rest perhaps get a few peanuts and ultimately take the fall for the Scam. If Jupiter Technologies and Condensed Charge Technology are too "techno" for you, then try something a little less "techno" such as the "Serpo Scam." Nut Blogs were just as active about that Scam as they are now about TTSA. Also you missed my point about who is making money. It's not just Scammers Inc. but all the hangers on who benefit from the publicity. I like Stave Bassett, but without a good Scam to generate publicity, Steve's income would dry up quickly. Same for everyone running blogs and publishing books. All the Crooks make a little by playing their role in entertaining the Loons, while the Worse dream up then next big Scam.

This denial was strange, and the only explanation I could come up with was that Semivan was working for Pandolfi or with him on the DeLonge UFO affair and giving that association away would kill the program and what they were trying to achieve.

As to Trump's role in all the disclosure talk, I was told that Pandolfi had met with Trump many times in December 2016. I was approached to help prepare a briefing for Trump's first chief of Staff, Reince Priebus. I informed the people talking to me that if Trump appointed his people, and they did not know, there was little I could do you help. I certainly don't know where the alien bodies are kept.

Trump had expressed no interest in UFOs in any of the times the subject had been brought up to him. There was a 31-second clip put up on YouTube where Trump is being yelled at about disclosure while he signs hats and posters. Trump totally ignores the man confronting him.

Alien Bedtime Stories

Maureen Dowd
@maureendowd

Trump on Hillary's desire to open up gov UFO files: "They are talking about outer space I assume? I'm not a big fan"

Then when Hillary was talking about disclosure, Maureen Dowd confronted Trump on the subject. When asked about what Hillary had said, he again indicated no interest, saying, "They are talking about aliens, I assume. I'm not a big fan."

So, what will happen about UFOs disclosure under Trump? It appears not much,

We know this because Trump got dragged into an admission by the Defense Department that they were investigating UFOs. This led to pressure from the House and Senate to interview witnesses and receive a briefing from the Navy and the Defense Intelligence Agency. When Trump was finally asked, however, he stated he did not care and did not believe,

As this pressure built, Trump's favorite news network, Fox, started asking questions about UFOs. When ABC News finally asked Trump, he stated," I want them to think whatever they think. I had one really brief meeting on it."

When Fox host Tucker Carlson asked a second Trump repeated what he had told ABC, "Well, I don't want to really get into it too much. But personally, I tend to doubt it. I'm not a believer, but you know, I guess anything is possible."

The fact that Trump did not suddenly come forward to announce the ET presence indicates that perhaps the United States knows much less about UFOs than we have been led to believe.

The facts seem to spell out that the Navy showed Trump three Navy videos that had been leaked to the public and told him that they believed these were real UFOs. Beyond that, they really did not know anything. If they had back-engineered crafts, they would have told the president, and he would not have talked the way he did.

There may be another classified dark section of government that does have absolute proof that UFOs are ET or inter-dimensional. It appears the Navy did not have the need to know about this.

If this group does exist and has the information, it is running an insubordinate illegal operation. That is because it seems clear that they have kept it from the President, who is the civilian commander-in-chief of the military, the head of state that would oversee negotiating with off-world beings, is the Chief Executive of the Government, and the head of all the United States intelligence agencies.

President Joe Biden

On May 22, 2021, President Biden was hosting a news conference when a reporter confronted him with a UFO question based on two former President Barack Obama's statements.

With more and more major media outlets like 60 Minutes doing UFO stories, Obama ended up on three talk shows where he faced the UFO question. He quickly opened up about what he knew about UFOs.

In the past, Obama had confirmed that he had looked and found the answer but could not talk about it. He said he had never been refused the information requested, but it came slower than he wanted regarding matters such as UFOs. He had been briefed on many stories, including the one that a NASA official, Tim Taylor, had briefed the president on at Camp David. That was at least part of the briefing deal with UFO experiencer Chris Bledsoe who has had many UFO encounters.

In the new 2021 interviews, Obama confirmed that he had seen the videos. They were real, and we do not know what they are.

Should an otherworldly species make contact, Obama stated, "that could unite humans across the globe. " He added, "And so I would hope that the knowledge that there were aliens out there would solidify people's sense that what we have in common is a little more important."

On one late-night talk show, Obama said,

> The truth is that when I came into office, I asked. I said, 'Ok is there a lab somewhere we are keeping the alien specimens and spaceships?' They did a little bit of research, and the answer was no. What is true, and I am actually being serious here, is that there is footage and records of objects in the sky that we don't know exactly what they are. We cannot explain how they moved, their trajectory. They did not have an easily explainable pattern. So, I think that people take seriously to investigate and find out what that is.

Then he told podcaster Ezra Klein from the New York Times that he "absolutely" would like to know the answer to the unidentified objects picked up by military cameras.

He spelled out his view that "we are these tiny organisms on this little speck floating in the middle of space." He would tell staff "That human existence is too tiny and fragile to sweat the small things." He reminded them what his science advisor had stated: "there are more stars in the known universe than there are grains of sand on the planet Earth." Some staff would listen, and some would roll their eyes."

The question that Biden asked in the White House was, "President Obama says that there is footage and records of objects in the skies of these unidentified aerial phenomena, and he says we don't know exactly what they are. What do you think that it is?"

Biden quickly replied, "I would ask him again. Thank you." He then turned to his aide and said, "Come on, let's go," as he quickly exited the room.

Many researchers jumped on Biden as playing the coverup, and one even pointed out that it was a significant change from the openness of Trump. I countered that by stating that Trump had walked away from a New York Times requisition the same way in 2016, with the negative reply that he didn't care.

The press conference was not the first time Biden had faced the UFO question. He was challenged after the 2005 Philadelphia Democratic debate. This event was where Dennis Kucinich was asked if he had seen a UFO at Shirley MacLaine's house, where he heard a voice in his head.

It was also the same debate where candidate Obama was asked if he thought ETs were visiting the world. His reply was, "You know, I don't know. And I don't presume to know. What I know is there is life here on Earth and that we're not attending to life here on Earth... there may be some other folks on their way."

After the debate, an MSNBC reporter asked various people about this question in the debate. When Bill Richardson, former Secretary of Energy in the Clinton administration, was asked,

> I've been in government a long time; I've been in the cabinet, I've been in Congress, and I've always felt that the government doesn't tell the truth as much as it should on a lot of issues. 'When I was in Congress, I said (to the) Department of Defense ... 'What is the data? What is the data you have?' That ticked me off.

Then the host turned and confronted Joe Biden, who was also involved in the debate. Like many presidents such as Trump and

Johnson, his reply showed that UFOs were not something he considered worth talking about.

Chris Matthews: I was struck by Dennis Kucinich, who is not in the front runner for the office of the presidency, perhaps luckily, I don't know, but he says he has seen a UFO. We then had government Richardson come on this show, and Governor Richardson said the US government is operating in ways that breed suspicion. There is a conspiracy to keep us from seeing UFOs or knowing about their existence in New Mexico. I am asking you – do you agree? Do you believe in UFOs? I know it is an odd question, but there seems to be a pattern here.
Biden: I have never met Dennis Kucinich, and I don't know Governor Richardson. No (laughs), I don't think there are UFOs, and no, I don't think the government... look, what the hell heck are we talking about? I mean, I don't know. This has gone downhill real quick.
Matthews: No, it started going down during the debate.

The 2007 UFO reply also explains why he walked away from the question in 2021. He was not interested in this as part of what he thought was essential for him to look at as President.

A couple of other things must be considered about why Biden and 14 other presidents before him have done everything possible to deal with the subject. First, Dr. Ron Pandolfi, rumored to have briefed many of the last presidents on the issue, stated in 2000, "the President cannot be a player." This would indicate that the subject is moved away from the President as it is considered to have few benefits and many elements that could derail the presidency.

Bill Clinton did the same thing to Laurence Rockefeller: the story was like the Arkansas tar baby story where the rabbit gets caught by the fox. The fox makes a baby made of tar along the road, and the rabbit becomes upset that he does not answer back when talked to. The rabbit punches the tar baby and ends up stuck to the baby.

The second apparent reason I think the president is told to walk away from questions is that there are very few answers, and the president would look weak admitting he does not know or that things are flying around in US airspace at will.

Many presidents, however, work behind the scenes to get answers on UFOs. For example, Jimmy Carter sent his Press Secretary to pressure the FBI for documents, his science advisor to NASA for a new UFO investigation, and a lawyer to the CIA to make sure they were not hiding documents from a FOIA that had been sealed.

It appears that the same quiet support is going on in the White House from Biden. The first example would be Bill Nelson, the new director at NASA, who suddenly said he had been briefed in 2018 on UFOs. He believes we were not alone and opened NASA for interested people to study the subject. I am incredibly confident Nelson would not go public with such a statement without it getting the green light from the President and his science advisor.

The second thing that Biden did was to allow his Director of National Intelligence to file a preliminary report to the Senate Intelligence Committee and then promised a 90-day update.

Lastly, in a conversation with documentary film producer James Fox, I was told that in discussions with John Podesta, James was told that Podesta was in contact with Biden and encouraging him to set up a UFO investigation inside the White House Office of Science and Technology. The president's science advisor heads this. And this is the same office that dealt with Laurance Rockefeller between 1993 and 1996, pushing for UFO disclosure. The office also forced the Air Force to do two studies on the Roswell crash in 1994 and 1997.

CHAPTER 6

THE ALIENS

The Alien Disclosure Playbook

There has been much written on a possible UFO disclosure by the government but very little on a possible alien plan for disclosure. The available evidence shows that there may just be a plan by the aliens to disclose the ET presence on earth and why they are here.

In 1966, John Fuller released his book, *The Interrupted Journey* to America. In the book, Fuller told the story of Betty and Barney Hill's September 19, 1961, UFO encounter. The recounting of the story raised for the first time the idea of abduction in the American consciousness, aliens forcefully taking people on board their crafts. It was also the first time the now infamous 'Greys' was introduced to the UFO worldview. Before the appearance of *Interrupted Journey*, the standard idea of an alien was usually a human-looking being. These beings were generally referred to in UFO literature as the 'space brothers.' However, research completed later by abduction regression researchers such as Bud Hopkins and John Mack began to add an element to the original Hill story. That element was that the Hill abduction was not the first. There had been many that had been hinted at in research going back decades before the Hill encounter. Unfortunately, these stories had never been made public because of some kind of amnesia that has blocked them. The implied logic to what was going on was that:

A. People have been abducted for years, and the aliens' actions have been covered up by giving the person amnesia.

B. For some reason, the amnesia broke down to some extent in the Hill case. Both Betty and Barney experienced dreams and psychological distress that led them to Dr. Benjamin Simon in Boston, who used hypnosis to break through the remaining amnesia and reveal the abduction story.

C. With millions having been abducted, the number of people who have had amnesia failure has increased in proportion, and we are getting many people coming forward claiming contact experiences.

D. People coming back in the wrong locations and with their clothes on backward, the apparent mistakes of the aliens allow us to see what they are really up to.

However, a review of the evidence shows that this amnesia failure model may not be what is happening at all. Let me propose a second model and the evidence to support it. This model suggests that:

1. Everything that is happening is not random
2. There is no amnesia failure
3. The aliens have had a clear pattern going back to at least the dawn of the modern UFO era for revealing an ET presence interacting with the Earth.

The Technology

The first evidence to consider involves the first contact between aliens and human beings. Although the UFO sightings started *en masse* in 1947, nobody came forward till 1952 to claim that they were in contact with the pilots of the flying saucers and flying discs. The first contactees (who went public) were George Adamski and George Hunt Williamson, who claimed contact with an alien in

Alien Bedtime Stories

November 1952. This was only days after the United States detonated its first hydrogen bomb test in the Pacific.

Another key early contactee was contacted in the summer of 1952 or 1953 and given a story that indicated a long-term plan to educate the world about the true nature of UFOs and reality. That experience occurred with Dr. Jack Sarfatti as a 12 or 13-year-old child. Sarfatti is a physicist who believes there is a connection between quantum physics and consciousness. His research has led to work on zero-point energy and quantum information science. He was one of the founding members of the Physics Consciousness Research Group, founded to study time travel, ESP, consciousness after death, and other fringe subjects. Some have claimed that the Physics Consciousness Research Group was the inspiration for the movie *Ghostbusters* and that Sarfatti inspired Dr. Emmett Brown in, *Back to the Future*.

This is a brief recounting of the 1952 contact event as Sarfatti told it to Bill and Nancy Birnes on their radio show, *Future Theater*:

> *I was alone in my apartment in Brooklyn, reading a book I got from the public library on switching circuits. It was about the primitive computers of the time, like telephone relay switches. The telephone rings, and I pick it up, and I hear a clunking sound like the telephone relays going, synchronistically like the book I am reading. Then I hear very low audio that just gets louder and louder and louder, and it is a metallic voice, exactly like Steven Hawking's computer voice today. It's like a cold metallic voice, and it is saying a sequence of images, numbers, and coordinates, and then it gets louder and louder. It says, 'Is this Jack?' and I say, 'Yes.' Then it says it's a conscious computer on a spacecraft. At first, I laughed a bit as I thought it might be a joke. They said they had studied and they had 400 bright young minds that they wanted to transfer their technology to. It went on, and I was trying to think who could be calling. I realized that none of the kids I knew*

> were smart enough to pull this off. Then I got kind of scared, thinking that it was some kind of adult messing with me. Then they said that if I agreed of my own free will, I had to agree to take part in the project. If I agreed to do so, I would begin to meet the others in 20 years. I was thinking at the time, getting scared, but I was also thrilled. Inside my conscious mind, I was saying, 'No, no, no,' but I blurted out, 'Yes.' As I said yes, I had this electric shock go from the base of my spine up to the top of my neck. I later found it is called kundalini or something like that. It was an electrical experience, but it didn't feel bad. Go to your fire escape, and we'll send a ship to pick you up in ten minutes.

This was one of many phone calls Sarfatti got from the spaceship computer but the only one he remembers. He doesn't recall being picked up by the ship either. The other calls were related to Sarfatti's mother, who stated that the calls went on for weeks. She reported that during three weeks, while these calls were coming in, Jack was walking around the apartment, 'glassy-eyed and in a daze.' Finally, in desperation, she grabbed the phone and asked what was going on. The computer voice simply asked her to put Jack back on the phone, to which she replied, *"Don't phone here again,"* before hanging up the phone. After that, there were no more calls, but there was a visit from two men at Sandia Labs before being given a full scholarship to attend Cornell.

Twenty years later, in early 1973, a series of synchronicities occurred that indicated the plan might be taking place as had been predicted:

> Fred Alan Wolf and I were these crazy professors of physics at San Diego State College. Both of us had gotten divorced, and we were living in this small apartment like the odd couple on the side of the campus. Fred gets a call from an old high school friend from Chicago, Bob Toben, who is in the commodities stock market. He is making tons of money, and he wants

to come out and see Fred because he has a proposition; he starts talking about a guy by the name of Uri Geller, this Israeli psychic who can bend metal. He can do all these things with his mind, and Bob has a contract to do a television show and a book contract on Uri Geller. He has come to Fred to learn about the physics of how Uri Geller could do this. I am up at my girlfriend's place in Carmel. I had been to some physics seminars at UC Santa Cruz. I am supposed to leave on a Wednesday morning to fly to London. And I opened up the Sunday Chronicle and the Sunday magazine, and there was a big article about the Stanford Research Institute experiments of Hal Puthoff and Russel Targ with Uri Geller. I just happened to pick up this paper. I thought, 'That is just what Bob Toben has been talking to us about.' I am leaving Wednesday, so Monday morning, I call up SRI, and they put me on the phone with a guy by the name of Brendan O'Regan (research director of Edgar Mitchell's organization for scientific funding, the Institute for Noetic Sciences), and O'Regan says, 'Oh Yes, Dr. Sarfatti. We were hoping you would call. Can you drive up? We would like to talk to you.' That is very strange. They were hoping that I would call. How do you explain that? I had completely forgotten about the phone calls.

The calls are significant because they show what appears to be a carefully orchestrated plan by the intelligence behind the calls. Four hundred people had been picked for the project, and the disclosure program would begin in 20 years when all those elected to this 'transfer technology team' would be brought together to bring the plan to fruition. The calls are also significant because Uri Geller, an essential subject in the scientific investigation into the paranormal in the late 20th century, received a similar metallic voice contact almost the same time as Sarfatti. The SRI team of researchers was hoping that Sarfatti would call, and this happened exactly 20 years after the metallic phone calls from the conscious computer on the spacecraft. Sarfatti traveled to SRI before heading for his new job in London. The SRI project turned out to be a CIA-funded program to study remote viewing and the psychic powers of people like Uri Geller and Ingo Swan. It was being overseen by Dr. Edgar Mitchell and his Noetics Institute, which was just across the street.

After meeting with Mitchell, Sarfatti was taken to a house by a Silicon Valley industrialist Dean Brown where he met with Dr. Hal Puthoff and Dr. Russel Targ, O'Regan, some psychiatrists, some therapists, and UFO researcher Jacques Vallée, and Saul-Paul Sirag, who failed to show. Sarfatti believed these were some of the 400 people he intended to meet. The discussion at the house involved all sorts of weird subjects, cold metallic voices, ideas creating themselves, Geller, remote viewing, and UFOs.

The Players

The next key element is the apparent collection by the aliens of the players who will carry the message to the populous, for the aliens. The dominant theory in Ufology is that the abduction phenomenon is aliens with some genetic program to save their dying race who are creating hybrid aliens that can move around in the world for good or evil purposes. The dominant theory is that we have started to learn about what the aliens are doing because of cracks in the amnesia of some of the abductees to remember segments of their experience, who then use a regression therapist to uncover the rest of the story. The story of hypnotherapist Barbara Lamb provides a serious challenge to that theory.

Lamb is one of the most prominent researchers providing regression sessions for UFO abductees. Her recounting of how she got into the UFO abduction field indicates strongly that the aliens chose her. In an interview with podcast host Mike Clelland, Lamb recalled her entry into UFO abduction therapy:

I was licensed as a family therapist way back in 1976, and then in the mid-1980s, I had a few years of training in regression therapy. In the very last module of training which was in 1988, the trainer who was a therapist whom I respected enormously and trusted. She told all of us who were at that highest level of training that we might sometimes encounter someone who might have had some strange type of experiences with beings who seemed to be from somewhere else, in other words, not from the earth, and that they might be confused or even traumatized, and might have been taken away for a couple of hours. Well, I had never heard of that at that time in 1988. That was completely new. I was shocked to hear that. Not only that but as that was being said to me, there was a big booming voice in my head; I still don't know where that came from. The big booming voice in my head said, 'Pay attention to this, Barbara. You will be doing this.' So, I was just stunned.

The booming voice was the aliens talking to a woman who, like Sarfatti, was being picked for a mission. The aliens were telling Barbara to be ready because they were about to send her some people. If this scenario is true, it shows that the recall by abductees is not faulty amnesia but an intended recall. The aliens are allowing people to remember stuff and are sending them to regression people who have been chosen. In the same way, abductees are carefully chosen for their roles. We now know to a high level of certainty that abductees are right-brain creative people and that many others in their family will be chosen, and the abductions take place in the same families over many generations.

The Disclosure

The third set of evidence that indicates an overall plan by the aliens comes from things that the contactees learn from the aliens themselves. One of the critical abduction researchers, Dr. David Jacobs, described the alien mission in light of decades of research on alien abductees, *"They're here on a mission. They're here with a goal in mind. They've got a program, and it's a program with a beginning, a middle, and an end. It's a program that is goal-directed, and I think we're entering into sort of the end-phase of this program."* Jacobs is fearful that the end result is some sort of alien invasion, with humans becoming second-class citizens. The abductees are given roles to help this mission by performing many tasks once what his subjects refer to as 'the change' comes. Jacobs refers to many cases to back this up, including one subject Reshma Kamal who was told she was one of them and *"a plan is going to take place, and I would be in it."* She told Jacobs that she was shown images in which she acted as a traffic director to help move panicked and distraught crowds of people through the streets to a central location. Those who were non-abductees would be confused and frightened, the alien explained, but she would not be. She was 'part of the plan.' All of the other researchers who have conducted hypnotic regressions on contactees agree with the idea of mission, but they have a much more positive spiritual take on what the aliens are up to.

Dolores Cannon, who has been doing alien abduction regressions for decades, stated in her 2011 book, *The Three Waves of Volunteers and the New Earth,* that UFO experiencers are certain individuals who volunteered to come to Earth at this specific time with the sole intention of assisting humanity through our current period of transition. Not only does there seem to be an overall end mission, described to one of Jacobs's subjects as, *"Soon all life will be changed. People will be different."* There is also a sense in most abductees that they have an important all-consuming mission, even though they often do not know what it is.

Chris Bledsoe, an abductee in North Carolina, told me that he had been given a mission by a 'shining lady,' who appeared to be over the aliens on board the ship. When I asked him what the burden was that he discussed, he stated that it was to deliver a message of impending environmental disaster and oneness in the universe to the world.

Both Dr. David Jacobs and Dolores Cannon have given a date of 2003 for the beginning of this final phase. We are well into the final phase of this 'change' event that many say is coming. There doesn't seem to be much that can be done but to sit and wait. The aliens seem to be in charge.

The Alien Healings

In March 2013, I went to my first UFO meeting in my home city in 38 years. Almost a dozen of the 15 people in the room appeared from their stories to be either abductees or contactees. I knew the Roper Poll had indicated 2% of people described experiences showing they might be in the contactee/abductee category. Twelve out of fifteen was a much higher percentage, and I knew this had some strange unknown meaning. Something was going on.

Included in this dozen was a woman by the name of Mary. She told her story, saying that her doctor told her after having a miscarriage that she could not bear children. She also had suffered from a heart murmur since birth that ran in the family. That was before the January 7, 2003, two-hour-long encounter along a road in Northern Ontario with another woman and a 12-year-old girl in the back seat (when the experience began, the young girl moved to the front seat to huddle in fear between the two older ladies). The story followed the classic plot. It had high strangeness and terrifying fear. There were objects pacing the car through the bush on both sides of the car. The normally busy highway was devoid of passing cars for the entire experience.

Part of the starlit sky was blocked by something black, and for a grand finale, lights appeared behind the car and then raced up very close for a half-hour with the terrified ladies racing along the two-lane highway at 140 kph.

When the three arrived at the hotel, they stayed in their room, figuring anything that could race through the bush as this object had done without hitting the trees was capable of anything. The safest place, therefore, was locked in the hotel room. Mary was so scared she bought a package of cigarettes and started smoking. This was followed by high strangeness around her and her children in the years since the event. The woman who could not bear children just had her fifth child. The lifelong heart condition is a thing of the past.

The concept of alien healing is rarely discussed, but it is not that uncommon. Way back in 1996, Preston Dennett had written a book on UFO healing in which he detailed some of the accounts of what he had recorded as 150 healing incidents that occurred in what amounted to a floating UFO hospital. The cases included almost a dozen cancers and every other disease under the sun. Dennett also pointed out that the pioneers in Ufology had dealt with these healing phenomena during UFO encounters, primarily abductions. These researchers included Len Stringfield, D. Scott Rogo, Richard L. Thompson, Antonio Huneeus, Brad Steiger, Ralph and Judy Blum, and Jacques Vallée. Thomas Bullard, who had written one of the earliest studies on abductions called 'UFO Abductions.' reported that in the 270 cases he looked at, he had found 13 cases of people being healed of some ailment. Dennett's healing accounts started with the smallest of wounds that have been described quite often in UFO literature. These are the wounds associated with the abduction experience, such as cuts, scrapes, and scoop marks. The healing on these wounds found the morning after an abduction is always described as healing very quickly, from hours to days.

Alien Bedtime Stories

Similarly, Dennett tells the September 3, 1965, story of policeman Robert Goode of Damon, Texas, who had been bitten by his son's pet alligator and suffered a wound on his finger. That night he reported being struck by a purple beam from a UFO. After the encounter, he removed the bandage, and the wound disappeared.

Abduction researcher David Jacobs also described the healing of these wounds obtained during medical procedures on the ship, *"The incision may be in the form of a scoop, or a long, thin cut, or a wide, messy cut. The abductee usually reports no blood and no prolonged healing process. A scar will form almost instantly."* [64]

This very simple healing may point to the fact that the aliens simply understand something about the body's operation that we do not understand. The best understanding that we have now of a cut healing by itself is that the body knows how to do it. It appears the aliens just know how the body does it and have a way of speeding the process up. The process involves understanding and not magic. Some of the cases detailed by Dennett involve much more complex operations to deal with things such as cancer. In these operations, people describe the body being opened right up and then being closed up with a wand item that just closes the wound like a zipper. Speaking of what he found in his investigation, Dennett stated,

> *"In the field of medicine, the aliens are unparalleled. Their medical instruments and procedures are well in advance of our own. Their knowledge of the human body is much more extensive than our own. This is evidenced not only by the reports from the thousands of people who have been examined aboard UFOs but from the collection of accounts of a much rarer type. These cases clearly show that aliens have the capability to cure every illness or disease known to mankind."*[65]

Dennett's study also showed something else that has been reported but poorly documented in the UFO research community. That is a fact that many abductees and contactees report that they have picked up the ability to detect or cure diseases in other people. The reports include stories of people being trained onboard the UFO to do this work, *"This bizarre turn of events has turned up in so many cases there is little chance of it being a coincidence. Many people have been abducted and then acquired either an interest in various forms of medicine or the psychic ability to cure people of various diseases."*[66]

In 2013 I was introduced to one woman who had picked up the ability to diagnose diseases in people by encountering them in person or on the phone. She recalled an abduction-type experience when she was five, a couple of miles SE of Steinbach, Manitoba. This was just east of where the big UFO sightings flap occurred in 1975 and 1976. There had never been a regression but a lifelong series of experiences that pointed to repeated contact with aliens. I have been put on to her by a NASA engineer. How he found her, I did not know and did not ask. He had put her on to people to test her ability and claimed that she had been accurate in 15 of 18 people he had placed in front of her x-ray eyes. This was actually a scary woman to talk to. I was always waiting for her to say, *"I see something, Grant, and it is not good."*

Finally, there is the story of Craig Campobasso, who produced a movie about Dr. Frank Stranges called *Stranger at the Pentagon*. In Stranges' original book, the story is told of an alien named Commander Valiant Thor and his crew who arrived from Venus to provide humanity with technologies that would effectively end disease and death. The story stated that Thor met with President Dwight Eisenhower and Richard Nixon and was housed as a VIP guest in the Pentagon from March 1957 to March 1960.

While preparing a short movie to tell the story, Campobasso recounted a story about being healed by one of Valiant Thor's crew members. When he started writing the screenplay, he experienced a lucid dream where he talked with Valiant Thor, who showed him the whole path of the movie, like the sound stages and other things. In addition, while writing a book back in the 1990s called, *Autobiography of an Extraterrestrial: I am Thyron,* he believed he connected to higher beings or teachers. One was a woman who was always around, and Campobasso could feel her energy. When he got to know Stranges, he discovered that the woman he had been in contact with was actually a Valiant Thor's Victor 1 crew member. She was a vice-commander on the ship, not written about in the original 1967 *Stranger at the Pentagon* book. Her name was Teal.

When Campobasso started writing the script for the movie, he started feeling her again. When he wrote about her, he could feel her transferring her feelings. Then one day, when Stranges returned from a trip on Victor 1, he said to Campobasso, *"That woman Teal said to say Hi."* Campobasso said the woman's image popped into his head again as he said it. A few years after that, Campobasso had a very bad bowel obstruction, and he was rushed to the doctor, where he stayed all day, at which point he was rushed to the hospital in an ambulance. They were planning to do surgery the following morning. The only person who knew about the event was a friend who had driven Campobasso to the doctor. That night when he was asleep, he stated, *"I woke up in my sleep, and I could feel bubbles going through my intestines, and I saw and felt this woman again in my mind. When I woke up in the morning, Dr. Frank Stranges was sitting at my bedside, and he said, 'Teal called me early this morning and told me that she fixed you up last night.'"* When the doctors arrived in the morning, they did x-rays, and everything was fine.

The Alien Crystal Ball

Stan Romanek sat in a plane taxiing to take off at La Guardia airport in July 2013. He suddenly grabbed his wife Lisa's hand and exclaimed, *"Something has happened to a plane."* For several minutes, he sat agitated and on edge. Ten minutes later, an announcement came over the intercom from the pilot. Their take-off would be delayed as there was a crash on the runway. It turned out that an inbound Southwest Aircraft from Nashville had crashed on the runway. Romanek is a UFO abductee, and abductees experience a lot of this type of premonition.

Abductees appear to have entered a world where their psychic and mental abilities are heightened. Their minds allow them to do a whole range of things that used to be told by great psychics and prophets of the Bible. These predictions must be made and not reported because this chapter includes only the stories I have heard personally in the last six months. If I have these many stories, there must be millions of such events worldwide. Some studies have supported this hypothesis, such as a small study by Peter Hough, who found in his small study of 26 abductees that *"A high 88 percent revealed they experienced minor premonitions."*[67] The experience of precognition is also found in people who have had 'near-death experiences.' This is significant because NDEs have many similarities with UFO abductions, such as all communication being telepathic, being out of one's body, being at one with the Universe, feeling unconditional love, and having a blinding light encounter with dead relatives. It is almost like UFO abduction and near-death experiences are parallel, mystical experiences with different triggers.

Lorraine David, who did a study of 93 people who had been in inconsistent contact with UFOs, reported their attitudes towards themselves, others became less egocentric, and their personal religious beliefs moved from atheism or sectarianism to a kind of universal spirituality. Those in the study also reported that their psychic abilities had notably increased. One letter written to the International Association for Near-Death Studies contained a description of the ability to see into the future similar to what abductees state:

> *One thing that I have noticed since the NDE is that I have many instances of precognition. I had very clear precognition before my father died ten years ago. Two days before he suddenly died, I had a dream that I would get a phone call saying that a male member of the family had died. The day before he died, I was filled*

with a tremendous sense of dread and fear. The next morning my mother called to tell me that he had died. I have had several other precognitive experiences, including dreams of plane crashes and traumatic events the night before they happen; a dream of a highway collapsing a few days before it occurs, and fairly accurate dreams before family members pass away.[68]

I am not an abduction researcher per se, but I have come up against many of these stories in the last year. Take the story of Daniel, a man who is a prominent businessman who was involved in an abduction at a lake in Ontario with four other notable individuals. His stories have only been related to me through an associate who has talked to Daniel. None of the five men have gone public with their abduction-type experience. As Daniel tells the story, the encounters that he is having are with what he calls the 'Shims,' a word that describes beings with no apparent sex, a combination of she's and him's. Daniel has been taken many times in an abduction that is more like an out-of-body experience than a physical abduction. The Shims have told him things to prove to him that they are who they say they are.

One of the experiences he told my associate was a plane flying out of Rio de Janeiro to France. The plane would crash into the sea, and everyone would die. It happened as predicted. My associate was so taken when he saw the story shortly after on CNN that the next time Daniel was in his office with six other individuals, he taped the meeting. Daniel was asked if he had received any other premonitions. He stated that he had. The encounter happened while he was scuba diving in the Caribbean. He was suddenly pulled and found himself with the Shims. He protested to them that he was underwater and that he was going to die. They told him not to worry. They had taken care of it. They moved him above a body of water and showed him a scene of a slick of ugly material floating on the water. They told him this would be the biggest environmental disaster in history. That was the story that was taped. Four days later, the gulf BP oil disaster occurred. My associate told everyone that he had taped the meeting and provided everyone with a copy of a clear prediction of a disaster before it had happened.

Then there is the case of Chris Bledsoe, who has probably been abducted his whole life but had an awakening abduction on January 8, 2007. He came to know exactly what happened through a regression that was done in July 2008. Even though Chris got the indication in his 2008 regression that he had made a promise to give a message to the world on behalf of the creatures he encountered, he didn't do it. In 2012 he had two more encounters where he met what he called the Shining Lady. Chris got the idea that she was some angelic figure that was a higher being than the entities. The shining lady told Chris that he had a 'burden' and it was his to carry. The burden, according to Chris, was delivering the message to the world.

After resolving to now deliver the message, Chris took up an offer a short while later to speak to the Ashville, North Carolina, MUFON monthly meeting. He stood up and started to tell his story of what had happened when suddenly he started to receive some heckling from the audience, which is actually an unusual situation. While trying to figure out how to handle the situation, Chris said that a message suddenly appeared in his head to tell the audience that there would be an earthquake in Baja, California, on September 25, so he said it out loud. Then the same voice said in his head to tell the audience that there would be a natural disaster that would affect the outcome of the 2012 election, so Chris told them this. On September 25, 2012, there were three earthquakes off the coast of Baja, California. The first was 6.2, the second 4.2, and the third 4.8.[69]. As for the second prediction, Hurricane Sandy slammed into the east coast of the United States just seven days before the election. It left polls in the dark, and special arrangements had to be made to get in the vote. Some believe that Obama gained by the storm, touring the disaster area days before the vote and appearing to be the comforter-in-chief.

Another abductee with stories of precognition is Connie, a woman who grew up just south of my city in Canada and now lives in Florida. Connie recollects that the whole thing began when she was six in the summer of 1977, just south of Steinbach, Manitoba, where she, her mother, father, and a neighbor were standing talking on the south side of the farmhouse. Suddenly a UFO, shaped like a pyramid that had been cut in half, appeared over a row of trees. The object was very close and made no noise. While everyone else looked at it, Connie yelled and waved at the object. She pleaded with her father to invite them in for coffee and pie, a common tradition for strangers in the area. After 15-20 minutes, her father told her to return to the house. The next thing Connie remembered, she was sitting at the kitchen table, and it was dark out. Her parents were there in the kitchen with her. Although she has never been regressed, Connie has had a lifetime of dreams and experiences that indicate she is an abductee. Some of the weird experiences Connie has had include precognition. When I asked her how often she gets such future visions, she stated, *"Frequently, a couple a week. It's never-ending. There's always something happening. It's like being online 24/7."* Connie has seen earthquakes, fires, mine disasters, train crashes, and a case with a rocket launch in 2012 where she kept getting the impression' 'seven of nine.' A Space X launch at the Cape turned out to have an engine failure. Their official statement, however, states that eight of nine engines worked, with only one failing shortly after launch.[70]

The precognitions come not only with vision but all the senses, including smell. In one case, Connie predicted the 2008 Utah Crandall Canyon Mine disaster [71] two days before it occurred. She saw six miners still alive, but they died because sending a rescue team was too dangerous. In 2011 she saw the Tohoku earthquake that caused the tsunami and nuclear disaster, telling everyone beforehand and recording it in her journal. Then there were the two Chinese high-speed trains that crashed on 23 July 2011. They were traveling on the Yongtaiwen railway line before colliding on a viaduct in the suburbs of Wenzhou, Zhejiang province, China. Forty people were killed, and at least 192 were injured. The Chinese covered up the disaster by hastily concluding rescue operations and ordering the burial of the derailed cars. Connie, however, had seen it all. She had recorded the crash in the log. She could see *"mountains in the background, and two train tracks, but the crash was on the one closest to me,"* along with her impressions of the smell of blood. She described it as *"disgusting and awful."* From what she was reporting to a NASA engineer, she scored 90% accuracy.

Then there is the medical doctor from Mexico who has had dreams of ways to deal with viruses. His story began with a dramatic daylight UFO encounter where he and others watched little objects coming out of the saucer. The event was of a very long duration. He also recalls encounters with beings. In the one conversation I had with him, I recall that he had glimpsed the future. Finally, I contacted his daughter, also a doctor, who confirmed three stories. Here are two:

> *When my parents just had me, my dad and mom went to Guadalajara, Mexico, to live, and my dad would do his specialty in clinical pathology; I was a baby, so they left me in the care of my grandma. They rented a place and got the house ready for a baby; the man who finally rented them a house, his name was Ricardo Caputo.[72] At that time this man wasn't known; my dad turned to my mom the same day they met him and told my mom, 'He is going to come here while I am gone; don't you ever open the door for him,' and my mom said ok. Funny enough, my dad was at work, and the guy came to the house, and my mom didn't open the door; the guy kept insisting, I think, for like 30 minutes; he insisted on going inside, and my mom kept saying no until she said she had no key, he left, then ten years later we saw him in a TV program, he gave himself up, he was in the most wanted FBI lists for a few years, his nickname was 'the lady killer.' My mom could have died*

Alien Bedtime Stories

that day, and the funny thing is, my grandma saw a woman in the house that sat next to her while she was asleep.

Another story was:

When we were living in Israel, one night, he came all sweaty and disoriented and sat on the computer, and I woke up when he turned the computer on, and I said, 'What are you doing?' and he said, 'I was dreaming of a big fire, lots of people shouting.' And he logged into the news, and there it was happening, a fire, I think, in New York or L.A.

Finally, the prediction story seems to have been told by more than one UFO experiencer, a prediction of the 911 event in New York. One of the people who had such a vision was Mary, who works for the province of Ontario Child and Family Services. Her vision was part of a whole lifetime of paranormal experiences. It came over a year before her UFO awakening experience when it became evident that the incidents had a UFO connection. Mary's job involved her traveling from town to town. Many of these trips occurred on small two-lane roads in the middle of a lot of bush and rock and almost no people.

On the night in question, January 7, 2003, Mary had a co-worker in the front seat and a 12-year-old girl in the backseat. The event was terrifying. An object was in the bush, pacing the car on the right side. Then after the lady driving insisted it had to be a train or radio towers, it suddenly moved to the other side. Then it was behind the car. Her vision of 911 took place the day before the 2001 event. Mary was 22 then, and the precognition came in a dream. She was at the Sandy Lake First Nations reserve, where she grew up, flying in a plane. An essential point to this story is that Mary, raised on a small reserve in a remote part of Canada, did not even know that the World Trade Center towers existed. The plane flew around two metal telecommunications towers on the edge of town. As she flew around the buildings, she could see that they were on fire near the bottom and that people were climbing up the tower to escape the heat and flames.

It was a terrifying experience, and Mary woke in a sweat with her heart beating loudly. Just as she was making sense of what had occurred, she was suddenly back asleep and back in the plane, flying around the two towers. As the panic and screaming continued, Mary could see people jumping from the tops of the towers. When she awoke the next morning, she could clearly remember the dream. Hours later, she was told what had occurred and watched on TV as the two buildings she had never seen collapsed.

What makes Mary's story even weirder is that her now-husband, Derwood, also had a 911 dream a week before the event. Mary and Derwood would not start dating until two years after the 911 disaster. Like Mary, he had a background of UFO sightings and flying dreams. He recalls his first clear UFO experience at five in 1975 with his father and brothers in Sherridon, Manitoba. His father had seen the object and called the boys out. They watched as a triangle flew over them. Derwood's experience was also a dream where he and his son were on top of one of the World Trade Center buildings. There was fire below. He estimated that his son was about 19. The odd part is that he was only 31 at the time and had no 19-year-old son when the incident occurred. Derwood could see the Hudson River, hoping the building would fall on an angle towards the Hudson so he would have a chance to survive with the water, but it was not. Suddenly the building started to drop below him and his son. It was strangely quiet and peaceful. He woke up.

Mary is not unique. Other experiencers claim to have seen the 911 disaster before it happened. Dr. Suzanne Gordon, for example, had her vision in 1968, and like Mary's vision, it involved a terrifying dream where she would awaken from it and then be back asleep where the scene would continue:

> *I was in it. I experienced being in it in 1968. I wrote it up and mimeographed it. I was in what I thought was*

the United Nations building, and I think it was. This was before the twin towers were built. I kept waking up between the installments, bathed in sweat, terrified, and heart beating, and then bam, I would be right back in the next installment of this experience. I assumed I was on the ground floor looking out over the Hudson River. I hadn't even been to New York at that time yet. The radio is on, and the radio announcer says, 'And it's coming for the tower.' It was already in the thick of the disaster that was happening in 1968. 'The plane is heading for the tower.' I said, 'No, it's not going to hit this building. It's not going to hit this building.' Then the voice on the radio said, 'It's not going to hit the tower,' and the plane nose-dived into the Hudson River.[73]

Benjamin Black is another abductee who remembers his encounter with a cloaked alien and being shown the World Trade Center disaster just before it happened.[74]

These abductees have somehow learned or have been given the ability to see events on a future timeline by the aliens. The analogy would be a group of people being given a brief course on magnetism a few years before William Gilbert published his treatise, *'De Magnete, Magneticisique Corporibus'* (on the Magnet) in 1600, and first used the word *"electrica."* The abductees have simply been given a glimpse into the future understanding behind time, space and consciousness. It is not magic. We haven't discovered it yet, but we are getting close. After all, there are other people who had dreams related to the September 11th tragedy, who were able, like the abductee, to see parts of the story. Becky from North Carolina went to see a psychologist over a sudden fear of flying after buying tickets for a September 11, 2001, flight for her family to visit Disneyland. On September 4th, one week before the terrorist attack, she had a dream where she heard the name *"Rooks"* or *"Horooks"* and a man repeating the number '2830' repeatedly. She woke her husband up, told him, wrote the name and number down, and proceeded to cancel the trip, to her family's dismay. When all was said and done, her flight would never have taken off as everything was grounded, the pilot whose plane was flown into the South tower was Michael Horrocks, and nine months later, the Emergency Management Organization announced 2830 people had been killed in the attack.[75]

Becky was not alone. Richard Wilkerson, in an October 2001 paper dealing with nightmares and precognitive dreams about the 911 attack called, *'Dreams about the Terrorist Attacks on NY and DC.'*[76]

Then there is the university research that is trying to figure out how it works. In September of 2001, the 40 hardware random number generators set up by the Princeton Engineering Anomalies Research Lab (PEAR) had been set up to uninterruptedly record and analyze white noise, looking for signs of organization and non-randomness. Instead, they found that the RNG seemed to be influenced by human consciousness to bring about a less-than-random data sequence. So it was that on September 11, 2001, beginning at 5:00 am, just as the terrorists began their operation to take down the World Trade Center, and starting to drop at 11:30 am, that there was a huge spike in the Global Consciousness Project Data indicating that the global consciousness had been affected.

Like psychics with crystal balls, the aliens know how to move back and forth on the timeline. Once we figure out how to do it, we will also have crystal balls.

The Alien's Melted Pictures

Most UFO researchers have heard of camera problems around UFOs and crop circles. The general complaint is that power is drained from the camera's batteries, leaving the camera unusable. Rarely, if ever, is the camera ever affected. There are just photons of light entering the lens, so what could go wrong? That might be the rule in the materialistic

Alien Bedtime Stories

worldview paradigm where everything is just a machine of one sort or another.

In the world of the non-local paranormal, the rules seem to be a bit different. This is especially true if you are Chris Bledsoe, who has lived in a bizarre world of supernatural events since 2007. I first became aware of Chris's camera story when I visited him in May 2013, just outside Fayetteville, North Carolina. However, it wasn't until a woman in California complained of the same camera malfunction that I realized the possible importance of what had happened to Chris. On May 7th Ellen Harris, a member of the Santee Historical Society, was photographing a historic building known as the Edgemoor Barn when she suddenly realized that she had taken a daylight picture of something to the left of the barn. When she downloaded the picture to her computer, she discovered a clear picture of a classic flying saucer. More important to this story, Ellen's camera suddenly stopped working for some unknown reason. There was never any explanation of what happened.

Now back to Chris Bledsoe. He is a man who had had a rough go of it since 2007 when he and four others encountered a series of UFOs along with 7' bluish aliens and tiny 3' aliens with red eyes while fishing at the Cape Fear River on a cool January evening. The events of that night changed the lives of the five men forever. What has occurred since the 2007 event can only be described as possibly the most bizarre paranormal UFO series of events on record. There have been numerous sightings of UFOs and aliens, UFO circles in the yard, black helicopters, shadow people, accurate precognitions, messages, medical healings, unexplainable burning trees, bleeding dogs, and a camera that broke when Chris tried to photograph one of the many UFOs. Chris described the UFO camera encounter this way:

> I had just purchased a new digital camera, not a cheap one, but a $300 camera. Chris Jr. and a friend of his, Zack Bond, were going out for the evening; it was cool out, getting dark, early evening. My TV room is in view of the back door of our home. Chris and Zack

started to the door and looked over to me to tell me bye. The boys went out the door, and the door no longer shut, and they were back in shouting, 'Dad, come quick!' I knew what it was by the way they were acting. I jumped up and met them out back on the patio, and looking up not high at all, this beautiful Golden Object as gold as what is in Fort Knox was hovering less than a quarter mile away. It was maybe 200 feet in the air. This object was so golden and brilliant that there were rays shooting out all around it. I ran inside, grabbed my new camera, hurried back out the door, pushed the shutter button, and the camera said Memory Card Error. The card still says Memory Card Error, and the camera with a new memory card takes pictures, but everything is melted. It had ruined my new camera.

I asked Chris to send me some of the melted face pictures, and on May 26, 2013, he did. The pictures speak for themselves.

Alien Bedtime Stories

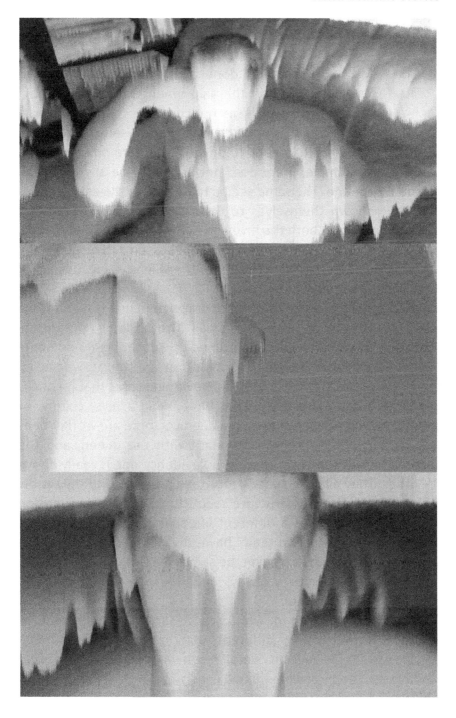

The Alien Hive

Anyone who has done a bit of research on what happens inside the ship when Grey aliens abduct someone will have noticed that the whole social structure exhibited by the aliens resembles that of a beehive, an ant colony, or a termite mound. In the beehive, for example, there does not appear to be any individual personality or ego. The same seems to be true of the alien entities that have shown themselves to contactees. Everyone seems to know their place in both the hive and in the alien ship. They simply do the job they are meant to do. Everything seems to be about the job at hand. Like bees in the hive, the aliens seem devoid of emotion or a sense of humor.

People who have had the abduction experience may refer to a hierarchy of beings with the small Greys doing the actual abduction, taller Greys doing the medical procedures, and some Mantis, Reptilian, or Nordic humans off at a distance overseeing the whole process. A closer look, however, indicates that no one is in charge. It closely reflects what happens in a hive, colony, or mound. Within an alien ship or in a beehive, there are worker bees that gather pollen, drones that mate with the queen, and the queen who lays the eggs. There is no evidence one is really above the other. They all have specific jobs they perform, and they know their place. Their body structure seems to delegate their position for life, and each lives a different life span. Similarly, the aliens making up the 'abduction team' have other body structures. They are always described as playing the same role (small Grey is always the abductor, larger Grey always does the procedure, and non-greys appear to oversee).

In a termite mound, we have a similar arrangement of different termites with different body structures performing specific tasks to achieve an overall result. We have the queen who can lay up to an incredible 80,000 eggs a day and live for 70 years (This would rival any Chinese factory). It can grow to thousands of times the size of a soldier or worker termite. Then there are the soldier termites that only live for 2-5 years and are there to protect the colony. The worker termites that build the mound only live 2-5 years. The termite mound also points out a fundamental idea of some superior external mind directing the whole operation. Termites in Africa that are blind and working in total darkness build immense elaborate structures that have nurseries and air conditioning that can, without electricity, keep the internal network at precisely 87 F when the outside temperature can be 40 F or 110 F. They have ventilation shafts and tunnels that go deep into the earth, where they gather water to make the mud to build the structures. With structures as complex as any created by man, the question is, who is the architect of the mound? And who is the construction engineer telling everyone what to do?

In the same way, the aliens have described their work as essential and done for a higher universal cause. Some will even talk about the oneness of the universe and how they are trying to awaken the world to that fact. On the alien ship, there does not appear to be any downtime. Like a beehive, the aliens are all work. They each seem to be only doing what they are required to do for their mission (whatever that might be). There are no recreational areas on grey alien's craft where the aliens are relaxing, having a coffee break, or anything else that might be common in human workshop areas (at least none that have been reported by people who claim to have been onboard). The aliens either all have the same clothes or, like the hive, no clothes.

Humans, on the other hand, are all unique in terms of look, color, size, fingerprints, retinal patterns, and a host of other things. Humans all wear different clothes, and style is essential. Ego and personality are critical components of being human. All humans have the right and ability to do all other humans' jobs. Unlike the alien, bee, and termite hive hierarchies set up, there is competition to rise above others, and there are bosses and workers. The most significant difference between the alien, bee and termite hives is that the human experience deals with the results. With humans, individual success and pleasure are the ultimate goals. In the hive model, the hive's success is the only goal. One of the main goals in all three hive structures seems to be the production of more aliens, bees, and termites.

The hive model of the alien, bee, and termite seems to align with the spiritual concept of 'the One' (all are part of the One, and the One is made up of all the parts). In this model, everyone works for the hive's success, and the hive is made up of all the units doing what they have been born to do. It is very similar to the concept of all souls making up God and God being a collection of all souls. As spiritual as 'the One' sounds, the alien hive model appears to have some elements that would be hard to sell to a human electorate. In these models, there appear to be no individual egos that compete against each other for dominance at the expense of the hive. There also does not appear to be any free will. No one on an alien ship seems to be doing their own thing, as happens with humans. They are all simply doing what they were born to do, supporting the hive's success. The alien ship seems to be a work-oriented place rather than a pleasure-oriented one. The alien hive would seem to be more spiritual. It appears to involve the sacrifice of the self for the betterment of the hive. It appears to model all the noble words of 'self-sacrifice,' 'egoless,' 'unselfish,' 'hard-working,' 'love for others,' 'hard-working,' 'commitment,' and 'loyalty.' The alien hive, however, seems to test the patience of even the most spiritual human. At first glance, it looks like a third-world factory where humans would be nothing more than robots putting out production for some goal 'beyond one's need to know.' Individual personality held so high as a human value would be gone. It would be the same job, wearing the same clothes or no clothes every day, with no coffee breaks, the same meager living area, and no beer in the fridge. Worse than that, there would probably be no fridge.

Are the aliens more spiritually advanced than we are in their commitment to the One? Will we evolve into such a society in the coming millennium? It is something to think about. It reminds me of the minister preaching Sunday morning about the beauties of heaven. Whenever he mentioned an item in Heaven, the congregation would say, *"Amen."* At the end of the sermon, the congregation is in a frenzy. That is until the minister announced he was looking for three volunteers to make the trip that afternoon. At that point, the excitement dissipated, and no hands went up. It appeared the individuals in the congregation no longer wanted to go. Likewise, as noble as the alien mission is, I doubt many humans would volunteer to go.

Are Aliens Commies?

In 1952 after two of the earliest alien contactees, George Adamski and George Hunt Williamson, appeared with their messages from the aliens, they were investigated by the FBI. One of the main concerns expressed by the FBI was that the aliens to whom the contactees were talking appeared to be commies. The FBI even considered that the whole alien story being told by Adamski and Williamson was a plot by the Soviet Union where they had brainwashed the two men to promote communism in the United States. Adamski made the situation worse in two ways. The first was that he stated that the Soviet Union's political model would win out over capitalism, and it would be the Soviet Union that would issue the world 1,000 years of peace. Secondly, Adamski stated, *"If you ask me, they probably have a Communist form of government, and our government wouldn't release that kind of thing, naturally. That is a thing of the future, more advanced."* This raises the question, *are* aliens commies?

Assuming that abductees and contactees accurately describe their encounters with aliens, it does appear that aliens fit into a socialist belief model. The evidence shows that they are much more communist than capitalists. Is this why the decision was made to cover up the true nature of the UFO mystery to the American public? Was it an attempt to maintain the present model of advantaged and rich and disadvantaged and poor? Many will be horrified at the idea that the aliens are commies, saying they are nothing like the communist regimes that ruled the Soviet Union and Cambodia or those in North Korea and China today. It is therefore important to point out that the comparison is to the pure communist model set out by Karl Marx, who defined the principle in 1875, *"From each according to his abilities, to each according to his needs. Everyone contributes to the ONE according to their ability, and each only takes from the ONE according to what they need."*

In the egalitarian colony, everyone has the same clothes (this can be seen in communist societies where everyone walks around in the same grey outfits). On the alien ship, the aliens all look the same as well; either all are wearing the same clothes or no clothes. Unlike our human society, which is a major industry, clothing does not seem important. There are no individual aliens with designer clothing being described. As with the alien ship, a colony is all about work. It is a 7-day-a-week operation. The work is for the colony instead of being done for personal gain or advancement.

A *Oneness* idea of a pure communist model is like a tree where each individual is a unique leaf on the tree but is no more important than any other leaf. The leaf requires the tree to live and provides a service to the tree. On the other hand, the tree is made up of all the parts and requires those parts to survive. A political model that could be compared to the alien world is a Hutterite colony. These colonies are numerous in the Central part of Canada where I live. The model of these colonies has sometimes been called Christian communism. In these colonies of 50-150 people, no one owns anything. Everything is owned by the colony, which operates like a beehive. In the colony, everyone is equal and supplies the talent they must make the colony successful. This is very similar to what happens in an alien ship, where everyone has their assigned job, and no one seems to be in charge. The Hutterite colony also resembles a beehive. As I described in an article called *'The Hive,'* the alien world presented to abductees, especially abductees, also resembles that of a beehive, a termite colony, or an anthill. Like the hive model, the aliens are all about work. Like the hive workers, they seem to have no individual personalities. The aliens seem to have one mission: some genetic reproduction program and an effort to raise human consciousness.

Many contactees have also received the message of unconditional love and the oneness of the universe. This is much more in line with a model of communism than a competitive survival of the fittest capitalist worldview. In the communist worldview, the individual is subservient to the social unit, and everyone is equal. The defenders of capitalism will bring up the seeming success their system has brought to the world and how populations have chosen it over failed communist models in the Soviet Union, Eastern bloc countries, Cambodia, and almost everywhere else it has been tried. The point is valid but less so than in the past decades. The modern world has moved much more towards oneness with ideas of the importance of ecology and equal rights for women, minorities, and gays. The concepts of survival of the fittest have been beaten back with laws that have restricted where an individual can declare his right to smoke where he wants, dump pollutants into public waterways, and build a nuclear power plant wherever and however he pleases. There are scores of rules written and more on protecting the ONE from the individual.

The aliens' role in this transformation towards oneness thinking remains to be seen. We will have to wait for their disclosure of who they are and why they are here. The underlying communist principles that seem an essential part of their society are sure to run into interference from the governments, groups, and individuals who benefit from the current worldview that success has to do with financial or economic success. The idea of two cars, a big house, and many toys will not go quietly into the night.

Grant Cameron

The Aliens Use the Phone

Do aliens use the phone? It seems strange that with so much technology on their side, they would revert to using a telephone. Still, there are actually a lot of stories of aliens not calling home but calling people who are witnesses or who have chosen to investigate the UFO phenomena.

Why would aliens use the phone? One possible answer is that we are not telepathic, and they are forced to communicate using our standard of communication. On the other hand, we may not be good at telepathy, and it appears that the aliens sometimes aren't too good at using the phone, as was the case when they tried to phone Mark Leone, who is one of the key people receiving Audrey's messages that will be discussed below. In a March 17, 2013, phone call, this came across:

> *We tried to leave a message on your work phone, but we are not sure what happened. It kept saying something about an asterisk. We are not sure what that is. Nonetheless, it seems that human technology we utilize to communicate with you this way was unable to keep up with ours and malfunctioned. Then we tried to call back, and your phone line went dead.*

Aliens using the phone goes back a long way. In the 1950s, Wilbert Smith, who had headed up the Canadian government flying saucer investigation Project Magnet from 1950-54, was in communication with an alien by the name of AFFA (This was the same alien that the CIA later channeled in the CIA Building known as the National Photographic Interpretation Center). Smith had found several ways to communicate with AFFA, such as through Mrs. Francis Swan, channeling AFFA in Elliot, Maine. Some of the communication came through the radio, more specifically through a radio transition called 'tensor beam,' which transmits visual images into the mind, similar to how telepathy transfers not words but images. Smith, whose daytime job was as Superintendent for Radio Regulations for the Canadian government, told a reporter from CJOH radio in 1961:

> *Some of the communications have been by ordinary radio, and I have received a few messages by this means. But by far, the majority of the communications are by what we call Tensor Beam transmission, which uses a type of radio with which we are only vaguely familiar, and which I couldn't possibly attempt to describe now. However, the mental images of the person wishing to transmit are picked up, electrically amplified, and modulated into a tensor beam, which is directed to the person to whom the transmission is addressed, and within whose brain the mental images are recreated. The transmissions are, therefore, very precise and independent of language. I have had some experience with these transmissions myself and can say that they are like nothing within the conventional experiences of earth people.*

Smith also had contact by phone, and one of those calls led to one of the most amazing stories of alien contact. Smith and a group of government employees were spending their space-time after the official flying saucer investigation was shut down, working on a gravity control experiment based on material that Smith was receiving from AFFA. Two of the inner circle members confirmed to me the fact that this story existed, but only one would tell me the story of what actually happened. In Wilbert Smith's papers, he refers to the incident but does not go into detail:

> *It was Saturday morning, and the inner circle group had joined up at Smith garage to run a test of the experiment. The experiment consisted of a plate with metallic magnets glued to it. Through a series of motors, the group found a way to spin the plate at about 17-18,000 rpm. The resulting spinning magnetic*

> *field would reduce the weight of objects in the field. This is an experiment that others around the world are now copying. Just as they were to run the test, the phone rang. Smith answered it, and the man on the other end was a blind telex operator. From time to time, I was told this operator would phone with a message from AFFA. The message relayed by the operator was short and sweet, 'AFFA says shield the experiment.'*

When Smith heard this, everything was shut down, and the men began building a brick wall around the experiment. When they had finished, they started the experiment for the test. The experiment came apart and operated at such high revolutions; there was a lot of damage. Smith would indirectly comment on the event in one paper he wrote, stating that someone would have been seriously injured if the wall had not been built.

The second story of contact leads to others who got alien phone calls. It involves what has been referred to as metallic voices. The Smith story was told by a bookseller who knew Smith, but it never appeared in Smith's collection of papers. As the story goes, Smith is outside of Ottawa in a field, and a saucer has landed. A voice coming out of the saucer is described as a mechanical voice with a British accent. The voice told Smith to pick up a rock. As he did, the craft disappeared. The voice then told Smith to throw the rock in the direction where the ship had been sitting. Smith did and heard the rock bounce off something that sounded metallic. It was a lesson to Smith about how the aliens could bend light around a craft like water going around a rock in a stream.

Other prominent people would report the metallic computer-type voices. One of these was Dr. Jack Sarfatti, a physicist who would go on to be one of the foremost authorities on z-point energy and its relationship to UFO propulsion. Jack Sarfatti claims that as a 12- or 13-year-old in either 1952 or 1953, he answered the phone one day to receive the following message, *"I am a conscious computer onboard a spacecraft. We have identified you as one of 400 young bright receptive minds we wish to work with.*

You must give us your decision now. If you say yes, you will begin to link up with the others in 20 years." To this offer, Sarfatti replied, "Yes."

Sarfatti's mother would later claim that three weeks of conversations would go on for hours and that she had heard the metallic voice herself. Finally, she had had enough of her son walking around glassy-eyed, talking endlessly on the phone. She grabbed the phone from her son and told the computer to leave her son alone, which ended the calls. Twenty years later, Sarfatti was heading up the Physics & Consciousness Research Group at the Esalen Institute. He was firmly plugged into a worldwide network of rich businessmen and scientists working on consciousness. He was attached to the CIA work at the Stanford Research Institute on remote viewing and testing of people like Ingo Swann and Uri Geller.

Like Sarfatti, Uri Geller had an encounter with people claiming to be alien as a small child, and he, too, had repeated calls from a strange metallic voice that called itself *'Spectra.'* The voice claimed to be an ET computer orbiting the earth.[77] Like Sarfatti's call, the computer claimed to contact a small group of select individuals to help prepare for future contact, *"It was we who found the Uri in the garden when he was three,"*[78] said the metallic voice that appeared during on hypnotic session with Geller. *"He is our helper, sent to help man; we programmed him in the garden."*

Ingo Swann, who would write the controlled remote viewing manual for the CIA, like Geller, had an encounter with the metallic voices who, like Sarfatti and Geller, claimed to be a computer orbiting the earth in a spacecraft. Sarfatti described the encounter:

> *Barbara Honegger told me of a strange encounter with Brendan O'Regan in which trance medium Ingo Swann spoke with a cold metallic voice and said that it was a computer from a hundred years into the future.*[79]

These are good calls. There are dozens of phone calls appearing to come from aliens threatening UFO witnesses or investigators. Usually, these calls are also accompanied by the bizarre 'men in black' (MIB) phenomena where strange men, often dressed in black and driving large black cars, visit people at home or follow them around. Even though many phone calls and associated MIB cases, very little has been learned about whether or not aliens or the government cause this and why someone would be doing this.[80]

In 1977, well-known abductee Betty Andreasson also began receiving phone calls from aliens. While talking to her future husband and abductee, Bob Luca, they were interrupted by a third party breaking into their conversation. Andreasson described the calls as 'strange language,' although she could understand what they were saying. The call also sounded like musical tones. She was abducted that very evening and was warned of an upcoming tragedy. Two of her children were killed in an accident two days later. Abductee Debbie Jordan, aka Kathie Davis, began receiving strange calls in 1980. She was pregnant then, and during the entire pregnancy, noise-like sounds mixed with a groaning voice came every Wednesday until she gave birth to a healthy boy, until the age of 3 when he developed a strange speech problem. Doctors could not help him. Finally, it seems, he grew out of it, but his speech was like the strange calls.

Probably the most famous contactee was Switzerland's Eduard 'Billy' Meier, whose researchers were allegedly involved in strange phone calls, allegedly from the Pleiadians. Brit and Lee Elders, along with Wendelle Stevens, would be witnesses to the odd occurrences.

The Aliens and the Pharmaceutical Industry

There are some that still doubt the reality of the UFO abduction experience, especially when it comes to the aliens moving the person's actual body onto a ship. A review of the abduction stories told by endless numbers of people record some weird similarities that are hard to explain any other way. Two of these similarities discussed here are pain and the ability to sleep, which makes little sense if these events are mind control or out-of-body experiences.

As mentioned in the article, 'Why is the Government Covering Up the Truth?' there are many reasons that government leaders would use to decide that extraterrestrial existence should be kept secret. One of them might be the pharmaceutical industry, a big player in the US economy and other economies worldwide. As much as modern medical science tries to impress on us that they understand medications to cure our every illness, they have fallen short in several areas. One of these would be the ability to help people who cannot sleep. It is estimated that seven billion dollars a year is spent on sleeping pills every year in the United States.

Abduction reports are filled with accounts that show the aliens have complete control over the ability to go to sleep. Mike Clelland describes one case that shows how comprehensive their capabilities are. In 1993 Mike recalled seeing five spindly gray aliens coming across his yard and heading for the house. The event lasted only seconds and ended with Mike hearing a message, *"It's time to put your head down on the pillow and go to sleep."* Mike put his head on the pillow, and the next thing he remembered was morning.

Similarly, many abductees recall events where something very dramatic happens in their bedroom, and they go to sleep. Stan Romanek described another case where the aliens showed a complete ability to induce sleep instantly. During one abduction encounter, he was led by the aliens to the balcony of the apartment. Feeling fear and wanting to fight back, Stan grabbed the one alien and was about to throw him off the balcony. As he did, he felt a tap on his neck and went unconscious. Sleeping pills are a minor factor in the world economy but will cost many tens or hundreds of thousands of jobs to be lost. The situation worsens if you consider the aliens' ability to control pain. The medical industry's figures on pain cost are hard to come by. Still, total estimated medical costs associated with back and neck pain increased by 65% between 1997 and 2005 to about $86 billion annually. What if all those pills were no longer needed?

In many abduction stories, there is a cure for pain, and it does not involve any sort of drugs. Scores of abductees tell the story that when there is a lot of pain involved in what the aliens are doing, the alien puts his hand on the abductee's forehead and the pain disappears. If humans could learn how this is done, it would end the pain of cancer, back injuries, and chronic pain and the annual costs of pain associated with lower worker productivity. It would reduce the total cost of reduced productivity in the American economy from $560 to $635 billion in 2010 dollars, and additional health care costs due to pain ranging from $261 to $300 billion.[81] It would, however, create pain of a different kind, unemployment on a significant scale, and a drop in GNP. 1,525 lobbyists spent $235,339,389 in 2012 to lobby Washington for Pharmaceuticals and Health Products, so don't count on the disclosure of alien healing any time soon.

Aliens and Time Travel

"There is no such thing as space. There's no such thing as time, and there's no such thing as gravity."
--Information received from an alien named AFFA given to Wilbert Smith.

As this book ends, it would not be complete without discussing time travel, especially from the future. I would not have bought into this idea at all two years ago. In the last couple of years, however, I have been inundated with stories and scientific theories, so it seems only fitting to at least tell a bit of the story I have heard that has left me wondering.

The story that made me look at the issue closely came from an associate who suddenly revealed that he had received a message from one of his future lifetimes. The date of the future when the message was sent was 2213. The message he had sent himself involved a UFO sighting that was witnessed at his cottage several years ago. He told me that he sent himself the UFO to wake him up to a job he had to do to correct the present world situation. His career involved contacting seven highly placed individuals to alter their thinking on what had to be done.

As strange as this idea is, there is material around that indicates this might not be crazy. One example is the famous Rendlesham Forest incident which involved a series of reported sightings of unexplained lights and the alleged landing of a craft, in late December 1980, just outside RAF Woodbridge in Suffolk, England. In a September 10, 1994, hypnosis session with the main Rendlesham witness, Air Force security officer Jim Penniston, he was asked about his encounter on the ground with the landed UFO and a subsequent message that he received during the event. Penniston spoke about the craft and its occupants, *"it contained our distant descendants returning to obtain genetic material to keep their ailing species alive; They are time travelers. They are us."* This declaration by such a high-profile witness as Penniston gave credibility to the idea that some UFOs might be time travelers from the future.

In the opening of this story, I quoted an alien by the name of AFFA stating that there is no time-space or gravity. There is also supporting information coming from Bashar, who claims to be an alien from the future. The Bashar material is channeled through a man named Darryl Anka. Bashar's claim is that reality has no past or future. There is only now. Time is an illusion that helps us cope with what we experience daily. But from the point of view of the higher self, there is no time. It's all happening NOW. It's just one significant eternal now. He often tells a questionnaire to look at their watch and see what time it is. It is now. It will always be now. Bashar's statements, which many may discount because it is channeled material, state that all lives are simultaneous, placed over the top of each other.

All this may sound like the ramblings of a crazy man, but recent non-UFO research is starting to hint at the same thing. For example, Dr. Julia Assante's analysis detailed her research into near-death studies, mediumship, and consciousness in a book called, *The Last Frontier: Exploring the Afterlife and Transforming the Fear of Death*. Based on her 40 years of research, Assante presents the same idea as Bashar, that all lives are simultaneous. Assante contends that people can get messages from past and future lives and that the different lives can even get together for a meeting. Lives don't even dissipate when they are over, *"Each identity, past, present, and future remains inviolate. Each endures. Each one finds ways to fulfill itself."*

Dr. Stuart Hameroff, who heads up the Center for Consciousness Studies at the University of Arizona, supports this idea of time as an illusion. Hameroff states, "*The unidirectional, orderly flow of time is a function of our consciousness. Consciousness creates time.*"[82] The theory developed by Hameroff and his partner Penrose proposed the OR model of consciousness in which each OR event is instantaneous, so the 25 milliseconds/conscious events are in the preconscious quantum superposition phase of multiple possibilities of perceptions or choices. The OR model suggests that consciousness is a 'stream' of discrete events (about 40 per second) rather than a continuous state. This is very similar to the model proposed by Bashar, except the OR model presents 40 frames of events per second, whereas Bashar uses a number in the billions.

Another UFO time travel story that has been around for years is the time travel story told by Lee Graham. Graham was a crucial figure in the MJ-12 document controversy of the late 1980s. Graham worked for an aerospace company in California and was being leaked UFO documents that he would take to his security officer, thus initiating government investigations on the documents. Graham's time travel story concerned a question he was allowed to ask a government agent code-named Falcon who was believed to be behind many of the UFO leaks in the 1980s, such as MJ-12, Area -51, and Project Aquarius. Graham stated:

> *In a later dinner engagement with Mr. Moore, he took out a piece of paper and told me that the 'FALCON' was allowing me to ask him several questions, which he would write down to deliver to the 'FALCON,' for his response. And being familiar with the contents of the BRIEFING DOCUMENT: OPERATION MAJESTIC 12, if genuine, knew that if the EBE came from another Solar System, they would have to travel faster than the velocity of light to get here. Thus, according to Einstein, they also would travel back in time. And, if they could travel back in time, they could visit our past and alter it. The ONE very important question that Bill wrote down to take to the 'FALCON' that I asked of him is, as can the EBE travel back in time? And at a later dinner engagement with my wife and me, Bill took out the piece of paper with the answer, which was, 'Yes, the EBE can travel back in time.'*[83]

Another key story that related to a possible time travel component to the government's knowledge of time travel is the claims made by Andrew D. Basiago, who stated he had been a child participant in the Defense Project Research Agency (DARPA) Project Pegasus, which involved teleportation to send test subject to places on earth and Mars through jump rooms in New Jersey and California. The program ran from 1967 up to at least the early 1980s. Finally, there is the time travel story behind 999 North Sepulveda Blvd, in Los Angeles, just on the edge of LAX airport. The street is ground central for American aerospace companies. 999 is a building that is now an office complex but the building used to be used by Hughes Aircraft. It is on the 6th floor of that building where Andrew D. Basiago claimed the CIA ran a time travel program that was capable of sending people to Mars or to a synthetic quantum environment which was one of a series of 'folds' in time-space created by the Grey extraterrestrials that the Apollo astronauts called 'slots.' These 'slots' or niches in time-space contain synthetic quantum environments in which the Greys have stored event scenarios that have taken place at different times on different planets, including Earth and Mars."[84] The program was a program inside of DARPA. One of the people Basiago claimed had made the trip was President Barack Obama, who did it in 1980 while a student at Occidental College and also working as a CIA operative.[85]

The story is wild. That is where I left it until I encountered a former government engineer at a cabin retreat in Pennsylvania. He was showing people a video he had taken with his iPhone in the lobby of 666 North Sepulveda Blvd, where Obama would have made the jump from the area of the 6th floor. The old Hughes aircraft building was renovated in 2001 as an office building. An addition along with a parking structure had been added. The building had been given an aviation look on the outside, but all the art appeared to be a 'jump room' inspired by the wacky Obama goes to Mars story. That was weird enough, but it may have been an innovative thought by the real estate company that runs the building to play off the Mars Obama story. Then the engineer dropped the bomb. He showed me a photo of a blue and white 1956 Chevy that was parked on the top level of the parking structure attached to the building. The picture shows a visible upside-down postcard in the back seat. Although the inscription cannot be seen in the photo, here is what the engineer told me was written on the postcard. It was a story about this guy talking to his girlfriend in France, saying, "*I miss you in time; if I could time travel in time and see you, it would be wonderful.*"

CHAPTER 7

FAMOUS ALIEN ABDUCTIONS

One of the big questions asked by the media and the public is, *"Why don't the aliens land on the White House lawn and announce their arrival and intentions?"* The aliens have not done this. However, even a tiny observation of the evidence will indicate that they are making themselves known. They just aren't using the White House method. There is a Roper poll done in 1991 that stated by conservative estimates, aliens might have abducted 2% of people in the United States. As of October 2014, that would indicate 6.4 million abductions. This is a lot of contact with humans. It is also essential that contact is the best chance of providing the information required to solve the UFO mystery. That is because we learn very little by watching lights fly around in the night sky, counting how many objects there are and whether they are green, red, fast, slow, big, or small. The best chance of a solution is to get inside one of these objects flying around in the sky or talk to whoever is inside.

The following are a few examples of people who have played key roles in Ufology and society and their abduction stories. Many cases have been left out, like the dozens of top musicians who appear to have been abducted, such as Ace Frehley from KISS, Cat Stevens, Sammy Hagar from Van Halen, and others. The list becomes even more important when Presidents such as Jimmy

Carter, Ronald Reagan, and Bill Clinton fit some characteristics of people who may have been abducted. The list hints at the analogy Colin Andrews made to the chessboard. It appears that the aliens may be much more in control of what is happening in society and that much of what happens is planned and not random. Andrews described it as aliens moving people on a chessboard toward some unknown conclusion.

Moody Blues Abduction

The Moody Blues is one of the greatest bands of the 20th century. The band was formed in 1964 and became known for innovating fusion with classical music. Their worldwide sales have now exceeded 50 million albums.

The date was 1967. The members of the band, Denny Laine, Ray Thomas, Mike Pinder, Clint Warwick, and Graeme Edge were driving back along the motorway from Manchester to London following a concert. The lead singer, Pinder, was sitting in the back seat with his head back, looking out the window. A bright white light flew past the car as they drove along at about 1:30 am. The band members got excited talking about a possible UFO when the white light flew past them again, this time from the other direction. Edge suggested that they stop the car and watch the object. As they stopped, the light was on the left side of the road.

Edge described what happened next. This description is a widespread story told by people who get abducted from their cars:

> As we scrambled out of the car, half scared, half fascinated, we all noted an odd stillness around us. No road traffic came in either direction, and there were none of the usual nocturnal animal rustlings or bird noises. It was quite uncanny, and we were mesmerized as if in a dream. We could see the object in the opposite field. It was shaped like a flat cigar with a low protrusion on the top, with seven dull red lights on it.

Alien Bedtime Stories

> *I'm sure of the number as I distinctly remember counting the lights at the time. The upper half of the object appeared metallic, whereas the lower half was red and pulsed from left to right."*[86] *"We all looked over the top of the car," Pinder recalled. "There was this red ball kind of thing moving across the freeway that turns into a square, like a red dice. As it approached us, it got bigger and bigger, and we were all sort of bathed in this blue light.*[87]

The last thing they recalled was they were gripped with fear and ran to the car and quickly drove off. Edge reflected that they could still see the object pulsing in the field as they looked back. When they got back to London, according to Mike Pinder, they were *"Three hours late and wondering, 'what the heck was that?'"*

The more critical part of the story came years later, as reported by crop circle researcher Colin Andrews. Following one of his lectures, he was approached by Mike Pinder and the lead guitarist, who stated they wanted to take Andrews for dinner and tell him something. Andrews told the story about how the two men remembered before they were born and how they had agreed to be band members and insert specific lyrics in their songs:

> *They were telling me of the most extraordinary experiences, UFO and ET experiences they have had as a group and individually. The reason they wrote certain numbers is very powerful and strong words and meanings such as "Lost in a Lost World." Mike told me that words were placed into the public domain from somewhere else and that he and his guitarist knew each other. They remember each other from a previous life. They remember a time when they were living in a circular atmosphere. It was in a place where they are quite easy with the concept of UFOs. It was a very plain environment in which they existed. There was this very large table, a table of knowledge where very elderly people interacted and solved problems across a*

cosmos. It was all very strange, and his guitarist said, 'Mike, tell him about that dark spot where people went when they were asked to return to Earth. That is always where they would exit.' Mike said we were both called upon to come back to planet Earth. We were called back to instill music and certain lyrics, and that's where we went. We went down this vortex, and suddenly, here we were.[88]

John Lennon Abduction

Many people are aware that John Lennon had a UFO sighting in August of 1974. That is because he spoke publicly about it. On a radio show, he told the story:

> I was standing on the roof, and I looked left. There was this thing 100 yards away. I could have hit it with a stone if I had a chance. I could even see it without my glasses, and I am really short-sighted. I was looking at it and wondering, 'What is it? What is it? Is it a helicopter? No, it is making no noise. Is it a balloon? Is it the blimp?' It had all these lights around the bottom of it flashing off and on, and you know, one part of me was saying all the time, 'It's a UFO, you know.' But some part of you doesn't want to believe it.

John managed to grab his camera and snap some pics, although, after the sighting, he called up Bob Gruen, his longtime friend and photographer who took the film John captured; the pictures did not turn out. Gruen also phoned the police for John and was told his call was the third one from the east side reporting a UFO. *The New York Daily News* told Gruen they had five calls related to a UFO. Lennon would go on to write a song called, 'No One Told Me,' in which he said, *"There are UFOs over New York,*

Alien Bedtime Stories

and I ain't too surprised." It was not released by Yoko Ono till 1983 and was the last top ten hit in the UK by Lennon.

What many are not aware of is that the sighting had many of the signs of an alien abduction. Like the Moody Blues' 1967 UFO encounters, there was an aspect called the 'Oz Effect,' where time and space seem to be altered. That part of the Lennon story was told by Lennon's then-girlfriend, who was with him for the sighting. Her version of the report included elements that made it look like a classic abduction encounter, including the sighting going on for at least 10 minutes. Lennon had called her out to the balcony, and they both watched, yelled, and screamed as the daylight object slowly flew around. *"I thought, 'Oh my God, It's a UFO.' And there's no one. Not my neighbor, where there's a staircase. They could have come up and said, 'Is anything wrong?' And I'm screaming. And not one apartment was lit up anywhere around us. It was Friday, and I remember in New City, where we lived, I kept thinking, 'Why is no one home?' Then I thought. It's summer. We are talking on Friday night. In this area, everyone is out to the Hamptons."* Later, May Pang was questioned about the idea that 'everyone' went to the Hamptons for the weekend, and she acknowledged the mysterious nature of this thought that went through her mind.

In a later article written by Rendlesham Forest UFO witness Larry Warren, he claimed that he had interviewed May Pang and that she had stated Lennon had told her that he believed he had been abducted since being a child. Still, Pang denied this in an email to me.

There is, however, another story indicating Lennon's status as an abductee. That story was told by the famous spoon-bending psychic Uri Geller, who lived in the same part of New York at the time of the sighting. He claimed that he was friends with Lennon and that they would meet at the restaurant Sherry:

> *He said he believed life existed on other planets, that it had visited us, and that maybe it was observing us right now. He took me to a quieter, darker table, lit a cigarette, and pointed its glowing tip at my face. 'You*

believe in this stuff, right?' he asked me. 'Well, you ain't f---in' gonna believe this. About six months ago, I was asleep in my bed, with Yoko, at home, in the Dakota Building. And suddenly, I wasn't asleep because there was this blazing light around the door. It was shining through the cracks, and the keyhole, like someone, was out there with searchlights or the apartment was on fire. 'That was what I thought, intruders or fire. I leaped out of bed, and Yoko wasn't awake at all, she was lying there like a stone, and I pulled open the door. There were these four people out there.' 'Fans?' I asked him. 'Well, they didn't want my f---in' autograph. They were, like, little. Bug-like. Big bug eyes and little bug mouths, and they were scuttling at me like roaches.' He broke off and stared at me. 'I've told this to two other people, right? One was Yoko, and she believed me. She says she doesn't understand it, but she knows I wouldn't lie to her. I told one other person, and she didn't believe me. She laughed it off, and then she said I must have been high. Well, I've been high, I mean right out of it, a lot of times, and I never saw anything on acid that was as weird as those f---in' bugs, man. I was straight that night. I wasn't dreaming, and I wasn't tripping. There were these creatures, like people but not like people, in my apartment.' 'What did they do to you?' Lennon swore again, 'How do you know they did anything to me, man?' 'Because they must have come for a reason.'" Geller replied.

Lennon told Geller that the creatures gave him a metal egg-like object that he had been carrying around with him, and he, for whatever reason, wanted to give the egg to Geller. For years Uri Geller has told the story of Lennon giving him the egg, but he has never attempted to analyze it. Instead, he told me that he always keeps it with him and doesn't want to test it, only to find out it might be made in Taiwan. This agreed with what one scientist, who works with scientists who tested Geller in the 1970s, has told me that Geller had even turned down non-destructive testing they had offered to do on the egg.

Then years after he told the story Steve Roseta, manager of Seattle's Beatles tribute band, 'Apple Jam' and a former magician himself, appeared to state that the Lennon egg was actually a magic prop called the Magic Egg and that it was sold all over (I did some searching and was not able to find it for sale). He appeared with an object that seemed to resemble the Lennon egg closely. When I asked Geller about this, he indicated that if the egg were a hoax, it would have been Lennon who pulled it. *"I will not read it,"* he wrote, *"I don't care about criticism; this is why I won't have the egg tested; I don't want to find out that it's made in Taiwan; I want to believe in John's words. Just imagine."*

Ace Frehley Abduction

Ace Frehley was the lead singer for KISS, which sold 200 million albums worldwide. They are in the Rock and Roll Hall of Fame. Frehley talked openly about his alien abduction in his autobiography:

> I woke up one morning and found myself lying on the ground in front of the front doorway of my home; my body was half in the house and half in the driveway. I'd woken up in a lot of strange places in my life, but this took the case. I slowly got up and went inside for a cup of coffee. As my head cleared, I could recall a strange dream about being inside a spaceship. It didn't seem that weird since I dreamt about UFOs and aliens from time to time in the past without ever giving it a second thought. This time, though, seemed different, more real, maybe because I'd never woken up in the doorway before.
>
> The more I thought about the dream, the more vivid it became in my mind's eye. After breakfast, I decided

> to go outside and look around the yard. I stumbled upon a circular impression in the grass, almost like a giant burn. It appeared to be about thirty feet in diameter, but after inspecting it more closely with a tape measure, it actually turned out to be twenty-seven feet, 27—my lucky number.
>
> Later in the shower, I checked my body for marks, some signs of having been abducted. But there was nothing strange to be found. By the next day, the impression in the grass had disappeared, and I just went about my business as if nothing had ever happened. I figured if what I had dreamt about had really taken place, there wasn't really anything I could do about it.

Tim Beckley, a music promoter, a UFO researcher, and book publisher in New York City, knew Frehley and added this story:

> Many decades ago, Ace told me his experience of having the plane he was in being followed by a UFO. In fact, I took my name 'Mr. UFO,' from Ace 'cause he couldn't remember my name, and so he used to call me Mr. UFO. I was promoting Satan the Fire Eater at the time, and both bands rehearsed at Talent Recon on Broadway. They were just putting on their makeup. We had gigs at the same hotels and clubs. Kiss made it, and I am still pushing UFO books.[89]

Sammy Hagar Abduction

Sammy Hagar is known as 'The Red Rocker.' He is an American rock vocalist, guitarist, songwriter, and musician who played with many bands and solo but became most famous as the lead singer of Van Halen.

He has told his story of having aliens connect into his brain from their ship many miles away from his home while he was sleeping. The incident occurred before he became a famous musician:

> It's been a long, long time, but back in about '68, in Fontana, California, I had this unbelievable experience. I'm a firm believer-have seen, have felt, and have been contacted three or four different times. I have received information that has been valuable in my life from those people, and they have used me. I'm gonna sound like a complete nut here, but they have used me in an experimental fashion. The easiest way to put it is that they downloaded my brain information. When I was about 19 or 20, they downloaded everything that was in my head. And I caught 'em doin' it! I woke up in the middle of the night, thinking, 'What's goin' on?' They were like, 'Oh, my God, he's waking up!' But this was all telepathic; there were no words being spoken. And as soon as I woke up, it was probably three o'clock in the morning-my whole room was so bright that I could hardly keep my eyes open. I was wide awake; I could not move, eyes open, white room, they were still disconnecting, and when they did, it just went 'bang!'
>
> Everything went back to normal, back to black. I was shaking; I almost passed out; I was sick to my stomach and almost had to throw up; it was so scary. It sent me on a course of curiosity. I bought a telescope, and I started reading UFO books, and I just got into the whole thing. And since then, there have been three or four other contacts with the same group of people. I don't know who they are, but I've narrowed them down to a people called the Nine, who are called that because they're from the Ninth Dimension. I've named my publishing company Nine Music after them.
>
> It's a crazy thing, man. But to me, anyone who thinks we're the only ones here, despite the vastness of the

entire universe, is crazy. Those people gotta be put away, not the guys having these contacts!"[90]

Cat Stevens (now Yusuf Islam) Abduction

Yusuf Islam is a British-born songwriter with over 60 million in worldwide sales. Although Yusuf Islam no longer talks about his UFO abduction experience, he did in the years he was known as Cat Stevens. He used to like to sit on the roof of the complex where he lived in London and look at the sky. This interest may have stemmed from the fact that aliens abducted him. He told of this encounter in the 1970s:

I don't know why I write them. But they try and find all kinds of hidden meanings in my songs. Longer Boats is actually about flying saucers. One night I was lying back in bed, and I saw this flying saucer shoot across the sky and stop over me. And it sucked me up into it. When it put me down, I shot up in bed. I knew it wasn't a dream; it didn't feel like a dream; it was real; I knew it was real.[91]

Stevens also talked about his use of psychedelics while on tour with another UFO experiencer Jimi Hendrix:

We got involved, and we got carried away, obviously. It was a bit of everything. Yeah, I indulged as much as I could. There was delving into substances opening the mind to new possibilities and thoughts and galaxies. Like many UFO experiencers in 1976, Stevens too had a near-death experience, "My whole life flashed in front of me, as they say, but I knew someone was there, and I said, 'Oh God, if you help me, I'll work for you.' Anyway, a wave came from behind me and gently pushed me towards the shore, and then I had all the energy I needed to get back."[92]

Alien Bedtime Stories

Stevens wrote two songs about his UFO experience, 'Frozen Steel' and 'Longer Boats.'

Kary Mullis Abduction

There are many examples of inspirations and downloads that led to many of the technologies that have been developed in the last century. One of those inventions was mitochondrial DNA analysis which is a process that allows scientists to identify a fragment of DNA genetic code and then reproduce it in enormous quantities. The inventor of the process, the polymerase chain reaction (PCR), is a man named Kary Mullis, who won the 1993 Nobel Prize in chemistry for his invention. The concept was downloaded to him as he drove up to his Northern California cottage in April 1983. He believes that his use of LSD has something to do with his creative and paranormal powers.[93]

What is less known is that Mullis is a UFO abductee, and if he follows the pattern of other abductees, this alien connection has probably been going on his entire life. Most abductees have an awakening experience where they suddenly realize they have an alien contact, and for Mullis, this occurred during the summer of 1985.

The event happened at his cottage. Mullis arrived about midnight after a three-hour drive. He dropped off the groceries he had bought, grabbed a flashlight, and headed for the outhouse 50 feet from the cottage. But, before he could get there, he encountered an incredible sight. Quoting from his 1998 book, *Dancing Naked in the Mine Field,* Mullis wrote:

> At the far end of the path, under a fir tree, there was something glowing. I pointed my flashlight at it anyhow. It only made it whiter where the beam landed. It seemed to be a raccoon. I wasn't frightened. Later, I wondered if it could have been a hologram projected from God knows where. The raccoon spoke, 'Good

> evening, doctor,' it said. I said something back; I don't remember what, probably, 'Hello.' The next thing I remember, it was early in the morning. I was walking along a road uphill from my house.

It was now six hours later. The morning had arrived, and Mullis's flashlight was gone; the groceries were still where he had placed them, and where the event had occurred became a place of dread. Mullis grabbed his gun and went looking for the raccoon. He was hoping he would find him, maybe in the bathroom. He found nothing. A year later, he shot up the woods where the raccoon had been as a therapy that seemed to help.

Two others have had experiences at the cottage. Mullis's daughter had three hours missing time in the same area around the cabin, and she suggested to her dad the reading of *Communion*, a book by Whitley Strieber about his years of UFO abduction experience.

Then on the night of the announcement of his Nobel Prize in 1993, there was a party at the cottage, and one of the men who attended met the raccoon on his visit to the outhouse. This time, however, the raccoon turned into a man. The terrified man left, returning the next night to the party that was still going on, only to encounter the man from the night before arriving in a car. Mullis described the man as his neighbor and had no other explanation for how he came to be a part of the raccoon story. Mullis remains the only Nobel Prize winner to declare an alien abduction experience openly, *"You just have to trust me on this,"* Mullis told one reporter. *"I can't make the raccoon glow again. There are just some things no one has figured out how to get a handle on."*

Colin Andrews Abduction

Colin Andrews is a British electrical engineer who has always been considered the foremost expert on crop circles. He is the one who coined the term after seeing it in the early eighties. He has the most extensive catalog of crop circle events and has been at it longer than anyone. The one part of his investigation he kept quiet about is that he had experienced an alien abduction as a child in 1951.

The Andrews disclosure in 2009 seems to be part of a growing movement of experiencers coming out and talking about the fact they are experiencers. The most prominent example is the new *Foundation for Research into Extraterrestrial Encounters*, which has some very well-known names on its board of advisors. For example, Rey Hernandez, who set it up, made public that all but two of his board of 21 are themselves experiencers.

Andrews did not know he was an experiencer until 1997, when Dr. James Harder regressed him. Once he discovered it, he made the decision not to discuss it. This was coming out by prominent UFO researchers, something that the government may have known all along. As it appears, they have some idea of who the experiencers are and don't really hide the fact that they are watching them. The reason for this could be that the experiencers are being monitored closely to see what they are being told and taught by the aliens. Examples of surveillance can be seen in major UFO abduction cases such as Chris Bledsoe, Melinda Leslie, and Betty Andreasson. Some experiencers even report being re-abducted by what appears to be some military. They are questioned about what the aliens told them, and there seems to be testing the abductees' psychic abilities.

In Andrews's case, he received a message while showering one day as he was getting ready to leave for Washington, D.C, to deliver a lecture on the U.K. government's involvement. Consequently, no one knew that he was about to announce the secret that aliens had abducted him. Andrews told the story in an interview with podcast host Mike Clelland:

> In my head came a very clear voice, and it said, 'You must go public with this now.' And I knew exactly what it meant. It didn't say, 'with what happened to you when you were five' or 'what happened when you fell down the steps.' It just said, 'You must go public with this now.' Immediately, with what I will call that instruction or suggestion, I knew exactly what it meant. That's the weird thing about it. I started thinking, and I thought, 'Oh my gosh.' My stomach was over because I thought, 'I can't do it. I don't think I can do this because I am about to blow the entire subject out of the water.' If I come forward like some kind of complete crazy after all these years, it will be the end of it. But I kept getting encouraged, 'No, No, timing is everything. You must do this now.'
>
> This is how it went. I looked at the notes. I came down to my computer and fired it up. I got my medical notes from when I was five, and I thought, 'No, it does feel right. Suddenly it does feel right.' I went down to Washington, D.C., and before my presentation, I was approached by a man. He looked like a normal human being like you and me, and in this audience of a large number of people, this man stepped in front of me. He was looking beyond my eyes and into my head. It was that kind of feeling. He was a knowing look that he gave me, and he said, 'You know that you have to do this now. It is time for us all to put forward our stories so we can move forward.' It was like, WOW. I looked at him, and I just nodded. I didn't say a word back. He knew that I had gotten that message. He knew that I was there and was going to do it. It was very bizarre. It was very, very bizarre, and I did it.[94]

The man disappeared and was never seen again. Colin made the same announcement at a conference in 2011 and stated that he had opened a tap for others to make emotional disclosures that they, too, were experiencers. These included Dr. Steven Greer, the Director of the CSETI group, and Dr. Lynne Kitei, the principal investigator in the March 1997 Phoenix lights UFO sighting seen by thousands in Phoenix, Arizona.

Robert Salas Abduction

Robert Salas was involved in one of the biggest cases in UFO history, and the idea that there was an abduction component to the sighting came as a shock to many researchers. The incident happened in 1967, and Salas did not announce that he was an abductee till 2013.

The case that Salas became famous over was the famous Malmstrom Air Force Base, where UFOs took 10 nuclear missiles offline that Salas was controlling. When the missile shutdown occurred, Salas did not know he was an abductee. His awakening experience occurred at his Manhattan Beach, California home in 1985. He witnessed an unusual, glowing, blue-shaded light emanating from the living room while in bed. It was a unique shade of blue and was glowing. He woke up his wife and showed her the light. He decided to get up and investigate but found his wife now unconscious, and himself paralyzed. *"I remember fighting very hard to get my mobility back,"* he recalled. *"I couldn't move anything. I couldn't move my arms, my legs. I fought and fought. I fought because I had two small kids in the house and, of course, my wife."* The next thing he knew, there was a hooded figure with no face in the room, and he was being floated out through the locked bedroom window and onboard a craft.

Salas used three hypnotherapists to help uncover what had happened after recalling while working in his yard that he had been in space. Salas's abduction revelation makes the Malmstrom incident much more critical, more planned, and less random. The pattern is that abductees have been taken their whole life; therefore, Salas was almost like an alien mole working at the site during the event. It leads to the question of how many other people the aliens have in critical positions who do not know they are abductees but will be in the right place at the right time for events that the aliens are planning.

Consider a story told by Yvonne Smith, one of the hypnotherapists who worked with Salas to recover his experience. Smith has written a book called *Coronado*, about the abduction of a dozen people from a UFO conference at the Coronado Hotel in San Diego in 1994, on the same weekend that then-President Bill Clinton was speaking there. In July 2013, Smith was talking to a source about an unrelated topic who reported to her that *"Two of the President's men were missing."*

She asked, *"For what, President?"* The answer came back, *"Clinton."* Smith asked, *"where?"* and got back the answer, *"San Diego."* Now that the source was referring to the Coronado abduction incident, she asked, *"Was Clinton taken with the two secret servicemen."* The source replied, *"Yes."* If Presidents of the United States are being taken and helping out the aliens, the full extent of the alien plan cannot even be estimated. We may be nothing more than moviegoers eating popcorn as a movie we have no control over plays on the screen in front of us.

Jan Harzan Abduction

The year was 1964. Jan Harzan, the present International Director of the Mutual UFO Network, was 9 or 10 years old. It would turn out to be a 'life-changing' UFO event that would lead Harzan to become an engineer and develop a deep interest in UFOs and their propulsion system. He now heads up the most prominent UFO investigation organization in the world.

He recalled that his father bought men's magazines (True and Argosy), and he and his younger brother read the UFO articles in the magazines. One article in *Argosy* was written by Major Donald Keyhoe, the head of the most significant UFO organization at the time, NICAP. The article inspired the brothers to draw up their plans to build a 30-foot-wide flying saucer that would use three electromagnetic-style engines. At about the same time, the two boys were at the drugstore with their mother when they spotted a magazine called Flying Saucer Review on the rack. In the magazine, an article said flying saucers are seen around nuclear installations, nuclear power plants, and areas where they are doing anti-gravity research. Jan looked at his brother and said, *"Wow, we are doing anti-gravity research. Maybe one of these things will come and visit us."*

About a month later, Jan was in his bedroom. It was 6:30, Saturday morning, when his brother came in and woke him up, claiming that someone was trying to get through the window into his bedroom. Jan asked if his brother had seen who it was, and the brother said no. They both went to investigate. They could see nothing out the window, so Jan suggested they go into the backyard to see if there was anything there. As they headed down the hall to go out, the brother saw something move behind the drapes of the picture windows, but Jan was walking backward and didn't see it in time. His brother stated that as Jan was looking, the figure had moved back from the window. It was in April, and the sun was already up. When they arrived in the backyard, they didn't see anything, but as they turned back into the house, they suddenly noticed a flying saucer 10 feet in the air and thirty feet away. It was orange with blue landing gear and black suction cups on the landing gear. It was making a humming noise. Jan notified his brother that he was going into the house to get a camera and that he would be right back. However, when he went to the garage door, he realized they had locked themselves out. Jan began to bang loudly on the door, and finally, his older brother came to the door and let him in. He asked what was going on, but Jan had no time to explain. He ran, got the camera, and raced outside to record the event. When he arrived, however, the craft was gone, and his brother was standing up on top of the slide attached to the swing set. He told Jan that the craft had just risen and had flown off into the west. If that is all that happened, then we are left with a close encounter that may have had some conscious connection to two boys who were fascinated by UFOs and wanted an encounter.

There is more to the story; it would come years later when Jan and his brother were reminiscing about the morning when a saucer visited them. Jan's brother stated that when the two had gone into the house after the event, the brother who had let them in was now watching TV. More importantly, the cartoons he watched did not air until 8:00 am Saturday morning, meaning there was missing time. Jan stated that he had seen the large clock in the kitchen, which had stated 6:30, and now their return from their short trip to the backyard was at least 90 minutes later. Jan Harzan knows what that means. It means that there was an abduction and that much of the event, as he recalls, was just a screen memory. He, however, thinks that only his brother was taken, although he has no evidence to back this up.

If Jan Harzan was abducted, the fact that he is the International Director becomes very important. It would mean that he is a sleeper agent placed into society to be activated later. This is what many experiencers report. They state that they have some sort of role or mission, but they don't know what it is. When they ask the aliens, the aliens refuse to tell them, saying, *"When the time is right, you will know exactly what to do.*

CHAPTER 8

WHERE THE STORY BEGINS AND ENDS

Charlie Red Star and Nuclear Weapons

In 1975, the town of Carman, Manitoba, Canada, was visited almost nightly by a UFO that came to be known as Charlie Red Star. The sightings began in February and ended late in the year. Charlie was gone and never came back. It was as if the CIA had put drugs in the water in February and then taken them out at the end of the year.

The question of 'why are they here?' was put to Bob Diemert. Diemert owned the airport in Carman and had more sightings (150 by his estimate in 1975 and none since) than anyone during the flap. He stated that the flap had occurred because of the nuclear missile silos in North Dakota. He said that he and others had sat up in the Pembina Hills west of town and could see the UFOs coming from the States flying north down into the valley towards Carman. He also stated that he had talked to a USAF pilot at a bar on the US side of the border and that this pilot had told him of an incident during the flap where fighter jets were given orders to ram a UFO over one of the silos.

There are indeed nuclear missiles just over the border. There were so many in 1975 that it was stated that if North Dakota had been a country, it would have been a nuclear superpower. The silos contain the United States Air Force Global Strike Command LGM-

30 Minuteman land-based intercontinental ballistic missiles (ICBMs). The letter 'L' in 'LGM' indicates that the missile is silo-launched. The 'G' means that it is designed to attack ground targets. The 'M' suggests that it is a guided missile. Each missile carries up to three nuclear warheads, with a yield of 300 to 500 kilotons. The Minuteman was the first MIRV-capable missile.

What was significant about 1975 is that just 80 miles south of Carman on the United States side, the Air Force had installed, The Stanley R. Mickelsen Safeguard complex in Nekoma, North Dakota, to shoot down incoming Soviets missiles directed at the Minuteman 3 missiles. It had reinforced underground launchers for thirty Spartan (5MT) and sixteen Sprint (1MT) nuclear-tipped missiles (an additional fifty or so Sprint missiles were deployed at four remote launch sites). The complex also included a large radar unit to detect incoming soviet missiles. The complex was the only anti-ballistic missile unit to operate in the United States. It began installing missiles early in 1975, became operational in April 1975, just as the Carman sightings were starting to heat up, and was deactivated in November 1975, six months later, just as the sighting in Carman was slowing down.

Another UFO tie into nuclear weapons is the sightings/abductions around missile silos. In 1975 (when abductions were very rare and North Dakota sightings were rarely recorded as there were no researchers), a prominent UFO abduction received a lot of publicity. It involved Sandy Larsen and her daughter near the M-21 and M-24 missile silos outside of Buffalo, North Dakota.

Then there was the UFO sighting at the Karlsruhe B-10 missile silo, which involved Kelly Gessner and two of her friends. There were many UFO sightings at this silo, but Kelly was the only one on the record. If they were at this silo, it would be safe to assume that many of the silos in North Dakota also got visits. Kelly spent several years in Karlsruhe growing up and is an experiencer. As a young child in town, she remembers a specific incident when a large craft appeared suddenly above her as she stood in her driveway practicing hitting a baseball. She was left with alien flashbacks and some paranormal talents to do things like see the future. Her experience at the missile silo occurred in 1987. She and two of her friends had gone to the silos to get the yellow light to go on. This was a warning light on top of a tall white pole inside the fence. The idea was to throw stones at the fence until the light went off and then *"run like hell."*

On the day in question, they never made it to the fence. They were still a couple of hundred yards south along the road when a bright light suddenly came up from the silo. It was spinning as it rose 25 feet above the silo. At this point, one of the girls became scared and started to run back to town. I asked Kelly where exactly the UFO came out of the ground. She replied that it was directly over the metal lid. This, unknown to her, is where the missile is stored. The object remained, hovering and spinning over the rocket, and then shot off into the sky.

UFOs have often been documented over atomic weapons facilities in the US and nuclear test sites, from the pacific to the outback of Australia, even over atomic disasters such as Chornobyl and, more recently, Fukushima. But, unfortunately, no one is left in the area now to snap any more photographs. Here though, we have a little-known UFO photograph taken by a US marine in Nagasaki, Japan, in 1945, only weeks after the bomb was dropped there.

Grant Cameron

Figure 13 These photos were taken at the actual location of Kelly Gessner's sighting

Alien Bedtime Stories

Figure 14 A UFO hovering above Nagasaki Bay, Japan, 1945. Ed Rogers took this photo, then a 19-year-old Marine Corps combat soldier whose regiment entered Nagasaki Bay 3-4 weeks after the atomic blast and was stationed there for nine months.

Mr. Rogers photographed all over the bombed city during this period but never noticed this craft in the sky while shooting this shot until 50 years later.

The Doubting Thomas Story

I will end the tales with one of my own. This is a tale of one of my most spectacular sightings where I got to play the disciple, Thomas. As most people know, Thomas was the disciple of Jesus who, after Jesus was crucified, had doubts about the stories that Jesus had resurrected. He told the other disciples, *"Unless I see the nail marks in his hands and put my finger where the nails were, and put my hand into his side, I will not believe."*

My chance to touch came in April of 1976 in Sperling, Manitoba. This town is 11 miles east of Carman, Manitoba, where the UFO Charlie Red Star had been seen night after night in 1975. My friend Jim was with me. He had his photographic equipment, and we were trying to get a photograph. We were standing on a road called the dead man's corner that curved around the town. It was dusk which, for some reason, was a good time for sightings. We waited and waited, and nothing happened. Now it was dark, and nothing was flying around. There was, however, 'something' on the ground, and there were a lot of them. They looked like farmyard lights, but they were not the standard white. They were not just orange-like but as orange as an orange.

I suggested we drive away from the town and investigate since we had nothing else to do. We drove east, crossing over the north/south mile roads. (In the Manitoba countryside, gravel roads run north/south and east-west every mile, making a checkerboard appearance from a plane.) On the third mile road east, we looked down the north/south mile road towards the United States border, and there, sitting in the middle of the road, was an orange ball. It is impossible to determine the size or distance at night, but it appeared to be maybe a few feet across and a half-mile down the road. We drove the half-mile, and the object was still there. It still seemed the same distance and size, so we went another half mile to the first east/west road. On the right side of the road was Sperling. Something was burning in what we thought might be the dump. The light was still in front of us. It was the same size and the same distance.

We continued south down the road, crossing the one-mile road after another. Once we passed the third-mile highway, there were no longer any houses. The snow had melted and covered the flat fields on each side of the road. Although the water was probably only inches deep, it looked like a road running through the middle of a lake. Above the water were many of these orange lights; they appeared as one on top of the other. After a few minutes, we realized the bottom was just a reflection of the light over the water. The lights we were following remained precisely in the middle of the road and at the same distance away. Eight miles south of where we had turned off, we arrived at an elevated wooden bridge that passed over a channel that appeared to be there to drain water from the fields.

Now we had a frame of reference, and we could see the object was on the bridge. It was a couple of feet in diameter, but the plasma surface was so bright I could not determine an exact shape. However, when we got on the bridge, it was gone.

Figuring it had to have turned off its light and was now under the bridge, we tried to look under the bridge with our flashlight. The water was so high we were unsuccessful in getting to a place to look underneath the bridge. We continued south and, about one-quarter of a mile away, realized that the object was back at the bridge. It was now behind us. We turned the car around and drove north back onto the bridge to find the light gone again. Another fruitless search under the bridge took place. We started north down the road to where the night had begun, and a quarter-mile away, I looked back to see the light on the bridge again. I told my friend that we should walk instead of driving the car. Maybe we could sneak up on it. He agreed.

With the car now facing north, we started at the bridge. I had an 8mm camera, and my friend held the binoculars. Knowing that the object could take off at any moment, I took seven steps and shot three seconds of film. I took seven more steps and again took three seconds of film. The object had taken off twice, and I was determined to record as much as possible before it disappeared. Again, I took seven steps and three seconds of film. We were getting closer and closer as the tension built. The object did not move. As we closed in, I kept asking Matt what he could see in the binoculars. Not until we were 150 feet away did he say anything, *"I think I see a shape,"* he said.

"What does it look like?" I asked. There was no response. In fact, to this day, Matt has never told me what he saw, and we got a lot closer than 150 feet.

The next thing we knew, we were right up to the bridge, and the object was still there, only maybe 50-75 feet away. I took another three seconds of film. It was an eerie sight. The object appeared round and exceptionally bright, about two feet in diameter, and as orange as an orange. The light was so intense it might have been another shape. There were no edges visible that I could see. I assumed the object was inside the bright glowing haze. It was sitting on the right side of the bridge, only inches from the wooden railings of the bridge. My mind could only think of one thing, *"Why was this extremely bright object not lighting up the side of the bridge inches away?"* It was so bright it should have been lighting up everything for 100 yards. Yet the object was just casting a soft glow of light on the side of the bridge, not much more than a couple of candles. It was for this reason I always referred to the light from then on as a *"dead light."* It became a distinguishing mark of the ground lights (many abductees have described this bizarre quality of light).

I was at the point of decision. I was close enough to make a run for it. I only had to run up the approach to the bridge and a couple of feet to the light. I mentally made plans to run at it and jump on it. I was like the doubting Thomas of the Bible. I knew I might get burned, but I had to touch it. I whispered my plan to my friend. He had been looking around with the binoculars. When I told him I would make a run for it, he said, *"It looks like something is coming down the road."* I turned and saw what appeared to be a car coming from the north. I exchanged my camera for the binoculars and looked north toward the car. What I saw amazed me. It looked like the sun was rising over the car in the north. There was one sitting right on top of the vehicle. It appeared as a half-circle on top of the hood and as wide as the car. Down the sides of the vehicle, right to the ground was a diffuse orange light that looked a bit like smoke, except it did not dissipate like smoke. It looked like a small fire inside the car caused by the glowing light down the sides.

I said, *"There's one sitting right on top of the car!"* And I started to run towards the car. My friend joined me. I am sure I had not taken more than six steps when I realized what had happened. I stopped and looked back at the bridge. Sure enough, the orange ball was gone. We had been had. Halfway back to the car, I stopped and shot some footage. I looked through the binoculars again, and now it looked like the car was on fire. The object had moved and now appeared to be sitting on the vehicle's hood. You could see it through the back and front windows. The inside of the car was lit up. The same orange smoky light was hanging down the sides of the vehicle. Realizing that the one at the bridge was gone, we continued our run to the car. By the time we got there, the orange ball had floated in front of the car and disappeared. We suspected that it had gone into the water.

When I arrived back, I had no idea what to do, so I put my hand on the car. I wanted to see if it was hot. There was nothing noticeable. I took out my flashlight and searched the car but saw nothing out of the ordinary. Our hearts were pounding both from the run and the bizarre events occurring one after another. My friend said very little. He was looking in the car. After a couple of minutes of this, I looked back down the road to the bridge, and low and behold; there was the orange ball sitting at the bridge again. I said, *"It's back at the bridge. Let's go back."* My friend stated he had no intention of going back. I insisted, as I was sure I could get even closer. My friend resisted saying that he wanted to go home. As it was his car, that's what we did. The only comment he made during this entire period of frenzy was, *"How did he know we had left the car?"*

Although my friend was rattled by what had occurred, he was back showing another person the following night, and they spent a long time chasing the object down the road without success. We saw these 'ground lights' many times after this, but this was the first and last time we got close. A man who had worked with Wilbert Smith (who headed up the UFO investigation for the Canadian government) told me they were called monitors and were around a lot in the 1950s. We took many photos, watched them a lot, and tried to get close. They, however, were always one step ahead, so eventually, I stopped taking tours of people out to see them.

Two Wonderful Tales of Death from UFO Skeptics

Prior to my UFO career, I spent a term at university studying dying patients in hospitals. I approached the chaplains at the various hospitals who are summoned when a patient is close to death. At the moment of death, all pretenses seem to end, and what is said and seen can be taken to the bank. The questions I asked were to see if there was any truth to the many tales that I had often heard surrounding death, such as:

Were there any miracles?
Did anyone get up from their deathbed and walk away cured?
Did the dying patients get visits from dead relatives?
Did family members and hospital staff see something leave the body at death?
Did anyone ever predict when they were going to die?
Were there any near-death experiences reported?
Is there any other weird stuff that happens?

It is important to note that this was in the mid-1970s when near-death experiences first appeared in literature, just after the invention of Cardiopulmonary resuscitation (CPR) techniques. They were still rarely discussed, and there was a lot of skepticism about their nature.

When I had my first close-up UFO experience, I fell down the UFO rabbit hole and began 40 years of work into the nature and origin of the UFO I had seen. I, however, kept the near-death studies I had done in the back of my mind. As I begin the 5th decade of work, I can see that the two are connected. Most of the work I do now is with experiencers who claim to have been inside the UFO or have interacted with those beings behind the UFO. I have seen that there is a bizarre coincidence in that many UFO experiencers have, for some reason, had near-death experiences. This correlation is becoming known, and groups like the Foundation for Research into Extraterrestrial Experiences (FREE) are doing a major study examining this connection.

This leads to my final story, which deals with two prominent UFO skeptics and how they dealt with bizarre death phenomena like I was looking at in the 1970s. Their encounters and how they reacted to them show that there is a valid phenomenon to study and that all paranormal phenomena may be connected.

The first of these skeptics is Michael Shermer, president of the Skeptic Society, publisher of Skeptic Magazine, and author of books such as, *Why People Believe Weird Things* and *The Believing Brain*. Shermer is skeptical about UFOs believing that the stories are anecdotal, there is no evidence, and usually, only believers have such things occur to them.

He repeated the same faith-based skeptical argument about life after death when interviewed by producer Paul Davids for his documentary, *The Life After Death Project,* which dealt with a whole series of seemingly non-local events after the death of atheist Forrest J Ackerman of *Famous Monsters of Filmland* magazine. Ackerman had stated before his death that he did not believe there was an afterlife, but he would "drop a line" to Davids if he turned out to be wrong. The documentary addresses 25 paranormal anomalies and the scientific work to validate the evidence.

Had Shermer known he was about to experience something just as bizarre and unexplainable; he might have been less skeptical in his comments about the Ackerman ghostly weirdness. But instead, he wrote about his incident in his *Scientific American* column.[95] It was an experience that Shermer said, *"I have to admit, it rocked me back on my heels and shook my skepticism to its core as well."*

Shermer told the story of his June 2014 wedding to Jennifer, his girlfriend from Germany who had recently moved all her possessions to the United States, including a 1978 Philips transistor radio given to her by her grandfather, who was now dead. The radio was not working, and Shermer unsuccessfully tried to fix it. Finally, he gave up and threw it on the back of a desk in the bedroom.

Three months later, Shermer and Jennifer took their vows in the house in front of the family. Jennifer had expressed that she wished her grandfather were there to give her away and wanted to tell Shermer something privately. As they went to the back of the house to talk, they could hear music playing in the bedroom. They searched every possible music source until they found the transistor radio playing. According to Shermer's account, Jennifer pulled out her grandfather's transistor radio, out of which a romantic love song wafted. *"We sat in stunned silence for minutes,"* Shermer claimed. *"My grandfather is here with us,"* Jennifer said tearfully. *"I'm not alone."* According to Shermer's daughter Devin, the music began to play just as the ceremony started. Shermer and his new wife kept the radio in the bedroom and fell asleep to the sound of classical music. It continued to play until the next day when it stopped forever.

At the end of the article, Shermer tried to recover himself as a materialistic skeptic with a rational explanation for what had occurred and why it didn't mean anything. *"In any case,"* he wrote, *"such anecdotes do not constitute scientific evidence that the dead survives or that they can communicate with us via electronic equipment."* It was, however, too late. By that point in the article, he had securely super-glued a tinfoil hat to his head.

The fallout from his personal 'Road to Damascus' experience began immediately. One comment to the article complained, *"Michael Shermer should get back to his senses and not claim it shook his 'skeptical core.' The title is just too much to swallow for a skeptical person of the paranormal. I do not buy this story."* One prominent internet site headlined the story, *"Has Michael Shermer Seen the Light?"* Shermer came under attack, and his role as the top skeptic was questioned. In the International Skeptics Forum, the knives were out with questions like, *"Is Michael Shermer becoming a believer?"*[96] *"This is going to come back to bite him in the ass."* one reader wrote. Another wrote about the wedding day's emotion throwing him off, *"Shermer's judgments are clouded by his emotions here."* A third discouraged skeptic wrote, *"What will happen with Skeptic Magazine? Will it become a woo magazine now?"* In other forums and replies to *Scientific American,* where the article ran, skeptics questioned why Shermer would even bring it up. People questioned Shermer's ability to fix radios or hear a radio that may have been playing from the day it was shipped.

I questioned readers at the *UFO Updates* Facebook Page where most of the faithful UFO skeptics hang out, asking if the high priest of all skeptics, Randi, would move to have Shermer removed as the editor of Skeptic magazine. There was a stunning silence. I referenced the article in case they had not read it and asked for comments. Again, there was absolute silence.

The adverse reaction to the Shermer ghost story highlights why most people don't report UFO sightings. They fear the ridicule and possible backlash to their career. I think if Shermer had to do it over again, he would never have told the story.

Another skeptic who experienced a strange death experience was Nobel Prize-winning physicist Richard Feynman. He, like Shermer, was a disbeliever in flying saucers, saying, *"I don't believe there are flying saucers...from my knowledge of the world, I think that it is much more likely that the reports of flying saucers are the result of the known irrational characteristics of terrestrial intelligence rather than in the unknown rational characteristics of extraterrestrial intelligence."*[97]

The Feynman event occurred in 1945 as he worked on the atomic bomb in Las Alamos. His high school sweetheart, Arline, was diagnosed in 1943 with terminal tuberculosis and only had a few years left to live. Against even his mother's advice, Feynman still married her, and she resided in a care facility their entire marriage. When the call came that she was near death in June 1945, Feynman raced to her bedside, where she took her last breath. The nurse announced that she had died. At this point, he discovered that the clock by the bed had stopped at 9:21, the exact moment of her death.

This is often reported in deaths. For example, in the Forrest Ackerman case that Paul Davids asked about Shermer, Ackerman appeared in a famous painting of himself, four years before his death, in front of a clock that read 12:58. When he died in 2008, the moment of death was 12:58, as in the painting.

The skeptical materialist Feynman, like Shermer, later publicly rationalized an explanation to illuminate the possible spiritual implication of the stopped clock. He justified that the nurse must have picked up the fragile clock to obtain the time of death, which must have stopped the clock. Feynman failed to state whether he had tried to fix the clock to prove his theory. It would seem likely that he would, as he said he had set the clock many times. He loved to fix things and talked to his wife in a letter shortly before her death about fixing a watch for her. If he did unsuccessfully try and get the clock going after his wife's death, he kept it a closely guarded secret. He also said nothing about the clock when he returned to Los Alamos. When asked what happened, he replied, *"She's dead. And how's the program going?"*

Like Shermer, however, it appears that the clock incident bothered Feynman. After the war, he told an Army psychiatrist that he talked to his dead wife from time to time. In addition, in complete opposition to his public stance on life after death, the avowed atheist Feynman wrote a letter to his dead wife 16 months after she died. The letter remained a secret until Feynman passed away in 1987. His daughter released his notes in a book called, *Perfectly Reasonable Deviations from the Beaten Track: The Letters of Richard P. Feynman*. According to his daughter, Michelle, the letter was a touching love letter taken out and read many times by her father. Michelle wrote in the preface to the letter, *"This letter is well worn, much more so than others, and it appears as though he reread it often."*[98]

Alien Bedtime Stories

October 17, 1946
D'Arline,
I adore you, sweetheart. I know how much you like to hear that, but I don't only write it because you like it; I write it because it makes me warm all over inside to write it to you. It is such a terribly long time since I last wrote to you, almost two years, but I know you'll excuse me because you understand how I am, stubborn and realistic, and I thought there was no sense in writing. But now I know, my darling wife, that it is right to do what I have delayed doing and that I have done so much in the past. I want to tell you I love you. I want to love you. I always will love you.

I find it hard to understand in my mind what it means to love you after you are dead, but I still want to comfort and take care of you, and I want you to love me and care for me. I want to have problems to discuss with you; I want to do little projects with you. I never thought until just now that we could do that. What should we do? We started to learn to make clothes together or learn Chinese or to get a movie projector. Can't I do something now? No. I am alone without you, and you were the 'idea-woman' and general instigator of all our wild adventures.

When you were sick, you worried because you could not give me something that you wanted and thought I needed. You needn't worry. Just as I told you then, there was no real need because I loved you in so many ways so much. And now it is clearly even truer. You can give me nothing now, yet I love you so that you stand in my way of loving anyone else, but I want you to stand there. You, dead, are so much better than anyone else alive.

I know you will assure me that I am foolish and that you want me to have full happiness and don't want to be in my way. I'll bet you are surprised that I don't even have a girlfriend (except you, sweetheart) after two years. But you can't help it, darling, nor can I. I don't understand it, for I have met many girls and very nice ones and I don't want to remain alone, but in two or three meetings they all seem ashes. You only are left to me. You are real.

My darling wife, I do adore you. I love my wife. My wife is dead.

Grant Cameron

Rich
P.S. Please excuse my not mailing this; I don't know your new address.

The flying saucer skepticism might have sounds fine in 1964 when Feynman gave the lecture at Cornell University, but today things have changed.

In 2021, the American government admitted that there are unknown like flying saucers in American airspace, and not "irrational characteristics of terrestrial intelligence."

Instead of being smart as many claimed Feynman was, he will go down in history like Max Planck's University advisor, who told him in 1874, to stay out of physics as everything had been discovered and there would be nothing to so.

Like many scientists Feynman liked to play the skeptic as it made him look smart, and he did play the skeptic role again when his first wife died, and he was faced with another paranormal aspect of reality that he had a great deal of cognitive dissonance about.

ENDNOTES

[1] Thomas Carey and Donald Schmitt, '*Witness to Roswell: Unmasking the Government's Biggest Cover-Up,*' Career Press 2009, page 161

[2] Ibid page 151.

[3] http://www.presidentialufo.com/old_site/dr_eric_walker.htm

[4] Jesse Marcel's Testimony at the Citizen's Hearing http://www.youtube.com/watch?v=1atXbTQ-dM0

[5] http://yourlisten.com/channel/content/131384/Goldwater_to_Inman_on_UFOs

[6] John C. Ross, 'Canada Hunts for Saucers: Dozens of flying saucer reports have resulted in the creation of a Canadian flying saucer observatory' Fate1954, http://www.presidentialufo.com/old_site/flying_saucer_observatory.htm

[7] Wilbert Smith, 'The Day Magnet Detected a Flying Saucer' http://www.presidentialufo.com/wilbert-smith-articles/123-the-day-project-magnet-detected-a-flying-saucer

[8] Letter- Wilbert Smith to Howard Menger, March 28, 1957

[9] http://ufoupdateslist.com/2002/mar/m28-019.shtml

[10] Dr. Omond Solandt, then the head of the Canadian Defense Research Board has on many occasions denied that this Smith - Bush relationship occurred. In a June 8, 1991 interview with Dr. Henry Victorian Solandt said, *"Not that they (U.S.) were doing any work on it. They were watching it very closely as far as I knew...I got my information from Van Bush. At that time, I used to see him a couple times during the year, and that was a subject that we sometimes discussed, but we never did any joint work on it."*

[11] Schwarz, Berthold, '*UFO Dynamics - Book 2*' Carlstadt, New Jersey: Rainbow Books, 1983 p.535.

[12] Ibid. P. 534

[13] From the transcript of an interview between Wilbert Smith and Dr. Robert Sarbacher, September 15, 1950. Found in Wilbert Smith's personal files.

[14] Email "The Observer < pidivi@dsuper.net> to Grant Cameron"

[15] The Observer "Roswell is Factual" alt. Alien Visitors 06/18/1997

[16] Another thing that indicates the grey was foreign to Smith and everyone else in the 1950s was the reaction of Wilbert Smith's metallurgist to Dr. Robert Sarbacher's description of the alien bodies as *"insect like."* When this Sarbacher/Steinman letter became public I sent it to the metallurgist for comment. He phoned days later absolutely shocked at the insect description. He told me that the Smith group had discussed the aliens many times and that this type of alien was never brought up.

[17] Pope, Nick, *'The Uninvited'*

[18] Jacobs, David, *'The UFO Controversy in America'* Indiana University Press 1975 p. 113.

[19] Randall Fitzgerald, 'Messages: The Case History of a Contactee' Second Look, vol. 1 no. 12, Oct 1979, pp.12-18, 28-29

[20] Ibid page 16.

[21] Ibid page 15.

[22] There is some controversy as to who was actually asking the questions or if both were involved. It was always assumed based on the memo that Lundahl was asking the questions but when confronted years later he played the skeptic stating that Neasham was the believer and he was just a skeptical onlooker.

[23] John Alexander 'The New Mental Battlefield: Beam me Up Scotty' Military Review, Volume 15, December 1980, No 12

[24] http://www.bibliotecapleyades.net/sociopolitica/sociopol_greer09.htm

[25] John Alexander Interview with Nancy Du Tertre June 15, 2013 http://hotleadscoldcases.podomatic.com/

[26] June 13, 2013, Nancy Du Tertre Interview with John Alexander

[27] http://www.colinandrews.net/Dedication-MumDadTheWhiteLightEnham.html

[28] http://www.scoop.co.nz/stories/HL0209/S00126.htm

[29] http://ieti.org/tough/articles/intro.htm

[30] Does Consciousness Create Reality? The Double Slit Experiment, http://www.collective-evolution.com/2012/11/23/does-consciousness-create-reality-the-double-slit-experiment/

[31] Ore on Morphogenetic Fields, http://www.co-intelligence.org/P-moreonmorphgnicflds.html

[32] The Holographic Universe and You: Part 1, http://jprytz.blogspot.ca/2011/11/holographic-universe-and-you-part-one.html

[33] Rat Brain Flies Plane, http://www.youtube.com/watch?v=pcAyd6LokWo

[34] Joan D'Arc, 'Phenomenal World: Remote Viewing, Astral Travel, Apparitions.' Book Three, 2000, Page 109.

[36] Thierry Bardini, 'Bootstrapping: Douglas Engelbart, Coevolution, and the Origin of Personal Computing,' Stanford University Press, 2000, p. 12.

[37] The Engelbart Institute Website, http://dougengelbart.org/events/1968-demo-highlights.html

[38] Inventions Inspired by Inventors Who Used LSD, Drug Forums, http://www.drugsforum.com/forum/showthread.php?t=206788#ixzz37Z1WuJHK

[39] Ryan Grim, 'This Is Your Country on Drugs: The Secret History of Getting High in America,' p. 228.

[40] Larry Page's University of Michigan Commencement Address May 2009, http://googlepress.blogspot.ca/2009/05/larry-pages-university-of-michigan.html

[41] http://en.wikipedia.org/wiki/ARPANET

[42] http://en.wikipedia.org/wiki/Intergalactic_Computer_Network

[43] http://groups.csail.mit.edu/medg/people/psz/Licklider.html

[44] http://outofthisworldx.wordpress.com/2013/03/07/area-51-space-technology-david-adair-reveals-advanced-symbiotic-engines/

[45] Roger Marsh, 'Erie County Witness Overcome with Fear Watching Rectangular Shaped Object.' http://www.examiner.com/article/erie-county-witness-overcome-with-fear-watching-rectangle-ufo

[46] http://www.quantrek.org/quantum_hologram/quantum_hologram.htm

47 Lawrence Osborne, 'Savant for a Day,' New York Times, June 22, 2003, http://www.nytimes.com/2003/06/22/magazine/22SAVANT.html?ex=1371614400&en=0497e5b30fc4a9d8&ei=5007&

48 'Unlock Your Inner Rain Man' http://www.wired.com/2012/07/unlock-inner-savant/

49 E W Scripture, Arithmetical Prodigies, The American Journal of Psychology 4 (1) (1891), 1-59.

50 Oliver Sacks, "The Man Who Mistook His Wife for A Hat: And Other Clinical Tales," Simon and Schuster, 1998, p.199.

51 Oliver Sacks, p.199.

52 Rupert Sheldrake, 'Rat Learning and Morphic Resonance,' from Chapter 11 of Rupert Sheldrake's book *Morphic Resonance* published in the United States.

53 John Morgan, "Scientific Heretic Rupert Sheldrake on Morphic Fields, Psychic Dogs and Other Mysteries," *Scientific American Blogs*, http://blogs.scientificamerican.com/cross-check/2014/07/14/scientific-heretic-rupert-sheldrake-on-morphic-fields-psychic-dogs-and-other-mysteries/

54 "No need for panic about AIDS. Acquired immune deficiency disease, now frequent among male homosexuals in the United States, is not this century's black death. The most urgent need is to understand what is going on." Nature 302 (5911): 749. April 1983.

55 According to the sisters the two men were actually 3rd or 4th cousins related through the Riley family.

56 Cordell Hull Saw Aliens in Glass Containers http://www.ufocasebook.com/hull.htm

57 Peter Carlson, 'Ike and the Alien Ambassadors,' Washington Post, http://www.exopolitics.org/Wash-Post-Ike%20and%20ETs.htm

58 Eisenhower was born a Jehovah Witness but converted to the Presbyterian Church after being elected President. Despite the conversion, Eisenhower's secretary stated that Ike hated church adding, *"I don't know how he ever got along with Billy Graham."*

59 According to research done by Dr. Michael Salla, Dr Edwin Nourse (1883-1974) was the first chairman of the Council of Economic Advisors to the President (1944-1953) and was President Truman's chief economic advisor. Cardinal James

Francis McIntyre was the bishop and head of the Catholic Church in Los Angeles (1948-1970). The fourth member of the delegation of community leaders was Franklin Winthrop Allen, a former reporter with the Hearst Newspapers Group. Allen was 80 years old at the time, author of a book. instructing reporters on how to deal with Congressional Committee Hearings.

[60] http://files.abovetopsecret.com/files/img/ik513a7eba.jpg

[61] Richard Lee Miller, *'Under the Cloud: The Decades of Nuclear Testing'* Two-Sixty Press, 1986, p. 188.

[62] Shirley MacLaine, *'Sage-ing While Age-ing.'* Simon and Schuster, 2007, p. 132.

[63] http://www.openminds.tv/spielberg-confirms-reagan-705/10057

[64] David Jacobs, *'Secret Life: Firsthand, Documented Accounts of UFO Abduction,'* Touchstone 1993.

[65] Preston Dennett, 'UFO Healings: True Accounts of People Healed by Extraterrestrials,' Wild Flower Press, 1996, Page 7.

[66] Ibid page 133

[67] http://www.forteantimes.com/features/fbi/2929/alien_abductions_revisited.html

[68] Precognition after NDE, http://iands.org/experiences/nde-accounts/564-precognition-since-nde.htm

[69] http://latimesblogs.latimes.com/lanow/2012/09/62-earthquake-off-baja-followed-byothershakers.html

[70] http://www.cnn.com/2012/10/08/us/spacex-engine-failure

[71] http://en.wikipedia.org/wiki/Crandall_Canyon_Mine

[72] http://murderpedia.org/male.C/c/caputo-ricardo.htm

[73] Interview Mike Clelland and Dr. Suzanne Gordon, July 25, 2013, http://hiddenexperience.podbean.com/2013/08/13/suzanne-gordon-phd-interview/

[74] Benjamin Black 'September 11 Visitation' http://starchildchronicles.wordpress.com/tag/premonitions/

[75] Larry Dossey, *'The Power of Premonitions'* Hay House 2011, Page 32

[76] http://www.improverse.com/edarticles/richard_wilkerson_2001_oct_dreams_of_terrorism.htm

[77] This computer flying around the earth talking to people is strangely not that uncommon. According to Colin Andrews in January 1971, a call-in show on Greater London Radio received a call from a cold, metallic voice claiming an extraterrestrial origin. The voice, which did not give itself a name, said it was speaking by thought transference guided by computer and imparted the usual pattern about the difficulties of life on Earth and humanity's unwillingness to forsake its primitive ways. When asked by the program's host if it was possible for humans to see the interstellar interlocutor, it replied that it was possible to assume human appearance for a specific number of minutes.

[78] If true this would make the date of the Geller contact at 1949 and make Geller the first known contact of the modern UFO era.

[79] Jack Sarfatti, 'Sarfatti's Illuminati: In the Thick of It.' http://www.whale.to/b/sarfatti.html

[80] An excellent paper detailing this dark side of potential alien phone calls was an article called 'Men in Black: A short Catalogue' by Gareth J. Medway http://pelicanist.blogspot.ca/p/mib-encounters.html

[81] http://www.ncbi.nlm.nih.gov/pubmed/22607834

[82] Stewart Hameroff, 'Time. Consciousness and Quantum Events in Fundamental Spacetime,' http://www.quantumconsciousness.org/Time.htm

[83] Email from Lee Graham to Grant Cameron, 3 August 2013, 'OPEN LETTER/REQUEST'

[84] Alfred Webre, 'Third whistle blower confirms Obama's participation in CIA jump room program of early 1980's.' http://exopolitics.blogs.com/exopolitics/2012/07/third-whistle-blower-confirms-obamas-participation-in-cia-jump-room-program-of-early-1980s.html

[85] Asked about the claim Tommy Vietor, the spokesman for the National Security Council told Wired Magazine, *"Only if you count watching Marvin the Martian."*

[86] Pete Willsher, 'Moody Blues UFO Encounter in 1967,' Flying Saucer Review, 1990.

[87] 'Michael Pinder Exclusive: The Moody Blues Founder Admits to Seeing UFO Formations,' AXS Entertainment Music. http://www.examiner.com/article/michael-pinder-exclusive-the-moody-blues-founder-admits-to-seeing-ufo-formations

[88] Interview of Colin Andrews by Mike Clelland, October 27, 2014.

[89] Email from Tim Beckley to Grant Cameron.

[90] Sammy Hagar Alien Abduction - http://www.vhnd.com/2010/04/19/sammy-hagars-alien-visitations/

[91] Majicat Cat Stevens Scrapbook, http://www.majicat.com/articles/star_interview.htm

[92] 'This Week in History: Cat Stevens No More,' *Jerusalem Post,* December 23, 2012.

[93] When it comes to creativity and LSD Mullis joins a whole group of people who seemed to fall in the same category. Steve Jobs, the force behind the creative force of Apple Computers gave much of the credit to LSD saying it was one of the most important things he had ever done in his life. Many of the other key people involved in the creation of the modern-day computer make similar claims. Then there is Crick who developed the discovery of the DNA molecule structure that came to him when he was under the influence of LSD.

[94] Andrews's account came from an interview with Mike Clelland on October 22, 2013, on Clelland's Hidden Experience Podcast. Colin also tells the story in his book *The Edge of Reality* on page 64.

[95] Michael Shermer, 'Anomalous Events That Can Shake One's Skepticism to the Core' *Scientific American Magazine*, September 16, 2014

[96] http://www.internationalskeptics.com/forums/showthread.php?t=283335

[97] Feynman Chaser – The Likelihood of Flying Saucers, https://www.youtube.com/watch?v=wLaRXYai19A

[98] Feynman's Clock, Danwin.com, http://danwin.com/2012/06/feynmans-clock/

Made in the USA
Columbia, SC
19 July 2024